No More Being Abused

I'M TAKING MY LIFE BACK

Mary C. Barron-Epps

DIVINE WORKS PUBLISHING, LLC.
ROYAL PALM BEACH, FLORIDA

Copyright © 2024 Mary C. Barron-Epps
NO MORE BEING ABUSED: I'm Taking My Life Back

All rights reserved. No part of this publication may be reproduced, stored in a retrieval system, or transmitted in any form or by any means, electronic, mechanical, photocopying, recording or otherwise without the prior permission of the publisher or in accordance with the provisions of the Copyright, Designs, and Patents Act 1988 or under the terms of any license permitting limited copying issued by the Copyright Licensing Agency.

The views expressed in this work are solely those of the author and do not necessarily reflect the views of the publisher. The publisher hereby disclaims any responsibility for them.

ISBN: 978-1-949105-69-8 (paperback)
ISBN: 978-1-949105-70-4 (eBook)

Library of Congress Control Number: 2024920334
Second Edition
Publication Date: September 26, 2024
Printed in the United States of America
Royal Palm Beach, Florida 33411

Divine Works Publishing books are available at special discounts when purchased in quantity for premiums and promotions and for educational and fundraising use. For details, contact: *books@DivineWorksPublishing.com* or call the phone number listed below.

Published by:
Divine Works Publishing
Royal Palm Beach, Florida USA
561-990-BOOK (2665)

www.DivineWorksPublishing.com

Dedication

This book is dedicated to women around the world who have or are currently experiencing abuse.
I pray this book gives you strength and the realization that there is joy on the other side.

ʊʒ

I'm Free

I'm Free - for once I'm in control of my own life

I refuse to live through another dreadful night

I'm Free -to not be the woman I became

For now I know my life will never be the same

I'm Free - I refuse to live in fear and shed another tear

For the pain and heartache you caused throughout the years.

I'm Free- from being scared wondering if I'll see another day

I lift my hands up, thanking God for making a way.

I'm Free - No longer scared for my life

With God, I shall Live and not Die!

- A Domestic Violence Survivor

A Message to domestic violence victims all over the world,

It's time to take your life back and be FREE....

Contents

Book 1: Maintaining My Dignity

Chapter 1   A Walk I Will Never Forget   1
Chapter 2   Determined to Graduate   9
Chapter 3   Gone, But Not Forgotten   13
Chapter 4   There He Goes Again   17
Chapter 5   Why is He at My House?   27
Chapter 6   I'm Too Nervous   35
Chapter 7   Stop Being So Nosy   39
Chapter 8   My Very First Kiss   47
Chapter 9   Just Wishing   53
Chapter 10   Family Is Everything   59
Chapter 11   He Put Me on the Spot   73
Chapter 12   Getting My Praise On   79
Chapter 13   No Pressure on Me   85
Chapter 14   The Yellow Envelope   95
Chapter 15   Telling My Family the Good News   101
Chapter 16   I Finally Made It   107

Book 2: I'm Nobody's Fool

Chapter 17   Can I Maintain My Dignity   117
Chapter 18   His Warm Embrace   129
Chapter 19   He Keeps Surprising Me   137
Chapter 20   A Bright Light   145
Chapter 21   Reaching My Goal   151
Chapter 22   Missing My Father   161
Chapter 23   I Gave It Up   171
Chapter 24   The Burning Sensations   183
Chapter 25   Honoring My Mom   189
Chapter 26   Caught in the Act   197
Chapter 27   His Apology   207
Chapter 28   How Could He?   217
Chapter 29   The Results   223

Book 3: I'm Taking My Life Back

Chapter 30 God Is Good To Me 231
Chapter 31 My First Slap 241
Chapter 32 You Heard What I Said 255
Chapter 33 Pregnant With His First Child 265
Chapter 34 Missing In Action 271
Chapter 35 Charmayne Still Loves Him 275
Chapter 36 Giving Birth to Your Son, Where Are You? 279
Chapter 37 Another of His Lies 287
Chapter 38 Ready to Go Home 291
Chapter 39 When Enough Is Finally Enough 299
Chapter 40 Enjoying My Bundle of Joy 305
Chapter 41 A Family Gathering 311
Chapter 42 Here We Go Again 319
Chapter 43 Can't Keep It in His Pant 327
Chapter 44 Abused By My Lover 335
Chapter 45 A Bitter Love 345
Chapter 46 Brought Back to Reality 353
Chapter 47 It Ends 355

Acknowledgments

My Lord and Savior, I thank you for giving me this gift and opportunity to openly share my story with other abused women around the world. I pray that I can help someone who finds themselves in an abusive relationship to realize that it's time to love themselves. Lord, you've been better to me than I've been to myself. Thank you for being there for me. Even when I wanted to die and give up, You never left my side nor did you give up on me. Lord, I thank you for your undying love. Your love has taught me my worth and in return I love you with every bone in my body and with every breath I breathe.

Mom, thank you for your encouraging words and the wise advice you gave me throughout the years. You've always led me to make wise choices and decisions in life. Although I've kept many things from you, I now wish I would have told you about my abusive relationship. I know you would have protected me from him. I do apologize for keeping you in the dark about what was going on. I cried many nights wishing and praying for someone to come and rescue me. I always kept a smile on my face trying to hide the pain and hurt I faced. I love you unconditionally and I dedicate this book to you.

My son, there are not enough words to express my love for you. Thanks for always having my back and being there when I needed you the most. You always urged me to follow my dreams and never give up. I love you--unconditionally. Always remember you can be anything you want to be, as long as you keep God first in your life.

My daughter, I thank you for your sage wisdom and advice and for helping me realize that I AM somebody. Having you and your brother in my life is a sheer gift from God. I am blessed to have you both in my life. I love you dearly. Thank you for blessing me with my adorable grandbabies. You all bring love and joy to my heart. I thank God each and every day for you. I love you all unconditionally.

To my god daughters, I wish you all the best in what you achieve in life. Reach for the stars and shine like it belongs to you. I love you all in my own unique way. I pray you will continue to put God first in everything you do. I promise you, He is right there when you can't find anyone else. Do not let a man hit on you. You are not anybody's punching bag. Remember that!

My sister, thanks for understanding and being there for me. You always had time to listen to me. You've never turned your back on me. You'll always be my best little sister. I love you.

My brother, I am so proud of you and how you turned your life around. I love you from the bottom of my heart. Keep on doing what God has destined for you. Remember to keep your queen smiling and loving her in every way you can.

To my nephews I love you all. Be the men God designed you to be. "He will never leave you nor will he forsake you." All you have to do is trust and believe in him. "The battle Is Not Yours, It's The Lord's."

To my nieces, Auntie will always love you. Even though we don't talk on the phone as much, you will always be in my heart. If you find yourself in a tough situation and you can't find your way out, fall down on your knees and call on the name of Jesus. He will come to your rescue.

My friends/sisters, you each know who you are. The moment we first met was an awesome connection between us. I cherish our friendship to the utmost and I respect you all. Thanks for all the good times we've had throughout the years. I thank God for having good friends like you all in my life. Yes, I got on your nerves, but it was for a good cause. Thanks again for being my friend/sister. I love each and every one of you. Keep your head up and don't become a victim like I was. My bestie, there's a lot of words I can say about you. One thing I can say, we share a closely-knit bond. No matter what I'm going through, you always find the right words to cheer me up. You always put a smile on my face. I can count on you for anything. Thank you so much for being there for me and being my friend. Nobody will ever understand our friendship and the love we have for one another. I can truly say, you are a TRUE FRIEND in DEED. I love you like a sister.

My Sister My Friends (Women's Group), there's not enough words that can explain the love I have for each and every one of you. We have prayed, cried, and laughed a lot. It's what's kept our love for one another strong. Thanks for playing a special role in my life and my children's life as well. I love you all……

My Pastor and family, I thank God for planting you both in my life. You both have given me encouraging and straight forward words. I appreciate the love you have for me and my family. I love and appreciate you both. I'm so glad to be a member of your Ministry. My faith has grown through your ministry. You both have shown me nothing but real and true love. Thanks for being there in my times of pain. My church family, I can only say, "My God, My God". We are an awesome family that loves everybody and we are there for one another. I love you all so much and there's nothing you can do about it. That's coming from the heart. Thank you for all the love and support you have demonstrated throughout the years. I love you all…

I thank God for my cousin who introduced me to this wonderful man. She picked the perfect man just for me. I love you unconditionally.

Who would have thought of me moving to another state to be with a man? "Well, I did." Not a day goes by that I don't appreciate you and the things you've done for me and gave me. "Baby, you're been my shelter in the time of my storm, a shield to protect me from the rain, an arm to cover me from my pain, a friend when I needed someone to talk to, a shoulder to cry on when I thought I was going to lose my mind, and a very supportive man to me. The love I have for you is unexplainable. You make me feel alive when I'm with you. You've never judged me; you are everything I wanted and dreamed of having in my life. Thanks for believing in me and never turning your back on me. I love you unconditionally. Thanks for loving me unconditionally. Thank you for supporting me in every positive thing I wanted to do in life and giving me wise advice through the years. I thank God for having you in my life. Even when I wanted to give up and throw in the towels, you wouldn't let me. Thanks baby!!!!!

Thanks to these two beautiful women, I couldn't have done it without you. You two ladies are the best. My teachers, thanks not only for everything you've done but also for the love you all have for me.

My friends/sisters, thank you for being my friend/sister and being an ear listening to me complain about this and that. We've had some good times in classes together. You all kept me on my toes laughing at the things you all did and said. You always had my back no matter what. You never took our friendship for granted. We've been through some good and bad times, but we came out with the good. Thanks for being my friend/sister.

To my family and friends, far and near I love each and every one of you in my own unique way. You all play a special role in my life. No matter how far away you are from me, I love you all. I thank each and every one of you for your undying love. You all are awesome. To my fans, especially women who are in abusive relationships. It is time for you to hold your head up high, fix your crown and know that you are loved. You don't have to remain a victim to domestic violence. Let this book be a sign to you that it is time to devise your exit strategy and put a stop to the hands that abuse you.

My publisher, Dr. Belinda John and the entire Divine Works Publishing team, thank you for giving me the opportunity to tell my story and publish my book. I appreciate your divinely guided help.

To all the readers of this book, a great BIG thank you for taking the time to read this book. I hope I've encouraged someone along the way to seek help. I love you all and stay blessed. Always remember to keep God first in your life and everything will go in your favor. Every footstep you take there's another footstep right beside you.

Chapter 1

A Walk I Will Never Forget

It all started on a hot summer afternoon. Charmayne had just completed her math homework and grabbed the phone to call her friend Sweet. She wanted to see if Sweet was interested in grabbing a burger together.

"Let me call my home girl Sweet."

Charmayne picked up the phone to call her friend Sweet to ask if she wanted to go grab a burger.

Sweet answered on the third ring.

"Hello."

"Hey girl, what are you doing?"

"I was about to call you."

"I guess we were both thinking the same thing," Sweet said.

After Charmayne and Sweet's girl-talk, they hung up the phone and prepared to meet up.

Sweet and Charmayne had been friends since elementary school and their bond remained strong throughout the years. They both participated in various activities within their community and played volleyball, softball, and cheered for a local basketball team.

In every neighborhood, there is always a spot where the teens go to hang out. For the girls, this restaurant was the place. It was where the local teens spent their free time and met up with friends to shoot pool, play video games, and listen to music on the jukebox.

Charmayne, Sweet, and some more of their friends played Space Invaders while some of their other friends listened to the music.

"Charmayne and Sweet, your food is ready," their friend Jan said.

Jan is one of Charmayne's friends who attends the same school and Jan's parents own the restaurant.

Charmayne and Sweet both walked up to the register to pay for their food.

"Girl, I can't wait to bite into this burger," Sweet said.

"Girl, me either. I was dreaming about this burger while I was sitting at my desk during second period."

Everyone busted out laughing at what Charmayne had just said.

"Charmayne you crazy," Fran jokingly chimed in.

While on their way home, amidst all their joking, they noticed several boys riding bicycles down the street.

"Girl, I wish I had a pink bicycle to ride," Camryn said.

"Why do you want a pink bicycle?" asked Charmayne.

"Inquiring minds like me want to know the answer to that question too, Charmayne," Sweet added.

"So, I can ride with the boys in the bicycle club."

They all started laughing at Camryn.

"Can somebody please buy my friend Camryn a pink bicycle?" Chuckled Charmayne.

Camryn, Fran, and Destiny were the type of friends who said the silliest things at the most unsuspecting moments. They didn't care what came out of their mouths.

"Hey, let's get us a girl's bicycle club," Lyric suggested.

"Can somebody please tell me why these ugly boys are following us?" Camryn exclaimed.

"I don't know why they're following us, but if they know what I know they better keep on riding somewhere else," Sweet teased.

The boys in the bicycle club rode their bikes a little closer to Charmayne and her friends.

"Dang, I know some of these knuckleheads from my neighborhood, but I've never seen the rest of them around here." Destiny added.

Charmayne's friend Destiny also knew three of the boys from the neighborhood.

"I remember Destiny used to date one of the boys back in the days. She's standing here acting like she never dated him. Girl, sit down somewhere, you're not fooling no one but yourself."

"Is there anything I can help you with?" Asked Camryn.

"Camryn, don't act like you don't know us," one of the boys said.

"No for real. What can we help you with?" Camryn insisted.

"How can we join the boys bicycle club?" inquired Charmayne.

"All you have to do is have your own bicycle and you can just ride alongside us," one of the boys replied.

"I never rode a huffy bicycle before."

"It's not that hard to ride a huffy bicycle," one of the boys answered back.

"If it's not that hard to ride a huffy bike then let me ride your bike," Charisma added.

"You're not in our bicycle club."

"Well, I will be in the bicycle club when I get my bike."

"You all looked beautiful walking to the park," another one of the

3

boys added.

"Dang you have good vision," Camryn said.

"Camryn, be quiet," Charmayne softly uttered. "They are just trying to be nosey, that's all.

"Girl… he's looking at you like he wants to snatch you up," Destiny said.

"Destiny hush. Nobody is trying to snatch me up. Besides, I'm not trying to date anyone, not at this moment. I have too much I need to accomplish in my life," Charmayne said.

"He wants to put you on his handlebars and ride you off into the sunset," Destiny teased.

"My friend is not trying to get snatched up by anyone," Sweet said. "So, you and your homeboys can keep riding off."

"He can be riding a ten-speed bicycle for all I care and I still won't date him."

They all laughed in sync.

"What's your name?" One of the boys asked Charmayne.

Before Charmayne could reply, Camryn intercepted and started asking questions.

"Why do you want my friend's name?"

"Don't do that Camryn. I can talk for myself. I don't need you to speak for me.

"My name is Charmayne. What's your name?"

"My name is Gram, nice to meet you Charmayne."

Charmayne already knew some of the boys, so she introduced them to her friends.

However, Gram's homeboys introduced themselves to Charmayne's friends.

"Hello everyone this is Gram."

"Hello Gram," they all said.

"It was nice meeting you all."

"It was nice meeting you too."

"What school do you go to, Charmayne?"

"Boy, why are you asking me all these questions?"

"I don't mean no harm. I'm just trying to be friendly, that's all."

"It's no problem. I was just wondering why you were asking me so many questions."

"My family and I just moved here from Wisconsin. My parents are trying to find a school near our home for my brothers, sisters and I to attend."

Charmayne intentionally never revealed the name of her school.

"It was nice meeting you, but I have to go and finish my homework." Charmayne said coyly, ending the exchange.

As Gram and his friends continued on their way, Gram looked back and waved at them.

"He seems to be a nice guy but he sure asks a lot of questions," Destiny suspiciously commented.

At that moment, Charmayne heard someone call her name, but she didn't see anyone. When she turned around it was Gram again.

"What color is your house?"

"Boy, you're not welcome at my house and neither are your friends."

"What street do you live on?"

"Why do you need to know all that?"

Charmayne and Gram kept hollering back and forth to one another.

"Do Gram ever give up? Dang, we don't know each other and he's asking way too many damn questions."

"Just in case I want to come over and see you." He added.

"Wow, this boy is not stopping until he gets to know you." Sweet said.

"This boy is truly desperate to be your boyfriend."

"Why are you smiling so hard Charmayne?" Asked Fran.

"I'm not smiling that hard."

"Yes, you are, Charmayne." Fran replied, calling her out.

Charmayne and her friends gathered in Sweet's yard and talked for a bit before heading their separate ways.

"We all need to get bicycles and ride alongside them," Camryn said. "I think it'll be fun."

"And why is that Camryn?" Asked Destiny.

"I just want to be popular like them."

"Riding a bicycle or being in a bicycle club does not make you popular," Sweet said.

"I don't have time to date or be in a bicycle club," Charmayne added. "I'm trying to stay focused on my education. And, I better get going. I need to go home and study for tomorrow's test."

"Yeah I'm about to do the same thing," Sweet said.

"I'll get up with you all later."

"Alright Charmayne, call you later," Destiny said.

Charmayne and her friends all went their separate ways.

When Charmayne got home, her parents were sitting in the living room talking.

"Hey Charmayne, come in and sit down on the sofa. Your father and I need to talk to you." Her mother beckoned.

"Yes ma'am."

"Charmayne, what are your goals after you graduate from high school?" Asked Charmayne's father.

After Charmayne told her parents what her goals were, they were very supportive of what she wanted to do.

"Charmayne, we know you can do it. There's a lot you have ahead of you. We need you to stay focused and stay away from negative people."

"Mom, you and dad taught me my core values. I'm not going to be around people who don't want the best in life. I want the best for me, my sisters and brothers."

"Listen baby girl, I want you all to be the best you can be. You have to have a backup plan just in case something goes wrong. Never fixate on one door being the only door you can enter into. There's always a side and a back door to go in and out of."

"Now, that's my baby girl. Always remember what your parents have taught you. Being a failure is not in our category. We are winners. We conquer what we set our minds on."

"Mom and dad, I want to help you out with the bills, do things with my sisters and brothers and put money aside for a rainy day."

Charmayne's father was the breadwinner of their home. He made sure the bills were paid and his family didn't want for nothing.

After eating dinner, Charmayne stored the food in containers and put them neatly away in the refrigerator.

Charmayne's sister Gracie and her brother Marc washed the dishes and put them away in the cabinet. While Rocky swept and mopped the floor.

Charmayne was getting tired. She walked into her room to get her pajamas. On this day, she decided to take a bubble bath instead of a shower.

"I think I'm going to take a nice soothing bath instead of a shower today. I need to relax my body and my mind."

Charmayne's mom startled her when she knocked on the bathroom door. She jumped up straight up in the tub.

"I'm glad I came out of that dream. I just met Gram and here I am having dreams about him already."

"It's me, Charmayne."

"Come on in ma. I'm glad you woke me up. I dozed off relaxing here in the tub."

"You need to go and lie down in bed."

Only if Charmayne's mom knew what she was dreaming about and who she was dreaming about.

Charmayne reminisced about the boy named Gram, who she met earlier while she and her friends walked towards the park.

Chapter 2

Determined to Graduate

One day, while in class Charmayne's guidance counselor, Mrs. Truth, called her name over the intercom to come to her office. As you know, when your name is called over the intercom people assume you're in trouble.

"Girl what did you do?" Asked Marin.

"An inquiring mind like me wants to know the answer too," Charmayne said.

When Charmayne walked in the office she noticed the expression her guidance counselor Mrs. Truth had on her face, which didn't seem good to her.

"Have a seat Charmayne," Mrs. Truth said.

When Charmayne sat in the chair, she noticed Mrs. Truth had some paperwork on her desk with her name on it. Charmayne knew she was in trouble.

Charmayne's mind raced wondering what she was about to tell her. Mrs. Truth picked up the paperwork from her desk and began talking with Charmayne regarding graduation.

"I wonder what Mrs. Truth wants to talk to me about. I see some paper on her desk with my name on it, but I can't read the top line. What have I done? I hope she quickly tells me why I'm here."

"Charmayne, I called you in my office to talk to you about your progress."

Mrs. Truth explained to Charmayne that in order for her to graduate with her class she needed to register for night school.

Charmayne and Mrs. Truth discussed all the alternatives for her to graduate.

"Charmayne, in order for you to graduate with your class, you will need to take some night classes. You will also need to do some extracurricular activities in school as well."

"Thanks Mrs. Truth. I thought I was in some serious trouble. You had me scared. I can feel my heart beating."

"Charmayne, I didn't mean to scare you. I'm so sorry if I did. Please forgive me for scaring you."

"It's okay Mrs. Truth. I did not know what to expect, that's all."

In high school Charmayne behaved badly. She didn't care what the consequences were. She fought teachers and students alike, and dared anyone to report her to the office.

Mrs. Truth was concerned about Charmayne's behavior and how she'd been acting out in school.

"Charmayne, you are an intelligent young lady." I have faith in you. I know you can do it, but you have to want to do it.

While listening to what Mrs. Truth was saying to her, Charmayne realized that she had positive people standing in her corner and cheering her on.

"My guidance counselor Mrs. Truth really cares about me." She's only looking out for my best interest and I appreciate it.

Thanks Mrs. Truth for being concerned about me. Noone's ever showed that kind concern for me.

"No problem, Charmayne. That's what I'm here for. Don't hesitate to come and talk to me if you have questions about anything."

When Charmayne got to class, she explained to everyone why she went to see her guidance counselor.

Charmayne was determined to graduate with her class and receive her diploma. She promised her family she was going to make them proud of her. When Charmayne got home, she shared the good news with her family.

My dad would tell me to never depend on a man to do anything for you. The mistakes you make in life, come with consequences behind them. Now, I see what my parents were trying to tell me.

"Baby girl, hold your head up," Charmayne's father said. "You don't have to hold your head down any more. When you walk across the stage to receive your diploma, I'll be cheering you on."

"Thanks Dad."

"I have the right gift in mind for what I want to give you."

"Dad, you don't have to get me anything. You've already done enough for me. You make sure I have food to eat, clothes to wear, shoes on my feet and a roof over my head. You don't owe me nothing Dad."

"Charmayne, why is your head so hard? I'm going to get you a gift and that's the end of the story. I'm so proud of you baby girl. You are doing something positive in your life. Your sisters and brothers are watching you. One day they are going to follow you in your footsteps. Be careful of what you do and how you do it in front of your sisters and brothers. Especially your sisters. They admire you a lot. They really look up to you."

"Yes, dad, I will make sure I do the right thing in front of them. I know they look up to me. I'm going to make sure what I do in life will always be something positive not just for me, but for them too."

"There are going to be people in this world and even in your family who won't understand what your plans are and what you're doing. You continue to do what makes Charmayne happy."

"Yes dad I know. Even some of my so-called friends won't understand what my goals are. I'm always keeping my eyes open regarding people who are not for my highest good."

"Don't let no one tell you anything different. Always keep your eyes open and pay attention to what's in front of you. You have to have a mind of your own. This world is full of people hating on their own kind. You are going to be introduced to different types of alcohol and drugs. I don't want you to get yourself involved with the wrong crowd. Be careful around the people who you call your friends. A lot of your friends are not your friends. You will see a different picture in life as you get older.

My dad must have paid a visit to the depths of my mind because I was just saying that to myself the other day. Some of my friends I had to let go because they were trying to make me do things that they were doing knowing I wasn't about that life.

"Baby girl, I just want the best for you, your sisters and brothers."

"I know dad. I want to be the big sister they can come to and depend on. Take care of them, because they are going to need your support. Your sisters and brothers are going to need their big sister. Teach them the right way."

Why is my dad talking to me like that? Is my dad trying to tell me something that I don't know about? Whatever my dad is saying to me, I'm going to take all of it into consideration.

"Dad, no matter what happens in my life, I will always be their big sister. They won't have to worry about anything. I'm going to be there for them."

Charmayne and her father talked for about thirty more minutes.

"Thanks Dad for the encouraging words. I promise you, I will be there for them."

"I know you won't let me down, baby girl."

Charmayne and her dad hugged one another.

"Love you baby girl."

"Love you too dad."

Chapter 3

Gone, But Not Forgotten

Charmayne was determined to make her parents and everyone else proud of her. She kept her grades up, stayed out of trouble, and attended night school. It had taken her a couple of weeks, but she was finally able to push forward. It wasn't easy for her.

As difficult as this already was for her, it seemed Charmayne had people coming at her from every angle. She felt like giving up on most days, but she knew she had to stay strong. No matter what the circumstances were or the outcome of the situation, she was determined to make the best of it.

One minute, Charmayne heard people saying all sorts of negative things about her, but that didn't let any of it stop her from getting her work done. The next minute, she'd hear people saying how proud they were of her. She did her best to remain focused and above the talk. Charmayne's friend Sweet would urge her to stay above it all..

I'm so glad I have a friend like Sweet. Sweet is always giving me solid advice and urging me to stay strong. I don't know what I would do without her in my life." Charmayne would repeat to herself.

"Girl, let people say what they want to say about you," Fran urged her to maintain her focus.

"You've come too far to turn around Charmayne," Sweet continued, "People are always going to talk, whether you do good or do bad."

"One thing I know, they have one more time to come at you the wrong way," Destiny added.

Before Destiny finished her sentence, Charisma interrupted her.

"Girl, Charmayne is not worrying about what anyone has to say about her,"

"I'm glad they're talking about me," Charmayne answered. "It's only making me stronger. As long as they're not saying it in my face."

"I know that's right," Sweet said.

"Don't let that bother you," Camryn continued.

"You all are the only ones complaining, notice I am not" Charmayne emphasized. "I'm not letting that mess stop me from what I'm doing. They know not to come my way."

"You are going to have negative people in your life who don't want to see you accomplish nothing. That's why I hang around positive people," Sweet explained.

"I'm with you on that Sweet," Camryn said. "I don't need friends who are going to be fake. I need friends who are going to keep it real with me."

"People are always going to be jealous of you," Marin pointed out to Charmayne.

"Girl I don't have anything for anybody to be jealous of. I'm struggling just like anybody else."

"There are some things you can say to people in a nice way and hurt their feelings at the same time," Destiny said. "You don't have to always curse them out."

"Hell, if they come at me the wrong way I'm going to curse them out," Fran added, "I don't care what nobody says."

"You sure can!" Destiny exclaimed, "If I got paid for all the things people have said about me, I'd be a billionaire by now. It doesn't bother me about the things they say about me."

"Me either," Marin said. "Even if you did everything right, they're still going to talk about you. So, whether you do it right or wrong they're still going to talk."

"Well I must keep the promise I made to my parents and family. If I let the old Charmayne come out, it will be pure hell trying to put her back where she belongs."

They all busted out laughing at what Charmayne said.

"Girl, I know that's right," Sweet related. "Whatever suits you, then I'm good. I refused to let some random female walk up in your face and I don't do nothing."

"Listen we're better than that," Charmayne said. "Any female is going to say what she wants to say. I'm not worrying about that. Talk is cheap."

"But this ass whooping I'm going to give them is a price," Camryn added.

"Yes, you're right," Fran said.

"Child, please," Marin teased Fran. "You too scared to do anything."

"Boy, lying," Fran said. "I don't take shit from anyone and you should know that."

"Girl, I know you not talking about being scared," Camryn joked.

"I'm not scared of anyone." They know not to take a ride this way. I'll send their ass back where they came from.

"Fran, we have seen you in action," Destiny said. "I remember when you beat up Chico. Girl you beat her so bad, I wanted to cry for her."

Charmayne's father passed away before he could see her graduate. This took a toll on her, she knew she had to keep pushing, but while grieving she wanted to give up on everything she'd accomplished.

Charmayne didn't want to do anything with her family or her friends. Going to school wasn't on her list. But then she remembered the promise she made to her father, mother, and family.

Charmayne was determined to graduate with her class and receive her diploma.

Charmayne's friends and teachers stood by her when she needed them the most.

My teachers and friends promised my mom and family that they would make sure I kept my head in the books and graduated with my class. They really care about me. Thank God for good people like them. I wouldn't trade them for nothing in the world.

Although it was tough during those years for Charmayne, she never gave up.

As the days, months, and years passed, it even became harder for Charmayne to stay disciplined. People came at her from every angle.

Charmayne tried her best to repress the hurt and pain she was enduring. She cried often and so much til she had no tears left to cry.

Charmayne missed talking to her dad for comfort. She remembered her dad advising her, "People are going to make you feel useless, but don't let that discourage you. You are someone special. You're special to me, your mom, your sisters and brothers. They are going to try to make you feel as if you're beneath them, but remember you are beneath no one. Let no one stop you from reaching your dreams."

Charmayne looked toward Heaven and said. "Dad, I will always love you. You will always have a special place in my heart. May you rest in peace, love you."

Chapter 4

There He Goes Again

One day while Charmayne sat in the living room doing her homework, she asked her mom if it was okay for her to start dating.

"If that's what you want to do, Charmayne. I don't have a problem with you dating as long as you keep your grades up."

I'm glad my mom and I have a good understanding. I know I can talk to her about anything. My mom knows I'm not the type of girl who will let someone take advantage of me. I know I have to keep up my grades in order to graduate with my class.

Charmayne's teachers gave her extra homework to do in order to help pull up her grades.

It's a good thing I have teachers who are looking out for my best interest. All my teachers gave me extra homework to do to help bring up my grades as well as my GPA. I'm so grateful for them.

"Mom, you don't have anything to worry about. I promise I won't disappoint you."

"I just want the best for you, your sisters and brothers."

"I know you do, mom. We won't let you down."

Charmayne started telling her mom about a young man she met the other day while they were walking to the park.

Charmayne's big mouth sister Gracie began blabbing and telling their mom about him.

"Gracie could've at least given me the chance to tell my mom about him." Charmayne thought to herself.

"He was asking her a lot of questions," Gracie continued.

"Mom, he wanted to know what color our house is," Miracle added. "Then, he asked her what school she attends."

"Well look at Miracle running her mouth too. Both of them are making me sick to my stomach. I wish they both would stop talking." Charmayne thought, she was not okay with this.

"Miracle, stop talking and let me tell momma what happened. You and Gracie getting on my last nerve."

"That's what you call nosey, Ty'Meisha said.

"I need for you and your sisters to stay in a child's place."

"Yes, ma'am," Miracle said.

" And what do you know about boyfriend and girlfriend?" Charmayne asked Gracie.

Charmayne's sisters were protective of her. They didn't want to see their big sister get mistreated by anyone.

Let me sit my sisters down and explain to them that there are some things they just can't say out of their mouth.

"Miracle and Gracie, I need to talk to you both." Come sit down on the sofa so we can talk.

Both Miracle and Gracie sat next to her on the sofa.

"Listen, there are some things you shouldn't let come out of your mouth. When you see two people talking, you should never interfere in their conversation. Whatever they are talking about does not have anything to do with you. So therefore, you should keep your mouth closed."

"Yes, Charmayne we understand." they both replied.

"Now if a person asks you a question, you should answer it in a respectful manner. You both need to stay in a child's place and speak when you are asked to speak. I don't want to have to stop you all from going anywhere with me, but if I have to then I will."

"We're sorry Charmayne and ma." We won't do that again.

"There's nothing you have to worry about Miracle and Gracie. Your sister Charmayne is a big girl. I can handle anything that comes my way."

"Okay Charmayne we understand," they both said.

"Each one of you has a special place in my heart. You will always be my little sisters. Nobody will ever take that away or come between us. I will always love each one of you in my own unique way."

Charmayne hugged her sisters to let them know how much she loved them.

"We love you too Charmayne," they again replied in unison.

"Well I have homework to do, I'll play with you all later."

After Charmayne finished doing her homework, she looked over it again to make sure it was completed. She cleaned up her room, and played dress up with her sisters and their dolls.

Just then the phone rang.

Charmayne overheard her mom say to someone, "Hold on while I get her."

"You have a phone call Charmayne."

Charmayne walked out the room to see who was on the phone for her.

"Hello."

"Hey Charmayne, what you doing?"

"Just got finished doing my homework, what's up?"

"I was calling to see if you wanted to go to the park and play volleyball."

"Hold on, while I ask my mom."

"Okay."

"Ma, is it okay if I go to the park and play volleyball with some of my friends?"

"Yes, you may go to the park for a while."

"We want to go to the park with you too," Charmayne's sister said.

"Dang, I hope I don't have to take my sisters to the park with me," Charmayne said to herself.

Charmayne wanted to hang out and kick it with some of her friends at the park.

"Every time I go somewhere, I have to take my sisters and brothers with her." I'll be glad when I can go to the park by myself and not have to take my sisters and brothers with me. Don't get me wrong, I love taking my sisters and brothers with me to the park, but not all the time. Sometimes I just want to chill with my friends and not with my sisters and brothers.

Charmayne's brothers Rocky and Marc wanted to stay home and play with their little buddies who stayed down the street from their house. They rarely went along to the park with them.

Charmayne's brothers didn't really like hanging out with their sisters like that.

"Make sure you keep your eyes on your sisters and hold their hands as they cross the streets."

"Yes ma'am."

Charmayne picked up the phone to inform her friend Sweet.

"Sweet, we'll be at your house in fifteen minutes. I'm bringing my sisters with me."

"Alright Charmayne, I'll see you then."

Charmayne and Sweet both hung the phone up.

Charmayne's mom gave them some money to get something to eat and drink.

As they were about to leave the house, there was a knock on the door. Charmayne peeped out the window. It was her friend Sweet and Destiny.

Charmayne opened the door and invited Sweet and Destiny to come in.

Charmayne, Destiny and Sweet discussed the math test they had to take during first period class the following morning.

"Hello Sweet and Destiny."

"Hello everyone."

"Mom, we'll be back soon."

"Remember what I told you about your sisters."

"Yes, ma'am, I will. We won't be gone long, I have a math quiz in the morning and I need to study."

"I'm glad you're bringing your sisters with you," Sweet and Destiny said.

"And why is that?"

"I have to stop at my house and get my sisters," Sweet said.

"Where are your sisters?" Charmayne asked Destiny.

"They are at Sweet house waiting for us to come get them."

"Oh boy we are going to have fun playing at the park," Ty'Meisha said.

"I'm surprised Marc and Rocky are not with you," Destiny said.

"Girl, my brothers stayed home so they could play with their friends. They like to stay home and play football in the yard with their friends."

"Girl, only if you knew. I'll be glad when I can go to the park without my sisters."

Charmayne whispered to Destiny and Sweet.

Charmayne didn't want her sisters hearing what she said to Sweet and Destiny.

"Girl, I feel the same way," Sweet said.

"Girl, me too," Destiny said.

As Charmayne and her friends walked toward the park, Charmayne's sister Ty'Meisha noticed several of the boys from the bicycle club walking toward the park as well.

"There goes the boys from the bicycle club."

"Yes, Ty'Meisha we see them. Thanks for giving us a head's up."

Charmayne's stomach started doing tricks. She was getting nervous.

Thank God their sisters walked ahead of them. They all had nosy sisters.

Charmayne, Sweet, and Destiny 's all began talking about who would have a car first and what kinds of cars they would have.

"As young as their asses are, they're talking about cars. They need to sit down some damn where and keep their heads in the books."

"Girl, they are too young to be worrying about who's going to have a car first and what kind of cars they're going to have," Destiny said.

"At least they got their heads together," Charmayne said. "It took me a while to know what I wanted to do."

"Here I am still trying to figure out what I want to do," Sweet said.

"Charmayne, looks like your man is headed toward the park with his homeboys," Destiny informed them.

"For your information, he is not my man, thank you very much."

Charmayne had a smile on her face. She wasn't sure if she was going to see Gram again. When they crossed the street, Charmayne made sure her sisters grabbed each other by their hands.

"My mom gave me permission to date Gram."

"Charmayne, are you serious?" Asked Sweet.

"Girl, my momma would be like 'Hell No, you're not dating no one.'"

"If we start dating, I don't want to rush into anything that I'll regret later."

"Girl, I know that's right," Destiny said. "Take your time with him."

Charmayne had a lot on her plate. She needed to remain focused on school and maintaining her grades.

"Girl, I promised my dad I would graduate with my class and walk the stage to receive my diploma."

"And you will, Charmayne." Nothing is going to stand in the way of achieving your dreams.

"Thanks Sweet. I'm proud of myself. I'm going to make my dad proud of me and that's a promise. I'm not going to let my dad down."

Even though it was hard for Charmayne not having her father around, she had to continue to do well in school and make her father proud of her.

"I can do this if I stay focused and keep a positive mindset."

"Charmayne, you are a smart young lady," Sweet said. There's nothing that would stop you. I have faith in you. I know you can do it."

"Charmayne, you are a go-getter," Destiny said. "I agree with Sweet. There are many days I was in your shoes. You are likable, outspoken, and smart. You have your mind already set on what you want to do."

"You're smart too, Destiny," Charmayne added. "Stop putting yourself down. We all are good, smart and talented young ladies. We just don't take no mess from nobody."

"I know that's right," Sweet insisted.

"There would have been a time when I would've given up, but I had to stay focused. I don't want the old Charmayne to surface."

"Charmayne, your behavior has changed a whole lot," Destiny said. "You don't play with no one."

"I thank God for having good people in my life, those who pushed me when I didn't want to be pushed. I'm no longer that rowdy person who doesn't care about anybody or anything. I take people's feelings into consideration. I just want people to respect me and not take me for granted."

"We all know how you can get," Sweet chimed in. "You know I got your back. I want someone to try you. They're going to regret seeing my face."

"They don't want the old Charmayne to come out," Destiny said.

Just as Charmayne and her friends were about to play a game of volleyball, several of the boys from the bicycle club showed up on the volleyball court.

"Can we play a game of volleyball with you all," Warner asked some of the older adults.

"Boy, you know you're not here to play a game of volleyball with us," Tiffany replied.

"What, you think we don't know how to play volleyball?" Trey challenged Tiffany.

"Girl, let's see what they all about," Marin said.

"Boy, we are going to send you back home with nothing to ride on with," Karin teasingly threatened.

"Well enough talking, let's get this game started," Gram declared.

Gram and his bicycle buddies knew exactly what they were doing on the volleyball court.

"Okay, I see they got a little experience in playing volleyball." Who taught them how to play volleyball?

Charmayne and her friends had a good time playing a game of volleyball against the older adults.

Just as Charmayne and her friends were leaving the volleyball court, Gram met Charmayne by the gate.

"Charmayne, can I walk you home?"

"Coming by my house would not be a good idea. I have to study for a math quiz for my first period class. I don't need no distraction. I need to pass this math quiz."

Gram understood what Charmayne was saying.

"I understand." Here's my number. Call me whenever you're ready too.

Gram wrote his number down on a piece of brown paper bag and handed it to Charmayne.

"Charmayne, if you don't mind, call me when you get home."

Charmayne smiled and put the piece of paper Gram wrote his number down on in her pocket.

"We'll see you and your buddies tomorrow," Destiny announced.

Gram and his friends rode away on their bicycles.

"Don't forget to call me too," Warner blurted to Sweet.

Gram and his friends rode off on their bikes.

"Girl, I can't wait for us to get bicycles," Marin said.

"And why is that?" Fran asked Marin.

"Me too Marin," Camryn said.

"Can you just answer my question?" Fran asked Marin.

"So we can hang out with them," Marin said.

"And why do you want to hang out with them?" Asked Fran.

"I think they are popular," Marin said.

"Riding a bicycle doesn't make you popular," Camryn said.

"Well to me it does," Marin said. "They get all the cool points."

"Girl, hush and let's go home," Charmayne said to Marin.

They all started laughing at how crazy Marin sounded.

Charmayne and her friends talked about how they beat the older adults in a game of volleyball.

"They thought they had the upper hand on us," Marin said.

"Yeah we had to prove them wrong," Destiny continued.

Charmayne and her friends enjoyed playing volleyball with some of the older adults. They especially loved to listen when the adults talked about their love lives with them.

It was not ever about who won or lost. Charmayne and her friends simply loved playing volleyball.

As Charmayne and her friends walked home, they noticed several friends from school walking their way. They all stopped to talk to one another.

"Girl, are you all ready for the math quiz we have to take tomorrow in first period?" Asked Trae.

"Girl, you already know I don't like math."

"Man, I do not like math," Sweet added. Math is not one of my favorite subjects.

"Mine either," Trae continued.

"You can give me anything else to take and I'd pass with flying colors, but not math."

"Well you don't have anything to worry about," Sweet said.

"And why do you think I don't have anything to worry about?"

"You know you're going to pass," Jazz chimed in.

"You know how the teacher is about his Charmayne," Sweet said teasingly.

"Well, I can't help it if I'm the teacher's favorite."

They all laughed at what Charmayne had said.

"Yeah we know you're the teacher pest," Camryn teased.

"What are you jealous? It's okay I have enough love to spread around." Charmayne clapped back.

Chapter 5

Why is He at My House?

It was a long school day for Charmayne. She was too tired to do anything or go anywhere. The pressures seemed to be catching u to her.

"Man, I'm so tired. I don't think I can function anymore. I just want to go home and crawl into my bed."

As Charmayne was getting off the bus she almost fell. Charmayne missed a step, but was able to catch her balance before anyone saw her.

Charmayne was glad nobody saw what happened. She was certain that if someone saw her misstep they would laugh at her.

I'm glad nobody saw me when I almost fell. If they did, I know somebody would've laughed at me. I know how my attitude is and if they definitely would've started laughing at me, I would have to curse them out from A to Z. I have zero tolerance when it comes to stupidity.

Before Charmayne was able to get settled in the house and relax her feet, her brother Rocky almost knocked her down.

"I'm so glad to see you," Rocky said.

Charmayne plopped down on the chair.

"Rocky, why are you so happy to see me?"

Rocky sat on Charmayne's lap.

Big as Rocky is, he got some nerves sitting on me. If he knows what I know, he better get off of me before I kick him on the floor. Tired as I am, I don't feel like being bothered by no one.

"Rocky, I just got home from school and here you are sitting on my lap. I know you have something up your sleeves. Besides, you're too heavy to sit in my lap. Get off of me before I push you down."

"You used to let me sit on your lap."

"Yeah that's when you were young. You're not young anymore. You probably can hold me."

"I'm glad to see you. How was your day in school Charmayne?"

"It was alright. Had a lot of tests to take in different classes. Your sister passed all her tests."

"Where is Marc?" Charmayne asked Rocky.

"He's down the street playing with his friends."

"Did you get an A on your math quiz?"

"No, I got a B on my math quiz."

Rocky was excited that Charmayne got a B on her math quiz.

"That's better than getting an F. I'm proud of you. See you thought you were going to fail, but you didn't. A job well done!"

Rocky gave Charmayne a big hug. "See I know you could do it. I had confidence in you."

"Well my body is aching, feet are sore, and my head hurts."

"Lay down and I'll take care of you."

"I appreciate everything you're doing for me, but I know you have something up your sleeve."

"Sis you deserve to be treated like a queen. You do a lot for us. You are always making sure we have this and that. You never complain about anything."

Rocky brought tears to Charmayne's eyes.

"You think you're slick but you're not. I know it's something you want me to do."

"You deserve to be treated like a queen."

"Boy, I'm on to your scheme. What do you want Rocky?"

"Can you take us to the park when you feel better? Some of my friends are going up there to play football."

"Did you ask momma if you can go to the park?"

"No, I was waiting for you to come home."

"Listen, you're not going to keep using me to take you to the park. You need to go and ask momma about you going to the park."

"You already know she's going to say we can't go."

"Well, I don't have anything to do with that."

"Please, Charmayne, will you ask mom if we can go to the park?"

"Give me a minute Rocky. I know you just saw me walking in the house. My feet are hurting me."

"My brother is too handsome. I'll do anything to keep him happy. My sisters and brothers love being around me. I'm their big sister and I have to protect them."

Charmayne laid back on the chair and propped her feet up on the table.

Rocky massaged Charmayne's head, rubbed her feet, and popped her fingers.

It felt so good to Charmayne, she dozed off.

Charmayne woke up when she felt a sharp pain in her stomach. She let out a loud scream. The pain started hurting Charmayne real bad.

"Charmayne, why are you holding your stomach?"

"Ma, I don't know. I just felt a sharp pain in my stomach."

"What did you have to eat at school?"

"I had a slice of pizza, a small salad and garlic bread. I don't know why my stomach is hurting."

Charmayne's mom gave her some aspirin to take for the pain.

"Take these two aspirin for pain. You'll feel better once you take these."

"Thanks ma."

Charmayne swallowed the pills with a cup of warm water.

She waited for a while before taking a shower. She wanted to wait and make sure she didn't have any side effects of the pill.

"After I get out of the shower, we'll walk to the storehouse."

"I don't have any money," Ty'Meisha said.

"Don't worry Ty'Meisha I'll buy you something," Rocky said.

"Well let me go take a shower so we can go to the storehouse."

Charmayne went into the bathroom to take a shower so she could take her sisters and brothers to the storehouse. They all had money except for Ty'Meisha.

"The water feels good running down my aching body. I try my best to teach my sisters and brothers about learning how to put money aside for a rainy day. But, for some unknown reason Ty'Meisha doesn't get the picture. She is always spending her money on foolishly instead of putting some to the side. I refuse to buy her something to snack on. She better thank her brother Rocky, because he just saved her."

Charmayne's mom went in the kitchen to fix some Kool-Aid for them to drink.

As Charmayne was taking a shower, she could hear her mom talking to someone.

"Who is it?" Charmayne's mom asked.

Charmayne couldn't make out the voice of the person. It sounded like Gram's voice, but she wasn't sure.

Charmayne's mom invited the young man to come in. They both introduced themselves to one another.

Charmayne couldn't believe Gram was actually at her house. Charmayne's knees got weak as she stood in the shower.

Charmayne heard her mom telling Gram he would have to come back later, because she had just got home from school.

"Yes, ma'am." he replied.

"I can't believe this boy is actually at my house. He got some nerve. Now that's what you call a bold ass person."

When Charmayne came out of the bathroom her sister Miracle ran up to her.

"That boy named Gram from the bicycle club came to see you," Miracle informed her.

"What did you just say Miracle?" My mom asked her.

Charmayne had to explain to her mom what Miracle meant by that.

"My big mouth sister Miracle always talks too damn much. She needs to learn how to stay in a child's place. That's why I don't like taking them anywhere with me. I can see why Sweet doesn't take her sisters to the park with her.

Charmayne's mom had a puzzled look on her face.

"Somebody better explain something to me. I don't want to stop the young man from coming here. He seems to be a nice and respectable young man."

"Mom, it doesn't mean that they are in a gang. It is a group of boys who like to ride their bicycles to the park. He's not in a gang or does anything dangerous."

"I was wondering what your sister Miracle meant by that."

"What did he say?" Charmayne asked Miracle.

"Momma told him he had to come back later because you just came home from school."

Charmayne's mom walked into the room Charmayne and Miracle were in.

"I think he's a nice young man with good manners. Miracle, go in your room and play. I need to talk to your sister."

"Yes ma'am."

"Ma, I don't know a whole lot about him or his family. All I know is they moved here from Wisconsin. He lives with his parents, brothers and sisters on Mind Yoke St."

After talking with her mom, Charmayne went into the room to finish getting dressed.

When Charmayne walked out her room, her sisters and brothers were all sitting in the living room waiting on her.

Charmayne's brother Marc was about to open the door when they heard a knock at the door.

"Who is it?" Charmayne asked.

"Charmayne it's me Gram.

Charmayne opened the door for Gram to come in.

"Wow, Gram looks good in his blue jean pants and white T-shirt. I don't know what kind of cologne he has on but it smells good too. He sure knows how to dress. Okay, I see you in your nice white sneakers. I guess he's trying to make his appearance noticeable."

Charmayne introduced Gram to her mom and her Uncle Smith.

"Mom and Uncle Smith, this is Gram."

"Hello Gram." Both Charmayne's mom and Uncle greeted him.

"We met one another yesterday while walking to the park."

"We heard a lot of great things about you Gram."

"Yes ma'am."

"What are your parents' names, young man?" Uncle Smith inquired.

Gram told my Uncle Smith his parent's last name and where they were from.

"It was nice meeting you Gram," Charmayne's mom said.

"I hope we can meet your parents as well," my Uncle Smith added. "I need to make sure my niece is not dating a criminal."

"Stop it, Smith," my mom said, addressing my Uncle.

"I'll see you all tomorrow," Uncle Smith announced.

""Nice meeting you sir."

"Nice meeting you too young man."

Charmayne didn't know who was more nervous, her or Gram.

Charmayne and Gram sat in the living room to talk for a bit.

"I'm going to go in my room so you all can talk," Her mom said, excusing herself.

Charmayne's sisters and brothers liked Gram.

"My sisters and brothers think they're slick. They like Gram because he buys them stuff."

"Would you like to take your sisters and brothers to the park while your mom is resting up?" Gram asked.

"I don't know. I have to ask my mom about that."

Charmayne got up and knocked on her mom's room door.

"Who is it?"

"Ma, it's me."

"Come on in Charmayne, the door isn't locked."

"Ma, is it okay if I take them to the park and run around for a while?"

"Be careful when crossing the street and make sure your sisters and brothers hold one another's hands."

"Yes ma'am, I will."

"You can leave my door open." I'll get up soon and lock the front door.

Charmayne walked out her mom's room and waved her hand bye at her.

Chapter 6

I'm Too Nervous

Before going to the park, Charmayne took her sisters and brothers to the storehouse. They bought snacks to have something to eat while at the park playing with their friends.

"Let's sit over here so we can keep our eyes on your sisters and brothers."

Gram made sure to keep his eyes on Charmayne's sisters and brothers.

Dang, Gram is making me nervous. I wish he would stop looking at me. My hands are sweating, and my legs won't stop shaking.

Charmayne fumbled her words while speaking with Gram.

"Is it okay if I walk you all home?" He asked.

"I would like that if you don't mind." She coyly replied.

At the park Charmayne sisters and brothers ran around with some of their friends from school.

I'm glad I can spend some time with Gram, while my sisters and brothers run around with their friends.

Charmayne's heart was beating so fast. She couldn't keep her eyes off of Gram. She stared at Gram from head to toe.

I love the way Gram smiles. He has such a handsome smile. Dang, Gram looked good sitting next to me. I don't know what kind of cologne Gram has on, but he smelled good as hell.

Miracle broke Charmayne's trance.

"I'm tired and ready to go home," Miracle beckoned.

Charmayne's sisters and brothers also stated that they were ready to go home.

When they arrived at Charmayne's house, their mom was sitting on the porch talking with one of the neighbors, Mr. Home.

"Hello everyone," Mr. Home said.

"How are you doing sir?" Gram asked Mr. Home.

"I'm blessed son and how are you doing?"

Charmayne introduced Gram to their neighbor Mr. Home.

"Goodnight everyone."

"Goodnight Gram."

"I'll call you when I get home."

"Okay, have a goodnight."

"Did you all have a good time at the park?"

"Yes ma'am, we did."

Miracle entered the house before everyone else.

When Charmayne walked in, Miracle was stretched out on the sofa sleeping peacefully.

Awww... Look at Miracle laying here sleeping peacefully. I need to wake her up so she can bathe. I know she's tired. After a shower, she'll feel much better.

After bathing Miracle, Charmayne put on her pajamas and laid her down on the bed.

"Don't go to sleep yet, Miracle, you have to eat."

"Okay, I want."

Charmayne opened the front door and called out to her sisters to come in and shower.

"Ty'Meisha and Gracie come inside so you can shower."

"Rocky, I'll come get you and Marc when they are finished"

"Okay," Rocky and Marc both replied.

After Charmayne's sisters and brothers got dressed for bed she went into the kitchen to fix them something to eat.

Charmayne's mom had cooked a good southern dinner. They had baked macaroni and cheese, baked chicken with brown gravy, cornbread, rice, pinto beans and fresh squeezed lemonade. They loved when their mom made fresh squeezed lemonade.

Boy am I tired. My body can't budge anymore.

Charmayne had to help take care of her sisters and brothers keeping her grades up so that she would graduate with her classmates as planned.

After making sure her sisters and brothers were put to bed, Charmayne headed to the bathroom to take a shower.

Charmayne's eyes were getting tired, but she fought to stay awake for when Gram called her.

The phone finally rang.

"Hey Charmayne, you sound like you're asleep."

"No, but I was about to."

Charmayne and Gram talked for a while before exchanging their goodnights.

When Charmayne's mom walked in the house everyone was sleeping in Charmayne's bed.

"Wow, my babies are all sleeping comfortably." I'm not going to move them, I'll just let them sleep.

"Goodnight my babies," Charmayne's mom whispered to them.

Chapter 7

Stop Being So Nosy

Charmayne's mom had to wake her up since her alarm clock didn't go off.

"Get up Charmayne you're going to be late for school."

Charmayne jumped up quickly.

"I didn't even hear my alarm go off."

"If you miss your bus, I'll take you to school."

"I think I still have time to get dressed."

Charmayne probably would have missed the bus if her mom didn't wake her up. When she got to the bus stop, her friend was waiting for her. They were waiting to hear the news about her and Gram.

"Tell me the news," Sweet said. I saw him walking to your house while I was cleaning out my mom's car.

"Wow, what would you like to know, Mrs. Nosey?"

"Everything and don't leave anything out. I saw you two walking together."

"Well, we took my sisters and brothers to the storehouse. If you saw all that, then you saw us walking toward the park too."

"Girl you are so dang nosey," Cleo chimed in.

"I know right," Charisma blurted out. "Every time you turn around she's up in somebody's business."

"I would be up in your business if you had any," Sweet teased.

"Oh I have business but you'll never know it," Charisma snapped back.

"Do you like him?" Sweet continued to pry.

"Stop it Sweet. Charmayne doesn't have to answer that question if she doesn't want to."

"Stop what Charisma? What am I doing?" Sweet persisted.

"You're really being too damn nosey for me." Charmayne pushed back.

Charmayne looked at Sweet as if she had lost her mind.

"Sweet, I'm not trying to sleep with him or any other guy. I'm taking things slowly with him. I'm not trying to rush into anything with him. I'm a virgin and I'm planning on keeping it that way. If he's that into me, then he'll understand and respect my feelings. I'm not ready to have sex, if that's what he's thinking."

"What did your mom say about him?" Sweet asked.

"Girl, why do you want to know what her mom said about him," Destiny asked.

"If I was you I wouldn't tell her anything," Marin said.

"Charmayne doesn't have to tell you whether her mom likes him or not," Fran added. "That's not any of your business."

"Well since you're all up in my business, let's talk about your boo thing."

"Yes Sweet, let's talk about your chocolate lover," Marin taunted.

"For your information Sweet, my mom knows I'm not going to do anything I'll regret later. She told me to take things slowly with him and don't let him take advantage of me."

"I know that's right," Cleo co-signed.

"I told my mom she doesn't have to worry about that, because I'm nobody's fool."

"That's what I like about you," Destiny remarked. "You don't take no mess from nobody."

"You got that right, Destiny," Charmayne agreed.

On Friday, Charmayne couldn't wait to get into some fun with her friends from school. The bus ran late as usual. Some of the students started walking home. It was an hour late and everyone was getting frustrated.

While Charmayne and her friends waited for the bus, Gram and some of his homeboys pulled up at their bus stop.

"Why are you still here?" Gram asked Charmayne.

"Well our bus is running late."

"Do you need a ride to school?"

"No Gram, my bus will be here soon."

Charmayne could overhear some of her friends in the background trying to figure out who the guy she was talking to was.

"Dang he drives a nice car," Lyric said.

"Does Charmayne know him?" Asked Kayla.

Charisma turned around to face Kayla.

"Dang you're nosey as hell," Charisma said. "For your information this is her boyfriend. Now close your mouth before something falls in it."

Charmayne and her friends couldn't do anything but laugh at what Charisma said.

"Girl you're crazy as hell," Charmayne said.

"Hey Destiny looks like your bus is coming," Trey said.

"Thanks Trey, I do have eyes," Destiny made known.

"Destiny, can I call you later?"

"Boy, be gone. You need to find somebody you can play games with, because I'm not the one."

Before stepping on the school bus, Gram winked his eyes at Charmayne.

"Gram, I'll call you when I get home."

"Have a good day in school, Charmayne."

They both waved at one another.

"Girl, I'm glad the bus came, because I almost got in the car with him."

"I was hoping you had so we could've all rode with them," Charisma said.

When Charmayne sat down in her seat some of her friends began asking a whole lot of questions.

"Dang I thought I was nosey, but you all beat me," Sweet said.

One of Charmayne's homeboys asked which school Gram attended.

"Why do you want to know what school he attends?"

"Because we beat them at every sport we play against them."

"What does that have to do with me? I can care less who beats who at sports. That has nothing to do with me. So what, our school beats them at every sport?

On Fridays, Charmayne really didn't do too much school work. In most of her classes they either watched movies, played board games or did trivia questions.

Charmayne had work study classes. If you had a work study class or a job, you could leave by noon. Since Charmayne was working at a department store she was able to leave at noon.

I'm glad I have this work study class. I can go home and get a little rest in before going to work.

Charmayne enjoyed working at the department store. It gave her the opportunity to learn the business and earn money to help pay for prom night, grad night at Disney World, and her cap and gown for graduation.

Charmayne was also able to buy her sisters and brothers a few things as well.

I'm so glad I can help my mom out with the bills. She's been carrying this load since my dad passed away. I can also do things for my sisters and brothers.

Several of Charmayne's friends had the same classes. On Fridays she was able to catch a ride with one of them.

Charmayne and her friend Fran stopped by a fast food restaurant to get something to eat. Charmayne paid for their food since Fran was giving her a ride home or to work.

Charmayne's parents always taught them, if someone does a good deed for you, make sure you do a good deed in return. You don't ever want to mess up things with good friends.

It's hard to find good friends like the ones I have. I cherished our friendship deeply.

"Thank you for bringing me home, Fran."

"No problem, Charmayne. That's what a friend does."

"Fran, you are one of my good friends. I don't know what I'd do without you."

"Talk to you later Charmayne. If you need a way to work, call me and I'll come and take you."

"Okay Fran, thanks."

Charmayne got out of Fran's car and closed the door behind her. Soon as Charmayne opened the front door, her sister Gracie ran up to her.

"Can you take us to the park please, pretty please?"

"Give me a minute to rest Gracie. I just got home and besides I have to go to work. There will be times when I can't take you, your sisters and brothers to the park. I have a job and it requires a lot of my attention." Charmayne pleaded.

"I understand," Gracie said.

"Just because I have a job doesn't mean we're not going to be hanging out together. I'm still going to play with you, your sisters and brothers. We're still going to do things we love to do together."

"Don't think you're going to the park every day to play with your little friends." You all have stuff here you can entertain yourselves.

"Yes Ma'am."

"You all have your bicycles you can ride on and games you can play with."

Charmayne's sisters didn't like the idea that they couldn't be with her like they were used to.

"I need to sit my sisters and brothers down and explain to them about my hours at work. They need to know why I'm not able to spend time with them like we used to. I know they hate it when I'm not with them. I have to spend quality time with them."

Charmayne explained to her sisters and brother that she had a job so she can buy them the things they need and to help their mom out with the bills.

"I need you all to know how important it is for me to work. I'm also involved with Gram. There will be days when it will just be me and him. Those days you all cannot hang out with us."

"We understand," Rocky said. "We like Gram and I know he makes you happy."

"Yes, he does make me happy Rocky."

"We know we can't be with you all the time, but please don't stop loving us," Ty'Meisha said.

Charmayne couldn't do anything but cry.

Charmayne could see that she was neglecting her sisters and brothers.

I don't believe Ty'Meisha just said that. I love each one of my sisters and brothers. It hurts me to know I'm hurting them by not doing the things we used to do together. I need to start paying closer attention to my sisters and brothers and their feelings.

"I will never stop loving either one of you. I don't ever want you to think I don't love you or don't want to be around you, because I do. I'm working so we can have a better life, I'm working so I can help momma out with the bills. I'm working so I can make sure you all have the things you want and need."

Charmayne started crying even harder.

"Don't cry Charmayne. I never meant to hurt you. I know you love us. I know you would never neglect us."

"We know you love us," Gracie said.

"You all mean everything to me. Nobody will ever take your place and don't you ever forget it. If I get off early today, I'll take you all to the park. I promise."

"We love you Charmayne. We're sorry for making you feel like this."

"No problem. I know you all are looking out for me. Your sister is a big girl. I know how to handle myself."

Charmayne, her sisters and brothers gave each other a hug. She made sure to kiss each one on the cheek.

"I'm very proud of you all. Understand that sometimes things can't always go your way."

"We understand Charmayne."

"Thanks for understanding the things I'm saying to you. Well, your big sister has to get ready for work."

After taking a shower, Charmayne went into the room to get dressed for work. As Charmayne was getting dressed, she heard her mom talking to Gram. Charmayne heard her mom telling Gram she was getting ready for work. When Charmayne opened her room door, she heard Gram telling her mom he could take her to work if she wanted him too.

"I'll take her to work for you if you want me too."

"Momma, are we still going to church tonight?" Asked Miracle.

45

"Yes, since Gram is taking Charmayne to work for me."

How does my mom know if I want Gram to take me to work? What if I wanted her to take me to work?

When Charmayne walked in the living room, Gram was talking to Rocky and Marc about football.

"Hey Gram, how are you?"

"I'm doing well, Charmayne."

"Gram said he will take you to work while we go to church."

Oh, so Gram volunteered to take me to work?

Charmayne looked at Gram strangely.

"Ma, did you just say Gram said he would take me to work?"

"Yes, he said he'll take you to work while we go to church."

Charmayne kissed her mom, sisters, and brothers on their cheeks.

"I'll see you all later. Have fun at church."

"Don't let them people work you too hard," Rocky said.

"Rocky, you know your sister has to work hard. That's what keeps money in your pocket."

"I know Charmayne. I was just playing with you."

"Ty'Meisha, if you want to go the park tomorrow, you better be good in church."

"I'm always good."

Chapter 8

My Very First Kiss

On the way to Charmayne's job, Gram and Charmayne laid everything out on the table about their relationship.

"Charmayne, would you like to date me?"

"I thought we were already dating."

Charmayne was glad they had pulled into the parking lot at her job. She did not want to answer Gram's questions.

I'm so glad we pulled into the parking lot at my job. Gram is asking me too many questions that I am unable to answer.

Before getting out of the car, Charmayne told Gram what time she gets off.

"I'll be here to pick you up," Gram replied without hesitation.

"Thank you," Charmayne replied.

Charmayne got out of the car and waved goodbye to Gram.

It was around eight p.m. when Charmayne punched out. Sure enough Gram was sitting in his car waiting for her. A big smile came across her face when she saw Gram.

I don't know what it is, but Gram got something on me. Every time I

47

see him, he just melts my heart away. I get a tingly feeling when I'm with him.

When Gram saw Charmayne walking toward his car he got out and opened the door for her.

Charmayne thought that was quite romantic of him.

"How was your day at work?" He inquired.

"It was okay. I like working here. It helps me out with stuff I need for school. I can now help my mom out with the bills."

Charmayne was in the eleventh grade. She had two jobs. She worked full time at a fast food restaurant and part time at a retail store.

"When do you graduate Charmayne?"

"I graduate next year. Why do you ask?"

"I'm just asking, that's all."

"I made some bad decisions in school and now I'm paying for my mistakes. I need one point zero credit to graduate."

"I'm glad you made the right choice in turning your life around."

"Well there may be days when you may not see me."

Gram looked at Charmayne as if she had said something bad.

Why is Gram looking at me like that? I'm just being honest with him. There will be days that we won't be able to spend time together.

"I'm here for you Charmayne. I will never pressure you into anything you don't want to do. I'm here for you whenever you need me. If that means I need to step back a little until you get things right, then that's what I'll have to do."

"Yes I know you're here for me. I know you won't try to pressure me or have me do anything I'm not comfortable doing."

"Charmayne, I'm not like that. I wouldn't do that to you. I wouldn't do anything to hurt you or make you feel uncomfortable."

"Listen Gram, if you're with me for sex I'm not the one for you. We can end this now before it goes any further. We can stop being friends and we can go our separate ways. I don't want to lead you on in anyway. I'm not ready to have sex. I hope you understand."

"Listen Charmayne, I'm not that type of guy. I don't want you to think I'm just with you for sex. Sex is not on my mind. I like hanging out with you and your family. I see good potential in you. I like you a lot and I want to be your boyfriend."

Gram assured Charmayne that wasn't like that and he simply wanted to get to know her better.

"Gram, I'm not that type of girl either. I don't want to give you the wrong idea about me as well."

"Charmayne when I first met you, I said to myself 'I think this could be the one for me.' I didn't stop until I had the opportunity to meet you."

Charmayne explained to Gram what her goals were and what she wanted to accomplish in life.

"I want you to know nothing is going to stand in the way of me reaching my goals."

"I agree with you on that Charmayne." I promise to back you up one hundred percent. I just want to get to know who you are if you let me. I like hanging out with you, your sisters and brothers. They keep me entertained. Besides, I enjoy their company.

"Well, my sisters and brothers like you a lot too. All they talk about is you. They always ask me when you're coming over."

Gram started laughing.

He talks a good game and he seems to be a gentleman. Why not give him a chance?

As Gram was drove, he noticed Charmayne was stuck in a deep daze.

"Are you okay, Charmayne?"

"Yes, I'm okay. I was just thinking about school and work."

Charmayne lied. She wasn't about to tell Gram what she was really thinking.

"Are you hungry?"

"Yes, I'm hungry."

Charmayne and Gram went to a fast food restaurant and both ordered a Deluxe Burger Meal with a sprite to drink.

While they ate, Charmayne noticed four girls talking and staring in their direction. One of the girls started laughing.

A little jealousy came across Charmayne's face, but she couldn't get mad.

Gram is a handsome young man with nice swag.

Gram made it known that he was with Charmayne. He wasn't thinking about any of those other females.

She was shocked when Gram got up from where he was sitting, and came and sat down next to her. He wrapped his arm tightly around her and it made her feel good. She felt he respected her.

"Baby, I'm with you. You don't have to worry about me looking at another woman. I want to be with you and you only."

"I'm not worried. A man is going to do what he wants to do. Those are your eyes. You can look at whomever you please."

"Charmayne I don't want to be with another girl or look at another girl. My eyes are only on you."

"If I wasn't with you, you were going to look at them anyway. Don't let me stop you from looking at them."

Gram was shocked at what Charmayne said.

But it was the truth. He was going to look at them if I wasn't with him.

"Gram, just be honest with me."

"Charmayne, I'm being honest with you."

"You're not with me just to have sex are you?"

"Baby I'm not. I really want to be with you. I would like for us to be a couple."

"I don't know you like that. I need to get to know you a little bit more before I can say I'll be your girlfriend. We need to take things a little slower and let mother nature take its course."

Gram agreed with what Charmayne was saying.

"I'm not going to rush you into a relationship or to be with me. I'll wait until you're ready to be a couple."

"I'm glad you understand about us getting to know each other and taking it slow. I need to get to know who you are and what your expectations are with me."

Gram didn't know what else to say to Charmayne. All he knew was that Charmayne was the one he wanted to be with.

Gram knew he had to change the subject quickly before things got out of hand.

"What would your mom, sisters and brothers like to eat?" he asked.

Charmayne told Gram what her mom, sisters and brothers liked to eat. Gram walked up to the counter and ordered their food. After receiving the food from the cashier, Charmayne and Gram walked out to his car hand in hand.

Charmayne noticed her mom's car wasn't in the driveway when they pulled in the yard.

"I would invite you in, but I'm not allowed to have anyone in the house while my mom's not home."

"I understand."

Gram sat on the porch while Charmayne took the food in the house. When Charmayne came back outside she sat down next to him.

When Charmayne looked up, she noticed Gram looking at her. A smile came across Charmayne's face.

"Why are you looking at me like that?"

"I was just admiring the way you look."

"Thanks for taking me to work and picking me up."

"No problem."

Gram grabbed Charmayne's hand and squeezed it gently.

The touch of Gram's hand feels so smooth. It's something about the touch of his hands. It makes me want to melt in his arms.

"Would you consider being my girlfriend, Charmayne?"

"Excuse me, what did you just ask me?"

Gram repeated it again to Charmayne. He wanted to make it known that he wanted to be in a relationship with her.

"Would you consider being my girlfriend? I know you're probably shocked, but I would like for us to be a couple."

I know Gram did not just ask me to be his girlfriend. What's wrong with him? He's forward with his words and with the way he feels about me.

Charmayne couldn't say anything. She was in disbelief at what Gram had just said to her. She tried to change the subject and talk about something else, but he wasn't taking no for an answer.

"I had a good time tonight. Thanks for buying me something to eat."

"Oh, that's nothing." *I believe in making my woman feel special.*

"Well, it's getting late and I need to get ready for bed."

Charmayne and Gram both stood up. Gram grabbed Charmayne's hands and started walking toward her. Gram kissed Charmayne on her lips. Charmayne's knees buckled.

Gram's kiss tasted like a smooth chocolate almond bar. I could've continued letting him slobber all over me, but I had to stop myself before it went any further. I have to maintain myself before I end up giving Gram my sweetness.

Charmayne pushed Gram away from her.

"I think we both need to stop before something happens between us. Don't get me wrong, I enjoyed every moment of it."

"I do apologize for what I just did. I don't know what came over me."

"There's nothing to apologize for. I wanted it to happen as well."

Charmayne and Gram both said goodnight.

Chapter 9

Just Wishing

After saying their goodbyes, Charmayne went into the house and closed the door behind her without waving bye at Gram. She was shocked that Gram kissed her. She lost herself thinking about their first kiss.

Gram shocked me when he kissed me on my lips. Go on boy with your bad self. Gram had no shame to his game.

Charmayne secretly wished and hoped Gram would continue kissing her. She knew it was wrong, but it felt good.

I wish Gram would have continued kissing me. His lips tasted like a sweet chocolate almond bar.

Charmayne wondered how it would feel having sexual intercourse with Gram. Her womanhood ached for Gram's touch.

What is this running down on my legs? Oh my God, I can't believe my sweet juice is running down my legs. Dang I'm just aching for Gram's touch. Better get up and go take me a nice warm shower. Maybe taking a shower will take my mind off having sex with Gram.

Charmayne headed to the bathroom to shower. She had to get her mind back to reality. While Charmayne was taking a shower, she heard the front door open.

I'm glad my mom didn't catch us kissing. I know my mom would've been mad at me. She probably would have told Gram he's not allowed back at our house.

Ty'Meisha started knocking on the bathroom door.

"Charmayne, it's me Ty'Meisha. Can I come in?"

"Ty'Meisha give me a minute and I'll be out."

"I just want you to know we're home."

"Okay, I'll be out in a minute."

Ty'Meisha opened the door without Charmayne's permission.

I know my little sister Ty'Meisha did not just open this bathroom door when I specifically told her I'd be out in a minute. Now, she's really looking for me to knock her ass out.

"Ty'Meisha close the bathroom door. Didn't your sister just tell you she'll be out in a minute? Don't make me go in my room and get my belt."

"Ty'Meisha you know better," Marc said. "You don't open the bathroom when someone is in there."

Ty'Meisha started crying.

"Ty'Meisha stop crying. I'm about to get out now."

Charmayne stepped out of the shower, dried herself off and put on her pajamas. She didn't want Ty'Meisah to be waiting on her long.

I don't want Ty'Meisha to wait on me too long. If she doesn't stop crying, my mom is going to beat her and make her go to bed.

Charmayne knew she had to calm Ty'Meisha down and stop her from crying.

Ty'Meisha was glad to see her big sister Charmayne. When Charmayne came out of the bathroom Ty'Meisha ran straight to her.

"Ty'Meisha listen, when someone is using the bathroom you have to wait until that person comes out and then you can go in."

"I was just trying to let you know that we were home that's all."

"I have a surprise for you all in the kitchen."

"Charmayne, what did you get us?" Miracle asked.

"Go look in the kitchen and you will see."

"Hey mom, how was church?"

"We had a glorious time."

"How was your day at work?"

"It was okay. We weren't that busy. I sold at least twenty-five pairs of shoes. Gram brought some food for all of you. The food is in the oven."

"I was just about to go into the kitchen and fix some peanut butter and jelly sandwiches for us to eat."

"Well you don't have to do that."

"That was very nice of Gram."

Charmayne sisters Ty'Meisha and Miracle were happy to play with the toys they found in their happy meal bags.

"Thank you," each one said.

"You're welcome."

Charmayne's sister Miracle started asking her a lot of questions.

"Charmayne, what did you do at work today? Were the customers nice to you? Did you take a break? How many pairs of shoes did you sell?"

"Miracle, why are you asking me all these questions?"

"I was only trying to see how your day was at work."

"How was church? Did you cry in church? Did you sit by your friends? Did you sing with the choir?"

"Stop asking me all those questions, I'm only six years old."

Charmayne and her mom couldn't do anything but laugh at Miracle.

"Well Miracle, I guess you know how it feels when someone asks you a lot of questions."

"I'm about to go to bed." I'm tired, my feet hurt and my body is sore. I've worked extra hard today.

"Alright baby, go lay down." We're finished cleaning up.

"Goodnight everyone."

"Goodnight Charmayne."

After Charmayne's brothers and sisters finished eating their food, they all chip in to clean up the kitchen.

"Go in the room, put on your pajamas and get ready for bed."

"Yes ma'am." They all responded.

Charmayne was so tired she forgot to pray with her sisters and brothers. Her sisters and brothers walked in her room without knocking on her door.

"Charmayne, wake up," Marc pleaded.

"Why are you all in my room?"

Charmayne couldn't figure out why her sisters and brothers were looking at her strangely.

"Why are you all looking at me like that?"

"I'm mad at you," Rocky said.

"Why are you mad at me? What did I do this time?"

Miracle looked at Charmayne with an attitude.

"Since Rocky is mad at me, what is your excuse, Miracle?"

"You forgot to pray with us."

"I'm so sorry Miracle, I forgot."

"Are you going to pray with us before you go to sleep?" Charmayne apologized to her brothers and sisters, because she had forgotten.

"Can you all forgive me? I totally forgot to pray before going to bed."

I really forgot to pray with my sisters and brothers. I'm glad they reminded me. I just love my sisters and brothers.

"Yes, I am going to pray with you."

They all got down on their knees and begin praying. Before going to bed, they always made sure to kiss one another good night and pray

"Before going to bed, my parents always made sure we prayed together as a family.

After praying, they kissed one another on their cheek.

"I love you," Marc said.

That made Charmayne feel good.

"I love you too, Marc." I love all of you.

"Goodnight Charmayne," they all said.

"Goodnight everyone."

Charmayne turned on the radio and listened to some soft music to go with the mood she was feeling.

Charmayne felt her body getting tired. She could still feel the warmth of Gram's arms around her waist and his lips gently but passionately touching hers. Her body impulsively began throbbing and repeating the same rhythm Gram moved in.

I've never been with a guy before. My friends always telling me how bad and painful it is when you first have sex. The touch of his hands caressing my body and his lips touching mines was amazing. He knew exactly what spot to touch to make me call out his name. His hands were caressing my breasts. His fingers entering my womanhood. I can feel the wetness flowing down my legs. I began to moan and call out his name. I wanted him to enter inside my womanhood. I was ready for Gram to make love to me. I wanted him to make me feel like a woman. Gram was pleasing me in a way I've never experienced before. I begged him to enter inside me.

"No, I want to make sure I'm pleasing you and you're being satisfied.

"I can't take it anymore Gram." Baby, please give it to me.

Gram kept pleasing Charmayne in every way he could. He began to put his manhood inside her. Charmayne begin to rock to Gram's rhythm moving in a slow pace. Charmayne started crying and calling out Gram's name telling him to go faster and deeper.

"Baby why are you crying?"

"It feels good. Don't stop, please keep going."

Gram started squeezing Charmayne more and more. She felt herself about to explode. Charmayne screamed out for Gram's to go deeper and give it to her good. Gram definitely hit the spot. Hitting the right spot made Charmayne call out his name.

"Baby, I'm coming."

"Baby, I'm coming too."

Charmayne and Gram both climaxed together. It made Charmayne body jerk a little. After making love, Charmayne and Gram both lay in each other arms reminiscing on what had just occurred between them.

Charmayne woke up to the smell of eggs, grits, bacon, and toast. Miracle ran in to Charmayne's room to wake her up so she could eat breakfast.

"Get up Charmayne, momma is cooking breakfast."

"Okay, I'm about to get up."

"Get up and go wash your face so you can eat with us."

"Yes, momma Miracle."

Miracle thought that was funny. She couldn't stop laughing.

"I'm not your momma. Momma is in the kitchen cooking breakfast."

Miracle always knew how to make Charmayne smile.

"Well, let me get up so I can go and wash up. I'll meet you in the kitchen, Miracle."

Charmayne felt a wet spot on her sheets.

What the hell? How did this spot get on my sheets?

She suddenly remembered where the spot came from.

"Wow, my dream felt like it was real."

She rushed and changed the linens on her bed. After that, Charmayne headed into the bathroom to shower up before having her breakfast.

Chapter 10

Family Is Everything

It was a Saturday morning. The wind felt nice and warm. After taking a shower, Charmayne noticed that her mom and siblings weren't home.

Now how is Miracle going to tell me to go wash up for breakfast and they're not even in the house.

Charmayne opened the front door and noticed they were all sitting on the porch eating breakfast without her.

"Good morning everyone."

"Good morning," they said in unison.

No matter what, my mom always cooks breakfast for us. She made sure we always had a good breakfast in the morning and a well balanced dinner at night.

Charmayne went into the kitchen to fix her food. After fixing her food, Charmayne went outside and ate breakfast with her family on the porch. The street was filled with children riding their bicycle, roller-skating or skateboarding. A lot of the neighbors were either washing their clothes or hanging them out on the clothesline to dry, washing their cars, mowing their grass or just sitting on the porch eating breakfast and drinking coffee with family or friends.

"Charmayne, you must have had a hard day at work last night."

"No, everything was good. Why would you say that?"

"When I was going to the bathroom, I kept hearing you saying something in your sleep."

Charmayne had to come up with a quick lie to tell her mom. She wasn't about to tell her mom what she was really saying in her sleep.

"The customers were aggravating me a lot, but I kept my cool."

"What happened last night at the store?"

"The customers would ask me to get them certain types of shoes to try on and then at the last minute they changed their mind."

I hate lying to my mom. I know it's not right, but I wasn't about to tell her what really was on my mind.

"I was so busy in the shoe department, that's probably why I was tossing and talking in my sleep."

"I know you work hard at what you do. Don't let people take you out of your character. You are better than that."

Charmayne tried her best to keep her customers happy and satisfied. She wanted the customers to keep coming back to the store and buy things.

"Yeah because you almost woke me up out of my sleep," Gracie said. "That's how loud you were talking."

"I was trying to figure out what was going on in your room," Rocky said. I started to come in there"

"The only way you can come into my room, if you knock on my door and I tell you to come in. If either one of you comes into my room without my approval, I'm going to knock you into next week, so don't try me."

"How can you knock someone into next week?" Asked Ty'Meisha.

"Come in my room and you will find out."

"Okay everybody better close their mouth, before I cut some butts."

"Yes ma'am," they all said.

Boy, I'm glad it was only a dream. Having sex was way out of the question for me. I have goals and I'm determined to reach them. My goals are to walk across the stage with my class, receive my diploma, land a good job and attend college. I wasn't about to let nothing or no one stand in the way of achieving my goals. I promised my dad he would be proud of me.

Charmayne's life growing up wasn't complicated, it was good. After her father passed away she had to help raise her sisters and brothers.

"My mom is all we have." We have to make sure we're there for her. Nobody and I mean nobody is going to disrespect my mom in no kind of way. If they do, than they will have to deal with me. I promise you that. Try my mom and see what will happen to you.

Charmayne, her sisters and brothers would be lost if it wasn't for their mom. Sometimes when Charmayne walks past her mom's room, she'll see her mom crying and on her knees praying for her children. Her mom is saved, sanctified and filled with the Holy Ghost. Her mom was always praying for them, asking God to protect them and not let them make bad decisions in their lives.

I'm going to always be here for my mom, sisters and brothers. My family means everything to me. My mom means the world to me.

"Mom, no matter what I'm always going to be here for you. . I promise to protect you and help you out with the things you need. I'm going to help you out with the bills."

After they ate breakfast, Charmayne's mom reached for their plates and cups to wash.

"No momma, you sit down, I got this. You're always doing things for us. Now it's our time to take care of you."

"Thanks, but I can do this, it's no problem."

Charmayne and her sisters went into the house to wash the dishes. Charmayne gave her sisters and brothers chores to do around the house.

"We all need to start paying attention to mom and making sure she doesn't have to keep cleaning up behind us," Charmayne said.

"You're right Charmayne, Momma is always doing for us. We never stopped to think about what mom needs. It's time for us to be here for her." Rocky said.

"Since Dad is no longer with us, we need to put mom's needs before ours. Momma is going to need us more than she ever needed us before. She's so use to daddy paying all the bills and making sure we had the things we need." Ty'Meisha added.

"I totally agree with you on that, Rocky," Gracie said. "It is time we start paying more attention to mom. We shouldn't have to wait for momma to tell us to clean up. We should already know what to do."

"As of now, each one of us will have a chore to do around the house. I expect each one of you all to perform your duty. I better not see either one of you slacking around the house. If I catch you not doing what I've asked you to do, you will have to deal with me. I promise you, it won't be anything nice." Charmayne was serious.

"We all are giving you our word about helping out around the house."

"I'm telling you now, I meant what I said."

Charmayne's brothers dusted the furniture, swept, and mopped the living room floor. They all wanted their mom to relax and enjoy her day. Their mom deserved the best, they all agreed. After the chores were all done, Charmayne asked her mom if it was okay if she could take them to the park.

"Ma, is it okay if I take them to the park? We think you should enjoy your day and relax."

"Just be careful when crossing the streets."

Charmayne made sure the house was sparkling clean and nothing was out of place.

"You better behave yourself and listen to your sister while at that park. Charmayne better not come home and tell me either one of you wasn't listening to her."

"Yes ma'am," they all said.

Just as Charmayne, her sisters and brothers were getting ready to walk out the door, Gram was standing there with his fist balled up getting ready to knock on the door. Charmayne and Gram both smiled at one another.

"Hello Charmayne, how are you?"

"Hello Gram, what are you up too?"

"You must have known I was thinking about you."

"And why is that Gram?"

"I couldn't sleep last night. All I could do was think about you. I had to come see you. The smile you have on your face makes my day."

Charmayne's sisters and brothers started laughing at Gram.

"Oh Charmayne, I couldn't sleep last night," Rocky said. "Baby, you were heavy on my mind. I had to come and see you."

Charmayne started laughing at Rocky's comment.

"Rocky, you need to stop mocking Gram."

"We're getting ready to walk to the park, you're welcome to tag along if you want too."

"Is your mom home?"

"Why do you want to know if my mom is home?"

"We're having a cookout/birthday party for Warner's son."

"Charmayne can we go to Warner Jr. birthday party?" Asked Rocky.

"He did mention that his parents were throwing him a party," Gracie said. "It would be nice to show our support for him."

"Gracie, I know you have a crush on Warner Jr. We boys talk all the time. Besides, he asked me if you had a boyfriend."

"And what did you tell him, Rocky?"

"I don't want none of my sisters dating any of my friend's brothers."

"And why is that Rocky?" Asked Charmayne.

"Because you have to make sure your homeboys don't mistreat your sisters. I don't want to have to beat up my homeboys because of the things they're doing to my sisters. I rather for my sisters to date someone I'm not that close to."

"You're right about that, Rocky," Gram said. "I'm the same way when it comes to my sisters. I'd hate to beat up any of my friends as well. I understand where you're coming from. When it comes to my sisters, I don't play no games."

"See Gram, that's what I'm talking about. You understand what I'm saying. My sisters think I'm being too hard on them." Rocky divulged.

"I have to ask my mom if it's okay for us to go. I totally forgot about the cookout/birthday party Marin and Warner were having."

Charmayne went into the house to ask her mom if they could go to a cookout/birthday party for one of her friend's sons. She knocked on her mom's room door.

"Come in."

"Mom, I forgot my friend Marin and Warner had invited us to their cookout/birthday for their son Warner Jr. I wanted to know if it was okay if we went."

"Yes, I know Warner Jr. His mom wanted me to come and help her with the decorations. I'm too tired to go anywhere."

"Come on mom and get dressed. We all can go together."

"You all can go. I'm going to stay home and rest while you all are at the cookout. Make sure you keep your eyes on your sisters and brothers. I want you all to have a good time with your friends."

"Yes ma'am. I'll keep my eyes on them. They are going to be happy knowing we're going to the cookout/birthday party. They had forgotten about the party just like me."

"Make sure you call me when you get there."

"Yes, ma'am."

Charmayne turned around and walked over to where her mom was lying at and kissed her on the forehead.

"See you later ma."

"Have a good time." Don't drink anything someone gives you unless you see them pouring it for you with your eyes.

"Yes, ma'am I will."

Charmayne made sure everything was shut off and all the windows were closed and locked.

When Charmayne walked outside, Gram was throwing the ball to her brothers.

Charmayne's sisters were talking to their friend Charmin from down the street.

"Did you ask momma if we can go to the party?" Asked Gracie.

"Yes we can go, but just be careful. If you all don't listen to me, I will tell ma."

Charmayne, brothers and sisters were excited about going to Warner Jr. birthday party.

They all loaded in Gram's truck. Gram had a truck with three rows in it.

Marin and Warner have a son name Warner Jr. and a daughter name War'Neisha. They all are friends with Charmayne and Gram.

Charmayne never thought those two would get together and have kids. Warner and Marin always had a love for one another.

Charmayne used to tell Marin that she and Warner should be a couple.

"I knew one day Warner and Marin were going to be together. They always were talking about one another and calling each other names. I can remember they used to pass love licks while playing around at the park."

Marin always thought Warner was handsome, but aggravating. She always use to tell Charmayne that one day they were going to get married and have kids together.

On the way to Warner and Marin house, Charmayne and Gram talked about the love Warner and Marin had for one another.

"I'm so proud of my friend," Charmayne said. "My friend was in love with Warner, but was too afraid to let him know how she felt about him."

"Marin should've said something to Warner," Gram said. "Well, Warner had a crush on Marin as well. He used to tell me some nice things about her."

"Oh he did?" What did he say about Marin?

"Man, I want to date Marin, but I don't know if she likes me. She reminds me of my grandmother and how sweet she was."

"What does his grandmother have to do with them liking one another?"

"Come to think about it, Marin does remind me of Warner's grandmother.

"What do you mean about Marin reminds you of Warner's grandmother?"

"Marin is humble and sweet. You will never catch her in a bad mood or have an attitude with someone. That's how Warner grandmother was. Nothing nobody did or said about her would get her upset. She always kept a smile on her face. I'm glad those two are in a relationship and are doing well."

"Yeah, me too." Marin is very sweet. I'm so glad to have her as a friend. Who would have thought those two would be living together and having kids? They both shocked me.

"Well I knew he wanted to be with her. He told me that he wasn't going to stop until he made her his wife."

"Are you serious? Marin used to tell me the same thing. Well, I guess they both got what they deserve."

"They deserve one another."

When they arrived at Warner's and Marin's house, there were a lot of cars in their driveway and alongside the road.

"It's a lot of cars here, Ty'Meisha said.

"Well, it's a party Ty'Meisha" Marc said.

"You don't think I know that."

"Listen, both of you need to be quiet before I take you back home."

"Okay Charmayne," both Marc and Ty'Meisha said.

"You all better act like you have some sense." I hate to take you back home and miss out on the party.

"We will Charmayne," they all said.

They all got out of Gram's truck. They were ready to have fun and play with their friends.

Warner met them at the front door just as they were about to knock on the door.

"Charmayne, I'm glad to see you," Warner said.

"Why are you glad to see me, Warner?"

"You need to help Marin. She needs help with the decoration and help putting up the balloons."

"So, why didn't you help Marin put up the balloons?" Asked Sweet.

"Sweet be quiet and go help Marin put up the balloons," Warner said.

Charmayne and her friends burst out laughing at what Warner had said to Sweet. They all went in the house to help Marin with the decorations and help put up some balloons.

Marc and Rocky went to play with Warner Jr. and the other boys who were playing basketball in the backyard.

Charmayne and her sisters went into the house to help Marin put up balloons for the party.

"Hey Charmayne," Destiny said. "I'm so glad you're here."

"Yes, we need help with these balloons," Sweet said.

"I knew my bestie would come and save the day," Marin said.

"So, I guess you all need my help."

"Help is not the word," Fran said. "I don't think I have enough air in my body to blow up another balloon."

"Me either Fran," Charisma gasped, "No more air for me."

Charmayne began blowing up balloons to help her friends out.

"The decorations look good, Marin."

"Thanks bestie. Do you think I need to put up some more decorations?"

"No, everything looks good, bestie. You did a wonderful job."

"I know who to call to decorate my house if I have a party," Sweet said.

"Yes Marin you did a marvelous job with the decorations," Charisma said.

After helping decorate the house, Charmayne and her friends went outside to put balloons around the gate and fence.

The kids were having a ball playing musical chairs.

Everybody was having a good time at the cookout/birthday party for Warner Jr.

Gram and Charmayne sat next to each other talking and enjoying the festivities.

"Charmayne, there's something I need to say to you."

"What is it that you need to say to me Gram?"

"Charmayne, I just want you to know how much I care about you."

"I care about you too, Gram."

"I would love to spend the rest of my life with you. You mean the world to me."

"Gram, where is all this coming from? I know you love me, but you're going too fast for me. You need to stop your brakes a little."

"Charmayne when we're together, I can see the happiness in your eyes. I don't know where all this is coming from, but you mean everything to me. My heart beats a double beat when I'm around you."

"Gram you mean a lot to me too, but we need to take it slow. Love doesn't grow overnight. The words you're saying are powerful."

"Charmayne, I don't care how long it takes, I want us to be a couple."

"Gram, you're scaring me."

Gram reached into his pocket and pulled out a ring. He wanted Charmayne to be his girlfriend.

"Charmayne, this is a promise ring I would like for you to have."

Good thing no one was looking at what Gram had given Charmayne.

"I can't believe this boy is really giving me a ring." What the hell?

"Gram the ring is beautiful, but I can't take it."

"I know, but I want you to have it. It's just a promise ring."

"Why are you giving me a promise ring?"

"It symbolizes the love we have for one another. Charmayne, I would love for you to be my girlfriend."

"Gram, I can't take this ring. You keep saying you love me, but we barely know each other."

"Charmayne, I really do love you and I don't care who knows it."

"What do you mean you love me? You don't even know me like that to say you love me."

"I know we don't know one another like that, but I know where my heart is. My heart is for us to be together."

"Gram, can you please tell me where all this is coming from?"

"Charmayne, I just feel in my heart that you're the one for me. I can't see myself with anybody else but you."

Good thing everybody was doing their own thing and not paying Charmayne and Gram any attention. They probably would have forgotten about the cookout/party for Warner Jr. Knowing Charmayne's friends, they probably would have told her to go for it.

"Gram you need to bring it down a notch. I think we need to talk about this later. For you to give me a ring and then say you love me, you're really scaring me."

"Charmayne, I'm not trying to scare you. I'm just letting you know how I feel about you. I don't mean to put any pressure on you."

"Gram, just let me think about what you're saying. I need to make sure this is something I want to do. Don't get me wrong, I care about you as well. When we're together, you make me feel special. You make me laugh and you keep me on my toes. Besides all that, my family loves you as well."

"Charmayne, it's the truth. You mean a lot to me. Nothing is going to change the way I feel about you. I definitely don't want you to feel any different about me."

"Wow, this is a lot to take in all at one time."

Charmayne was silent. She couldn't say a word.

Yes, I believe I love Gram as well, but it's too soon to get serious with him. I really didn't know what to say after all that. He took my breath away. What have I done for him to say he loves me?

After Charmayne and Gram had their little conversation, they went on to party with their friends.

"Girl, I was looking all over for you," Sweet said.

"Yeah me too," Charisma said.

"Well evidently you weren't looking that hard. Gram and I were over in the corner talking."

"Marin was looking for you as well," Destiny said. "She's trying to put the leftover food in containers."

"Okay, let's go in the house and help her out. I know she's going to need our help. We have a lot of decorations to take down and put away."

Charmayne helped Marin clean up the house while Fran, Destiny, Sweet, Charisma and Cleo put the food away.

The kids were still outside playing. They were having a ball. Everyone at the party was just like family, although they are all actually friends.

The guys were playing a card game called spades. They reminisced on the good old days.

Charmayne's sisters and brothers were getting tired. They were ready to go home.

"Charmayne I'm getting tired," Ty'Meisha said.

"Okay, we're about to leave. Go tell your sisters and brothers to go get in the truck."

Charmayne and Gram thanked Marin and Warner for inviting them to the cookout/birthday party.

"Warner, I just want to say thank you for inviting us. We had a wonderful time."

"Gram, you're my boy. I couldn't leave my homeboy. You already know how we roll."

"You got that right. Warner, you know I'm here for you when you need me."

Before leaving Charmayne, her sisters and brothers made sure to say goodnight to everyone.

"Good night everyone."

"Goodnight Charmayne," everyone replied back.

"Marin thanks for inviting us, we had a blast."

"Charmayne thanks for coming over. I couldn't have done it without you. You are a lifesaver. I know I can count on you to come through for me."

Charmayne and Marin hugged one another goodnight.

"Well I guess I need to head out before someone starts blowing up my phone," Sweet said.

"Yes, before he starts thinking you're cheating on him, Trey said. You should have been my woman."

"Boy, stop playing with yourself. When I wanted you, you was too busy chasing a hood rat."

Charmayne and her friends started laughing at what Sweet had said to Trey.

On the way to Charmayne's house, her sisters and brothers fell asleep.

"I see they had themselves a good time with their friends," Gram mentioned.

"I'm glad they did. They might as well wake up, because we're almost home."

"Charmayne, did you think about what I said to you?"

"Yes Gram, I thought about what you said. We still need to take it slow and get to know one another. I would love to be your girlfriend, but you need to let me make that decision, not you."

"I understand Charmayne. I'll wait until you give me your answer."

"Thank you. I appreciate you not rushing me into giving you an answer, when I don't know the answer. I want us to make sure that this is what we both want. Who knows, you might find someone else who can give you what you need and want.

"What do you mean about giving me what I want and need? I need you and no one else."

"We'll talk more about this tomorrow." Don't want to talk about this in front of my sisters and brothers.

Charmayne had to wake her brothers and sisters up.

"My sisters and brothers need to wake up, because I refuse to carry them in. Hell, they need to carry me in the house tired as I am."

Charmayne wanted to give Gram a kiss, but she didn't want to disrespect her sisters and brothers.

"Gram, thanks for taking us to the party. I had a good time with you and our friends."

"I had a good time with you too. Goodnight, baby."

"Goodnight Gram."

Gram helped Charmayne with her sisters and brothers and made sure they all got in the house safely.

Chapter 11

He Put Me on the Spot

When they walked in the house Charmayne mom was sitting in the living room reading her newspaper. "Did you all enjoy yourself at the birthday party?"

"We had a good time ma," Miracle said. "We played musical chairs. I won ten dollars."

"Good for you baby."

"Ma, I won this at the party," Marc said. "Nobody could beat me in throwing the football through the hoop."

"Marc won a trophy at the birthday party. He was the only one who can throw the ball through the hoop."

"Because that's your favorite sport," Rocky said. "You deserve it. Nobody could beat you at that."

"Well, did anybody else win anything?"

"Yes, just some little goodie bags," Gracie said. "I was busy playing with some of my friends from school. I didn't want to play any games."

"Gracie, what did you and your friends have to talk about since you didn't play any games?"

"I wanted to play some games, but my friends and I started talking about a project our teacher gave us to do about family. I let everybody tell me what they were going to do. I wasn't about to let them know what I was going to do. That will spoil the fun."

"Gracie, you're a mess," Ty'Meisha said.

"No, I'm for real Ty'Meisha. You know when you start telling your friends your business, they start telling someone else what you had said."

"Girl, you're always in somebody's business," Rocky said to Gracie.

'Well let me see if I can get in your business."

Everybody started laughing.

Gracie is twelve years old and she keeps everyone on their toes laughing at the things she says and does.

"Momma, I'm tired," Ty'Meisha said.

"Go get your pajamas so you can take a bath."

"Yes ma'am."

Charmayne's sisters and brothers went into their rooms to get ready for bed.

"Ma, can I go in your bathroom and take a shower?" Rocky asked his mom.

"Go ahead Rocky. Make sure you clean out the shower when you're done."

"Yes ma'am, I will."

Charmayne and her mom have a great relationship. She doesn't ever want to start telling her mom lies.

I need to have a talk with my mom. I need to tell her about the ring Gram wanted to give me. I was going to keep it a secret and lie to her about it, but I can't. I have to tell her the truth.

"Ma can we go outside? I need to talk to you about something."

"I want to come outside with you Charmayne," Miracle said.

"Miracle go in the room and get your pajamas like I said."

"Yes ma'am."

"When Ty'Meisha comes out the bathroom, I need you to go take a shower and get ready for bed."

Charmayne and her mom went outside to talk.

I have to make sure my sisters and brothers don't hear the conversation I'm having with my mother. I'm glad we went outside to talk because my sisters and brothers are very nosy.

Charmayne began telling her mom about the ring.

"Did you take the ring from him?"

"No ma'am. I told him that we need to get to know one another."

"What is his purpose in giving you a ring?"

"I don't know ma. All he said to me is that it was a promise ring and nothing more. I don't want to lead him on about anything. I'm still in high school trying to maintain my grades. I have a lot I want to accomplish. Besides, I owe everything to dad. I promised dad before he died that I would make him proud of me."

"Charmayne, I shouldn't have to tell you what to do or say. You're old enough to know right from wrong. You have to remember to stay ahead of the game. Don't let anyone influence you into doing something you're not supposed to be doing."

"I know ma, that's why I didn't accept his ring. God will send me the man he desires for me to have. Even if it's not with Gram, I still want us to be friends."

"You're right Charmayne, God will send you the man he desires for you to have. He might send Gram to be your husband, who knows. Are you prepared to accept what God sends your way?"

"Yes ma'am. I am prepared for what God sends my way. I know he sees all and he knows all. I know he won't put any more on me than I can bear. God knows I'm a nice young lady. He knows I'm dedicated to him."

"If Gram is not the one for you, are you prepared to move on without being his friend?"

"Ma, I don't know. Gram and I are good friends. It feels like he knows everything about me."

"What do you mean he knows everything about you?"

"It's like he knows what I'm thinking or feeling. Gram makes me smile, even when I don't want to smile. He knows how to say things to lift my spirit. I care about him a lot. I don't ever want us to stop being friends, even if we're not together."

"Charmayne, are you listening to what you're saying?"

"Yes ma'am. I think I want to give Gram a chance to see if he's the one for me. If it doesn't work, it won't hurt me as it would Gram."

"What do you mean by that?"

"Ma, Gram has been putting a lot in this relationship. If anybody will be hurt, it will be Gram. I don't tell Gram to go out there and buy me things, he does it on his own. Gram cannot tell you or anybody else that I came out of my pocket and bought him things. My money is to help pay bills and take care of my sisters and brothers, not to spend on a man."

Charmayne's mom chuckled at what she had said.

"Charmayne, sometimes you should volunteer to pay for things. Don't let it all be on him."

"I don't mind paying for our food, but he is supposed to be handling that, not me. Daddy always told me that a man is supposed to take care of his woman. Besides, he's the one who is calling, asking if I want to go and have dinner with him. I can see if I called and asked him, but he be the one calling, not me."

"Yes that is true, but don't keep depending on a man to do this and that for you. Your dad made sure the bills were paid, food in the house and things that we all needed. He never wanted me to spend my money on anything. I used to sneak and do things without him knowing."

"So, I'm not wrong if I don't pay for our food or anything else. It would be different if I called him. He's the one who be asking me to let's go do this and that. So, when you ask me then you're the one who has to pay."

"Charmayne, you're every spit of your dad. Your dad said what was on his mind and didn't care whose feelings he hurt. You remind me a lot about him. I'm not going to always be with you, so you need to start making the right choices in your life. I can't tell you who to date or what friends you should hang out with or who you should trust. You're old enough to realize what friends are for you and what friends are not for you. But one thing I want you to remember is, never put your trust in a man or in nobody. Only put your trust in God."

"Yes, ma'am I know. Even though I have a lot of friends in school, I can count on one hand who is truly a friend to me."

"Come on and let's go in the house before your sisters and brothers start fighting with each other.

Charmayne and her mom headed back in the house.

If my mom walks in the house and catches them fighting with each other, their butt is going to be on fire. Sometimes I hate to see my sisters or brothers catch a whooping. My momma don't be playing the radio when she's whooping you. She tells you to lean down on the bed and you better not move. If you move my mom will add two more licks to your whooping.

Charmayne and her mom both were shocked when they walked in the house. Her sisters and brothers were sitting in the living room with their pajamas on.

"How come you all are not in your bed?"

"We want to play a family trivia game before bed," Rocky said.

"I thought you all were tired from the party. You all came in the house saying, you were tired and ready to go to bed. If you're that tired, you need to be in bed."

"Taking a shower woke me up," Ty'Meisha said. "I'm ready to play a family trivia game too."

"Well, let me go to the bathroom and take a shower. When I come out, then we can play a family trivia game."

"I know what game we should play," Miracle said.

"Don't nobody want to play the *Name that Tune* game," Marc said. "That game is getting boring."

"I didn't say I wanted to play that game. If you are quiet, I'll tell you the game I want to play. You're always running your mouth at the wrong thing."

Oh Lord, I wish both Marc and Miracle would be quiet. If they keep arguing like that, my mom is going to snatch both of them up and whoop them. They better be quiet, if they know what I know.

"If neither one of you stop arguing, I will send you both to bed and put you on punishment."

"Yes ma'am," Miracle and Marc both said. "We're sorry momma."

Everyone had a good time playing Family Trivia.

"Okay, I think it's time for us to go to bed. We have to get up in the morning and get ready for church. I hope everyone had their clothes out for church. I don't need no one getting up in the morning looking for something to wear. You should already have your clothes lined out."

"'Yes ma'am we do," they all said.

"Ma, I made sure they had their clothes out." Marc and Rocky shined their shoes and ironed their clothes.

"Thank you Charmayne, I appreciate it."

"Well goodnight everyone, I'll see you all in the morning if it's the Lord's will."

"Goodnight mommy," everyone said.

Everybody said goodnight and went headed to their rooms.

Chapter 12

Getting My Praise On

It was around eight a.m. Sunday morning when Charmayne woke up. Charmayne's mom, along with her brothers and sisters were all still in bed. Charmayne tried not to disturb them as she got out of bed.

Charmayne tiptoed through the house trying not to make any noises. She grabbed her clothes, went into the bathroom and took a shower. The water felt good running down Charmayne's back.

This water feels so good running down my back. My body is aching from the party at Warner and Marin house. I did a lot of bending and that's probably why my body is aching.

Charmayne planned to cook a good breakfast for everyone. She really didn't know a lot about cooking. She sometimes watched her mom prepare dinner for them.

Charmayne knew how to cook simple things like eggs, fried sausage patties and bacon, and put biscuit in the oven.

Well at least I know how to scramble eggs, fry sausages and bacon, make toast and put biscuit in the oven. I really don't know how to cook grits, but I'll give it a try. I know my mom measures her grits before cooking them in the pot.

Charmayne decided to give it a try and surprise her mom, sisters and brothers with breakfast. Charmayne cooked grits, scrambled eggs, sausage patties, bacon and put some biscuit in the oven. As breakfast was cooking, Charmayne took out a couple of oranges and squeezed them to make fresh orange juice.

Let me taste these grits. Let me make sure it doesn't have any lumps in it. Oh yeah, it's on point. "Way to go Charmayne!"

Charmayne made sure she paid special attention to what her mom did in the kitchen. By the time Charmayne's mom, brothers and sisters all got up, breakfast was done and on point.

Sounds like my family is up. Let me start fixing their plates. I know one of my sisters or brothers is going to ask me, "Who taught you how to cook breakfast Charmayne?"

Charmayne mom, sisters and brothers walked in the kitchen. They all were surprised of what Charmayne had prepared for them.

And as if on cue, Miracle asked, "Charmayne, who taught you how to cook breakfast?"

I knew one of them was going to ask me that question. They are going to enjoy what I cooked for them. I'm surprised at myself. I think I did a marvelous job in cooking breakfast for everyone.

"By watching my mom in the kitchen, I always wanted to learn how to cook. I'm glad I did. So, here I am cooking breakfast for my family."

Charmayne's mom walked over to where she was standing and gave her a kiss on the cheek.

"Thank you for cooking breakfast for us."

"No problem, ma. I think it's time for me to start cooking. Sometimes I can cook dinner and let you relax for a while."

Charmayne, her mom, sisters and brothers all sat down at the kitchen table enjoying each other's company.

"Ma are we going to Sunday school this morning?"

"No, but we are going to church."

After eating breakfast, Charmayne's mom cleaned up the kitchen. Charmayne helped her sisters get ready for church. She made sure their hair was done, clothes were ironed and shoes polished.

My sisters love when I do their hair. Each one of my sisters has their own unique style. That's why I don't mind doing their hair for them. I make Miracle and Ty'Meisha look like little princesses.

Charmayne really didn't have to do too much with her brothers. They always had their clothes laid out for school and church.

Charmayne did Ty'Meisha and Miracle hair. She put pink bows on their ponytails to match their outfit.

"Charmayne thanks for doing our hair," both Miracle and Ty'Meisha said.

"You're both welcome."

Ty'Meisha and Miracle had a little time to color in their coloring book while their mom get ready for church.

Charmayne's mom came out her room wearing a black suit with silver accessories and black pumps.

Charmayne's mom looks like a model right out of Ebony Magazine.

"Wow, momma you look good," they all said in unison.

"Momma, do you like our hair?" Ty'Meisha asked.

"I love the way your sister did your hair. Your sister always does a good job in doing yours and Miracle's hair."

"Thanks ma," Miracle said.

"All of you all look nice."

"Thanks ma," Miracle said.

When Charmayne, her mother, sisters and brothers got to church, Sunday school was just turning out.

Every third Sunday, Charmayne choir have to sing.

Charmayne totally forgot about their choir had to sing this morning.

"Dang, I forgot we had to sing. I pray they don't ask me to sing my song today. I'm not ready to sing my song. Let somebody else sing.

Charmayne really wasn't prepared to sing her song, but she knew she had to do it. The choir were asked to give two selections. When they called the choir up to sing, Charmayne's heart started beating fast. As Charmayne started singing her song, the Holy Ghost took over her. Charmayne was in the spirit. She couldn't stop giving God the praises.

People were giving God the praises and shouting throughout the church. The spirit was so high in church it got a hold of me. I couldn't stop shouting and crying.

Charmayne's Pastor didn't get a chance to give his sermon. The Church was on fire with the Holy Spirit. Charmayne couldn't tell you what happened next. The spirit was all over her.

I don't know what happened to me while I was singing. All I know is, I was in the spirit.

After Charmayne got off the floor from praising God, she noticed people were on the floor slain out in the spirit. Some were jumping up giving God the praises. Charmayne never felt the Holy Spirit before, this was something new to her.

Charmayne was still crying and praising God. The tears were flowing heavily from Charmayne's eyes. She couldn't control it. After service people were still slain out in the Spirit, crying and praising God. Charmayne and her family walked out of church quietly, trying to not disturb the ones who were still in the spirit. When they got in the car everybody was silent. Nobody said a word. When they got home everybody sat down on the sofa still in silence.

"Why were you crying in church, Charmayne?" Asked Gracie.

Charmayne's mom had to explain to her why she was crying in church.

"When you're in the Spirit, things like this happen to you. God was anointing Charmayne through her song. He knew somebody's soul needed to be saved today."

"I never seen that happen in church before," Rocky said.

"I hope to feel like that one day," Gracie said.

Everybody was shocked at what Gracie had said.

They all started talking about how the Spirit came in while Charmayne was singing her song.

"Baby, you are anointed. God has given you a gift. You have a voice that knows how to set the atmosphere and bring in the Spirit. I want you to use your talent and let God use you."

"Yes, Ma'am."

"Charmayne, God used you today to sing that song for somebody who needed to hear his words."

"Ma the Spirit was so high, Pastor didn't get a chance to preach."

"Yes, Charmayne it was. That goes to show you that God is tired of his people playing church."

Charmayne's mom went into the kitchen to finish cooking dinner.

Everybody was still tired and exhausted from the service at church today. They all went into their room to relax before dinner.

My mom knows she be slaying it in the kitchen. She made everybody their special dish. My mom made macaroni with cheese, pinto beans, yams, collard greens, potato salad, fried chicken, BBQ chicken, ham, green bean, corn bread, homemade biscuit and a homemade lemon supreme cake. To top it off, she made homemade lemonade. Boy, were we full.

"Ma dinner was good," Rocky said. "I'm still full from the service this morning."

"Me too," Gracie said.

"Lord, I thank you for your grace and mercy. You've been better to me than I've been to myself. I give you all the praises."

"I'm going to go lay down. My stomach is full, besides I'm still feeling good from the service we had this morning. Ma, I appreciate you cooking this wonderful food for us. You're the best mom anybody can ask for."

"Thanks everyone." You know your mom doesn't mind putting it down in the kitchen.

"I'll clean the kitchen for you ma," said Marc.

"No, I got it. Just go in there and hang up your clothes when you take them off. I'll put them in the cleaners on my way to work in the morning."

"Yes ma'am."

Charmayne laid on her bed still feeling good from the service. She never experienced anything like that before.

Charmayne was used to seeing other people in the spirit, shouting and crying out to God, but nothing like this before.

"Lord I see how you move through other people while in the spirit, but I never thought this would happen to me."

Charmayne and her friends used to sit in the back of the church and pick on other members while they're in the spirit, shouting and praising God.

"I'm not going to sit in the back and pick at no one else while they're in the spirit. This has taught me a lesson. God you are so awesome."

Charmayne woke up around four p.m. still feeling tired and weak. Her mom, brothers and sisters were still asleep when she went to the bathroom. After taking a shower, she laid back down on her bed still feeling good about what happened to her in church today. She listened to one of her favorite artist's CD. The artist had a lot of good songs on his CD.

Charmayne dozed off again while listening to her CD.

Chapter 13

No Pressure on Me

When Charmayne woke up from her nap she noticed no one was home. Charmayne opened the front door and they all were sitting outside doing their own thing. Charmayne's mom was reading her newspaper, her sisters were riding their bicycles and her brothers were playing football with some of their friends. The wind was blowing nicely, but not too hard. Charmayne sat on the porch with her mom.

It feels so nice sitting outside with my family. The wind is blowing perfectly.

"Charmayne, would you like to talk about what happened to you in church today?"

"Yes, ma'am. I would feel better if I did."

"I know you've never experienced anything like that before."

"No ma'am. I haven't."

"See, the Holy Spirit can come in and change the atmosphere at any time. When we want things to go this way, God will come in and do things His way. Always remember to put God first in everything you do. Never put anyone before him."

"Yes, ma'am. No matter what I do, he is the head of everything I do."

"God always comes first in your life."

"I understand what you're saying mom. I know I'd be lost if I didn't have him in my life. I need him in every step I take."

"I'm glad we had this talk. I pray God will continue to use you in the way he did today. Charmayne you have an anointed voice. Continue letting God use you. Your life will be better than what it is now."

After talking with my mom, I feel a little more comfortable. Now I understand how it feels to catch the Holy Ghost. I've never been "in the spirit" before, but I can assure you it was the best feeling I've ever experienced.

Charmayne came from a loving and caring family. Her parents always taught them to never disrespect the elderly or talk back to them. Even if a person doesn't like you, still show respect and love to them.

I'm glad to have good parents like my father and mom. They always taught us how to love one another and not to look down on others.

Charmayne, her sisters and brothers knew that their parents didn't play with them. Their parents were quite strict with them. It didn't matter how old you were, you were never too old to get punished.

Charmayne came from a family that loved to sing. Everyone in her family was anointed by God. They could sing any Gospel song you asked them to sing.

"Charmayne go in the house and turn off the pots and the oven. I don't want the food to burn while we're outside talking."

"Yes, ma'am."

"Ma, I'm ready to eat," Gracie said.

"Me too ma," Marc said. My stomach is growling.

"Put the bicycles on the fence and the football on the porch."

"Yes ma'am."

"Go in the house and wash your hands. I'll be there shortly to fix you something to eat."

"Yes ma'am," they all said.

After eating dinner, Charmayne's two younger sisters, Gracie and Miracle, went into their room to play with their baby dolls and imaginary friends. They loved to pretend they have imaginary friends.

You would have thought they had about twenty people in the house with them. I love the way my sisters play with each other and get along well. They may argue from time to time, but they are there to protect each other.

Charmayne's brother Rocky and Ty'Meisha stayed behind to clean the kitchen, while Charmayne and Marc cleaned the living room. After everything was cleaned, Charmayne brothers and Ty'Meisha went to their rooms.

"Mom, can I talk to you for a minute?"

"Sure baby, what's wrong?"

"How do you feel if I start dating?"

"I don't mind you dating Charmayne. You have to make sure this is what you want to do. Whatever decision you make, just be careful with your decision."

"What do you mean by that ma?"

"Just because a person does things for you, it comes with a price. You're still young and you may or may not understand a lot about dating."

"There is a lot I don't understand about dating. This is my first time ever dating anyone."

"When a man buys things for a woman he already has it in mind you're his woman. A man doesn't care about anyone else, but their woman. You need to be careful in the things he buys you. A man can become very controlling and abusive."

"I understand ma. I be telling him to stop buying me things. He always says how he doesn't mind buying me things."

"What does he say when you tell him that?"

"That he cares about me and he wants to do things for me. It's kind of scary if you ask me. I like him a lot, but I told him we need to take it slow. I want to be in a relationship with Gram, but he needs to slow it down a little."

"Charmayne, be careful and take things slow with him. Don't rush into anything you're not comfortable doing."

"I know that ma. I'm not going to let no man pressure me into something I'm definitely not comfortable with or doing. You and dad taught me better than that."

"As long as you're happy with the decision you make, then I'm happy for you. I don't want you to ever feel like you can't come to me and talk. I'm always going to tell you the truth, that's what a mother does. You can come and talk to me about anything. There may be times when you may not like what I'm saying to you, but it's for your own best interests."

"Yes ma'am I understand. Thanks for listening and giving me solid advice."

"No problem." I love you.

"Love you too, ma."

Charmayne's parents taught them to be careful of the people they chose to hang out with and called friends.

Charmayne's dad would always say to her, "You don't have friends, you have associates."

Better go in this room and finish doing my homework.

Charmayne was in her room doing homework. She didn't even hear Miracle knocking on her door.

Miracle had to tap Charmayne on her leg to let her know Gram was in the living room.

"If you take off your headphones, you would have heard me knocking on your door."

"Excuse me, I was listening to my favorite artist. What did you just say?"

"Gram is in the living room waiting on you.

"Tell Gram to give me a minute, I'll be out after I'm done and put my homework away."

"Okay Charmayne."

"Hello everyone."

"Hello Gram. Have a seat. Charmayne will be out in a minute."

"Yes ma'am.

Charmayne walked in the living room where everyone was sitting.

"Hello Gram."

"Hello Charmayne." How are you?

"I'm good, what's up?"

Charmayne's mom told her sisters and brothers to go into their room and finish doing their homework. Neither one of them liked what their mom had said to them. But they knew not to disrespect their mom in any kind of way.

"Come on, let's go outside and sit on the porch so we can talk."

Charmayne told Gram all about the good time they had in church.

"Do you go to church Gram?"

"No, I don't go to church. I'm not ready to go to church yet."

Charmayne was silent. She looked at Gram in a strange way.

Do I want to date him? I need someone who doesn't mind serving the Lord like I do. He said that he doesn't go to church. Are you serious? You don't have to go to church every Sunday, but give God some of your time. It's not going to hurt you to get closer to him. I guess everybody doesn't serve God like I do.

What Gram said really stuck in Charmayne's head.

"Gram, would you like to go to church with me one Sunday?"

"I'll let you know when I'm ready to go with you."

"I understand that you're not ready to go to church, but it's good to be in church."

Charmayne didn't want to pressure Gram into going to church with her.

"I didn't mean it like that, Charmayne. Right now, I'm not ready. Who knows, I might be ready next week."

Charmayne could feel the tension Gram was giving her.

"I have something for you in the car and I hope you like it."

Gram went to his car to get what he had bought Charmayne. He handed her a brown teddy bear holding a heart box and a card in his hand.

"What is this Gram?"

"Just open it. I hope you like it."

"You didn't have to buy me anything. I already told you to stop buying me things. All I want is for us to get to know one another. Every time I turn around, you're buying me things. You don't have to do this."

Charmayne was shocked at what Gram had bought her. She stood up and gave Gram a hug.

One touch from Gram gives me the chills. I wish I could stay in his arms forever.

Charmayne had to remember that her mom, sisters and brothers were home. There's no telling who would have opened the door and caught them in each other's arms.

Charmayne wasn't about to disrespect her mom.

"Thank you for the gift Gram."

"No problem, Charmayne. I wanted to buy the girl of my dreams something nice."

Wait. Did he just say the woman of his dreams? Now, he really needs to stop. Don't get me wrong, I love the things he buys me but he's going overboard with it.

"Do you like it?"

"I don't like it, I love it."

Charmayne and Gram couldn't keep their eyes off each other.

Charmayne was silent. She remembered what her mom had said to her earlier about when a man buys you things.

"My mom just told me about when a man buys you things, he acts like he owns you. News flash, don't no man own me. I'm nobody's treasure, let alone his trophy woman."

Listening to what Gram had said to her about being the girl of his dreams, did not sit well with her. Charmayne was getting scared about what he had said to her.

"Would you like to come over to my house?"

"I can't. I have a lot of homework to do. I have a test in the morning and I need to study so I can get a good grade."

"I wish you luck on your test tomorrow."

"Thanks. I pray I pass this math test. Math is not one of my favorite subjects. I can do rock any other subject, but Math."

"Charmayne I have faith in you. I know you're going to pass your math test with flying colors."

Did he just say I have faith in you? This boy is crazy.

Charmayne couldn't believe Gram said he has faith in her.

"Gram, would you like to go out sometimes?"

"What do you mean would I like to go out with you sometimes?"

"I guess we're dating now. We can be a couple."

"I thought we were already a couple."

"What gave you the idea that we were a couple, Gram?"

Charmayne and Gram started laughing.

"I'm glad we're a couple now."

"Charmayne, you just don't know how long I was waiting for you to tell me that. You just made my day."

Gram got up and went to where Charmayne was sitting and gave her a kiss on her cheek.

Gram never pressured Charmayne into doing anything she wasn't comfortable doing. The feelings Charmayne was feeling for Gram were real, however she wasn't trying to make them known to him.

I don't want him to know how I really feel about him. If he knew how I felt about him, he would want to do things with me. I'm not trying to go down that lane not until I'm completely ready.

Charmayne didn't want to play with Gram's feelings. She wanted to make sure he's the one for her. Taking their time with would be best for the both of them.

Charmayne loved being around Gram, he was fun and full of energy.

I like being around Gram. He is so energetic and full of fun. He makes me laugh at the silliest things he says to me. I think I can get used to this.

Gram always knew the right words to say to Charmayne.

"Gram always finds the right words to say to me when I don't feel like being bothered by anyone." It's something about the words he says to me to make me love him more.

Gram would open doors for her and make sure she felt comfortable around him and his friends.

Gram would never put anybody before Charmayne or her needs. He wants to spend the rest of his life with Charmayne.

That's what Charmayne liked about Gram. He showed her so much love.

"Gram, let me ask you a question."

"Yes, you can ask me anything, Charmayne. What would you like to ask me?"

"Suppose you want to have sex with me and I'm not ready, what would you do?"

"Listen, I'm not going to pressure you into having sex with me or doing anything with me that you're not comfortable doing. That's not who I am. If that means I have to wait for you, then that's what I have to do. I don't want you to ever think you have to have sex with me because I do this and that for you. I'm not that type of guy. I want to spend time with you and get to know who you are. That's all I want to do."

"Well, I know it's going to be hard for you if we're not having sex. I'm not ready to have sex or do anything I don't feel comfortable doing. Having sex is not on my list for me to do."

"I can't get mad at you because you don't want to have sex with me. You think I'm going to force you to have sex with me. Listen, I want us to take our time with one another. Sex is not everything to me. I love being around you and your family. Being around you makes me a better person. I would rather hangout with you and not be around my friends all day long."

Okay, Gram is talking a good game, but I'm not stupid either. I can peep game when someone is trying to win you over and make you his woman. I don't know who he's fooling, but he needs to come correct. I'm used to how men talk to women about how they want to be with them. I learned that from the guys I used to hang around with when I was in a girl's gang. They taught me a lot. So, I hope he doesn't think he's winning me over.

"One day you might want to have sex with me and I'm not ready, what would you do?"

"Charmayne, I like you. I don't care about sex. That is not on my mind. I just want to spend time with you, that's all."

"I know girls are out there and you're going to be tempted, but are you able to control it? When you've been turned down so many times by me, eventually you're going to get tired and get it from somewhere else."

"Baby, you don't have anything to worry about."

"Well, I'm not ready to have sex. I don't know when I'll be ready. I think you should know this before anything goes any further between us. I don't want to stop you from being with someone else."

"If you're not ready to have sex, I can't force you to have sex with me. Sex is not on my mind. I want to be with Charmayne and Charmayne only. I don't want to be with anyone else."

"Listen, I don't want to hold you back from fulfilling your needs."

The look Gram gave Charmayne, she knew she hit a nerve.

Charmayne knew Gram was mad at her. He was silent for a minute.

I think I better change the subject before I end up losing him to someone else. He really cares about me and not just to have sex with me.

"Charmayne, if I wanted to be with somebody else, I would not be here sitting on your porch talking to you. Do you actually think I'd be wasting my time with you? I want to be with you. I chose to be here with you and nobody else. I never asked you to have sex with me. Where is all this coming from?"

"I'm just preparing myself for the worse. I don't want to stand in your way or make you miss out on what you need."

"Charmayne, I think we need to end this conversation, because I'm not going anywhere."

Charmayne nor Gram wanted to end their relationship. They both enjoyed being around each other,

"Charmayne, do you need help with your homework?"

"No, I have it all covered. I have to learn how to solve the problems by myself. If I let you help me with my homework, then I'm not learning it on my own."

Gram started telling Charmayne about a science project he had to do on planet earth.

"Well good luck with that. I can't help you on that one."

They both busted out laughing.

After talking for a while, Charmayne and Gram said their goodbyes.

As Charmayne and Gram parted ways a sudden realization washed over Charmayne. It was a feeling she couldn't shake and one she could not easily explain, but one that left her feeling uncertain.

Chapter 14

The Yellow Envelope

As time passed, Gram and Charmayne were still in a relationship. They were spending lots of time together. Their friendship was growing stronger. Charmayne loved being with Gram. They made sure to include Charmayne's sisters and brothers in most of the things they did together. Even though Charmayne was in a relationship with Gram, she never left her siblings out. Charmayne loves her brothers and sisters. She promised to always be there for them no matter what. All the time Charmayne and Gram spent together, he never once touched her inappropriately or tried to have sex with her.

"I know I'm not having sex with Gram, is he getting it from somebody else? I don't know what to think at this moment. Gram got to be having sex with someone else. Not one time has he ever touched me or tried to have sex with me. I believe he's having sex with someone."

Graduation was around the corner Charmayne knew something good was about to happen to her. She couldn't wait to walk the stage with her fellow classmates."

"I'm so glad to be graduating with my classmates." I can't wait to walk across the stage and receive my diploma. I am an official graduate. "Thank you Jesus."

Even though Charmayne father passed away two years before her graduation, it was a very difficult time for her.

Charmayne knew she had to make the best of it.

"I wish my dad was here to see me graduate and receive my diploma." I know he would be proud of me."

Two weeks before graduation, Charmayne's guidance counselor Mrs. Truth called her name over the intercom to come to her office.

I know I haven't done anything wrong, why is she calling me over the intercom to come to her house?" I know my friends want to know what I've done. To my knowledge, I was a good girl. I've stopped doing the things I use to do when I first started out, but now I've changed a whole lot.

When Charmayne walked in Mrs. Truth office she noticed her principal Mr. Digg in the office along with two of her other home room teachers. There was a man Charmayne didn't recognize sitting in her guidance counselor office as well. She was not sure what to expect.

"Have a seat Charmayne," Mrs. Truth said.

I hope Mrs. Truth is not about to tell me I can't graduate with my classmates. This will tear me apart, let alone my mom and the rest of my family.

Charmayne didn't know what they were about to say to her. She noticed one of her teacher Mr. Homie holding a yellow envelope in his hand. Charmayne sat down in one of the chairs and looked around the room trying to read the expression on everyone's faces.

Everybody in the room is looking at me kind of strange. What the hell are they about to tell me?

Charmayne head dropped. She knew she was in trouble.

"Yes I was bad in school and I did a lot of foolish things, but I've changed my ways."

When Charmayne decided to go to class, she did her school work and stayed focused in class. She never gotten into any more trouble.

See that's what happens when you play around in class and don't pay attention to what the teacher is teaching you. Now here I am sitting in this office with my guidance counselor, teachers, and people I never seen at this school.

"How are you're doing, Charmayne?" Asked Mr. Gate.

"I'm doing fine Mr. Gate. It will make me feel better if you tell me why all of you are here in Mrs. Truth office."

"Charmayne, graduation is about two weeks away. Mrs. Truth called you in her office so we can talk to you about your GPA," He explained.

Why do they need to talk to me about my GPA? The only person who need to be worrying about that is Mrs. Truth not them.

Mrs. Truth introduced Charmayne to the other individuals present in her office. Charmayne recognized several of the faces that were present, except for four whom she didn't know.

"You are an intelligent young lady Charmayne. Nothing will stand in your way in achieving your goals. I've been monitoring you and your progress while attending classes," Mr. Pain said. Charmayne looked at Mr. Pain with a strange look.

"What do you mean, you been monitoring my progress?

"You have come a long way Charmayne. Your grades have improved to where they were about two months ago. You have proved to us that you can do it, if you put your mind to it."

I try hard to do my best. I've made some bad decisions in my life and now I'm paying for it. My parents always taught me to treat people with respect. Sometimes I can get a little flip at the mouth, but it's not to hurt anyone's feelings.

"We're very proud of you and the young lady you've become."

"So am I, Mr. Pain. I believe I've made the best of it. I'm realizing some of the so-call friends I had really didn't mean me any good."

"You're doing good Charmayne," Mrs. Truth said. "We've noticed a significant change in you. Always remember to keep in mind that the way you talk to people affects not only you, but them as well."

"Yes, I think I'm doing a lot better. I've tone down my attitude and am more mindful of the people I chose to hang out with."

"Charmayne, I called you in my office to tell you I have some exciting news to share with you," Mrs. Truth said.

A smile came across Charmayne's face.

"So, I'm not in trouble?"

"No, you can breathe now."

By the tone of Mrs. Truth voice and the excitement on her face meant it was good. Mrs. Truth and the other teachers who were present in the office all stood up.

Okay, why are all of them standing up? What is about to happen?

Mr. Gate also stood up holding the yellow envelope in his hand. Everyone who was present in Mrs. Truth office started clapping their hands for Charmayne. Still puzzled at what was going on, Charmayne started crying.

Why is everyone standing up and clapping their hands?

"You did it, Charmayne." The man she didn't recognized said.

Mrs. Truth didn't want to spoil the other good news they had for her.

"What did I do?" Charmayne ask him.

"Charmayne this is Mr. Flowers," Mrs. Truth said. He has been following your progress for about a month now. We thought since you've been doing much better in your classes we decided to honor you with something else. We all got together and asked Mr. Flowers to come out here and honored you with this envelope.

Still puzzled, Charmayne was trying to figure out what was going on.

"Okay what have I done now?" They said I did it. What have I did? Somebody please tell me.

Mr. Flowers handed Charmayne a white envelope with a smiling face on it.

"What is this, Mr. Flowers?"

"Wait until you get home and share this exciting news with your family.

Charmayne gave Mr. Flowers a hug.

"Thank you for the envelope. I don't know what it is, but thank you."

"Congratulations," they all said to Charmayne.

Mrs. Truth also handed Charmayne a yellow envelope with her name on it. The envelope had Class of Nineteen Eighty-Six Ceremony written in black ink on it. Mr. Gate, Charmayne's teacher also gave her a yellow envelope with her name on it. Charmayne cried even harder.

"Lord, I thank you."

Charmayne looked toward the ceiling and held up the envelope.

"See daddy, this is all for you."

They all knew Charmayne father had passed away. Everyone in the office began to share the joy with Charmayne and her father.

"Charmayne, we know that this is hard for you since your father passed away. We wanted to do something extra for you and your family in honor of your father," Mr. Flowers said. I would like for you to give this special envelope to your mom, from all of us."

"I never thought people really cared about me like they do." Who would have thought I would be graduating with my classmates? Let alone having my guidance counselor, teachers and people I don't know supporting me one hundred percent like this? They really do care about me.

Each one of them hugged and kissed Charmayne on her cheek. That made Charmayne feel good knowing others really cared about her. Each one of them took the time out to make sure Charmayne performed good in school and stayed out of trouble.

"I'm determined to graduate with my class. Nothing is going to stand in my way or stop me from reaching my goals."

Charmayne went to school every day and did what she was supposed to do in class. She stayed out of trouble and got rid of the so-call friends that was causing her to get distracted.

If I want to graduate with my classmates, I have to do better in school. I have to stop thinking that I'm better than the next person, because I'm not. Here I am struggling trying to maintain a good GPA. I am ashamed of myself.

Charmayne enrolled in night school so she could get the extra credits she needed to graduate. When Charmayne walked in class, she still had tears in her eyes. Everybody in class was concerned about her.

"What's wrong with you, Charmayne?" Mr. Brown asked her.

Charmayne showed them the envelope that read "Class of Nineteen Eighty-Six Ceremony" written on it.

They all started screaming Charmayne's name. Some were even crying with her. That was the best news anybody could have gotten.

"Thank you Mr. Brown for not giving up on me. Thank you for pushing me even when I didn't want to be pushed. You saw something in me that I didn't see. Now, I understand why you stayed up in my face. You knew I have potential.

"I knew you could do it Charmayne," I was waiting on you.

Mr. Brown gave Charmayne a big hug and handed her another white envelope.

"Wait until you get home to open it."

"Thank you," Mr. Brown.

That day was the happiest day for Charmayne.

Charmayne couldn't wait to get home to share the good news with her family. She was excited to show her mom the envelopes she had gotten from her guidance counselor, her teacher, and Mr. Flowers.

Chapter 15

Telling My Family the Good News

When Charmayne got home, her mom was seated on the porch watching her sisters and brothers coloring the sidewalk with their colorful chalk. Charmayne approached them with a bright glow on her face.

"Girl, what's wrong with you?" Charmayne mom asked.

Charmayne handed her mom all of the envelopes she received from her guidance counselor, teachers, and Mr. Flowers.

"What is this Charmayne?"

"Mom, can you just open it?"

Her mom didn't notice the writing on the envelope. She opened the envelope and started reading the papers. She couldn't believe what she was reading. She threw up her hands.

"Lord, I thank you."

"Ma stop crying. You're going to make me cry."

"You just don't know how proud I am of you. You did it baby girl. When you thought it wasn't going to work in your favor, but look at God."

"Why is momma crying?" Asked Gracie.

"Momma is crying because I'll be graduating soon. That's why she is crying."

Charmayne told her sisters and brothers the good news.

"I'm happy for you, Charmayne," Marc said.

"I'm happy for myself."

Charmayne's sisters and brothers all ran up to her and gave her a big hug. They were all so excited for her. Charmayne's mom walked over to her and hugged her.

"I'm so proud of you, Charmayne. If your father were here, he'd be proud of you too."

"I know he would mom. I owe this to him."

"We miss him too Charmayne," Rocky said. "I miss him playing football with us in the yard".

"I do too," said Gracie." Daddy would always come in the room and make sure our homework was done before we went outside to play."

"Only if your dad were still here to see his children. He'd be so proud of each and every one of you all. I know your father would be cheering you on when you walk on that stage and receive your diploma."

"You're right ma, dad would be proud of me. It was like he was telling me to get myself together and stop hanging out with certain people who don't mean me any good.

Out of nowhere Miracle said to Charmayne "Don't cry Charmayne, Daddy will be there in spirit."

Charmayne cried even harder. She didn't know why Miracle had said that to her.

"What did you just say, Miracle?"

"Ma, I told Charmayne daddy will be there in spirit."

"How do you know that, Miracle?"

"Because daddy told me he was going to there when you walk on stage to receive your diploma. I talk to daddy all the time. He tells me how much he misses us and how much he loves us."

Everybody stopped what they were doing and started listening to what Miracle was saying. This was an exciting day for Charmayne, but not in her heart. She was excited about graduating with her class, but her dad wouldn't be there to share in all the excitement.

"Miracle you need to tell me everything your dad said," their mom said.

"Some things he wants me to keep to myself. He's all around us, can't you feel him."

"Ma, this is hard for me. I wish dad was here right now, so I could tell him all the good news. I know he would be proud."

Charmayne wanted her dad to see her walk on stage and receive her diploma.

I know I have to be strong for my mom, sisters and brothers. I can't let them see me fall down.

Even though Charmayne's dad wouldn't be there to see her graduate, but he'd be there in spirit. Hearing what Miracle said made sense. Charmayne would sometime feel a cool breeze brushed pass her while lying in bed. Charmayne never thought much of it. She just thought it was a window open somewhere in the house.

"Charmayne you can do it," Ty'Meisha said. "We all have confidence in you. When they call your name and you walk on stage we will be cheering you on. I'm so proud of you."

"Yes Charmayne, you're not alone," Marc said. "I'm going to be screaming your name on the top of my lungs."

"Boy hush," Gracie said. "They are going to put you out. This is a very important day for Charmayne. Don't ruin this special day for her. She's come a long way. She deserves this day not just for her, but for us as well."

"Yeah Marc don't ruin this for all of us," Ty'Meisha said. "Charmayne is our sister and we are going to support her no matter if daddy is not here with us."

Charmayne was proud of her brothers and sisters. They all showed their support of her. Charmayne brothers decided to take the spot of their absent father.

"I guess Marc and Rocky wants to be in charge over us. Yeah right, they better sit down somewhere before their feelings get hurts."

Rocky and Marc wasn't about to let no one disrespect their mom or sisters. They made a promised to one another to protect their family. Even though their father had passed away, Marc and Rocky were the only men in the house.

"Listen Rocky and Marc, I know you both are here for me. I know you want to protect me, but don't go overboard with your protection. I don't want neither one of you to ruin this special day for me."

"We're not going to ruin your big day Charmayne," they both assured her. "We know this means the world to you." Marc said. "You deserve to be honored."

"We love you Charmayne," Rocky said." We were just playing with you. Since daddy is not here with us, we have to protect you all.

"Boy sit down somewhere," Ty'Meisha said. "You can't even protect yourself."

"I know that's right. You let me run all over you," Gracie said.

"Yes, because you're my little sister. I don't want to hurt you. Besides, I don't put my hands on my sisters or any other female."

"Marc you will always be our little helper in the house," Miracle said.

They all started laughing at what Miracle had said.

"Charmayne, you did it baby girl." A mom's proud moment with her soon to be graduate.

"Thanks mom, I appreciate it."

Telling My Family the Good News

Chapter 16

I Finally Made It

A week before graduation, the seniors were out of school preparing for the ceremony. The graduates had to be fitted for their cap and gown. Charmayne was still overwhelmed about the excitement of being able to graduate with her class.

Thank you Jesus for giving me this opportunity to be able to walk on stage and receive my diploma. I owe all this to you.

The seniors had to rehearse how they were going to walk on stage, which hand they would use to shake the principal's hand, and which hand they use to receive their diploma. Charmayne and her friends were excited about graduating with their class.

"Girl, I never thought we would be graduating," Sweet said.

"I never thought this day would come for none of us," Charisma said.

They all agreed on what Sweet and Charisma had said.

"Who would have thought we'd be graduating with our classmates," Fran chimed in.

"Bad as we were in class, skipping school, fighting with everybody and cursing out the teachers. Who would have thought we're be graduating with our friends," Charmayne added.

"Girl, but there is a God who knows our hearts," Marin said. "He knew we deserved another chance to graduate with our classmates."

Charmayne and her friends kept saying, "God you are so awesome and everything we do, we do it in your name."

Charmayne started crying. She reached in her pocket and grabbed a napkin to wipe her tears away.

"It felt so good knowing I did it and didn't give up. God knows it was a struggle for me, but I held on to his loving hands. He never gave up on me nor did he turned his back on me. He was right there when I needed him the most. "Lord, I thank you."

"Yes, Charmayne you did it," Fran said. "You never gave up. I wish I had a determined mind like you have. I just want you to know how much you motivate me. You inspired me Charmayne. Thanks for pushing me to strive to be the person I am today."

"Fran, I only did what I would do for anybody else. I want my friends to be better than me. I try my best to be there for my friends/sisters when they need me. You all are like sisters to me. We may not agree on what we have to say to one another, but we are there for each other."

"Charmayne you are absolutely right," Sweet said. "I wouldn't trade my friends for nothing in the world. I love you all like you're my sisters.

After rehearsal, Charmayne and her friends all agreed to grab something to eat before they went their separate ways.

Charmayne made an appointment with her stylist. She had to get her hair done before her big day.

When Charmayne got home, her mom, sisters and brothers had bought her a beautiful black pant suit and a pair of black shoes to wear for graduation.

Miracle handed Charmayne a garment bag and a plastic bag.

"What is this?"

"Just look in the bag, Charmayne."

Charmayne started crying, but she was laughing at the same time.

"Don't cry," Ty'Meisha said.

"I'm crying because I'll be graduating with my class next week."

"Thanks you all for buying me something to wear to my graduation. I love the shoes as well."

"You're welcome," they all said in unison.

"It really was mom's idea," Gracie said. "Mom picked out the outfit while we picked out your shoes."

"You all have nice taste."

While Charmayne was in the room talking to her sisters, the phone rang. Miracle ran out the room to answer the phone.

"Charmayne telephone," Miracle yelled out to her.

Charmayne walked out the room to talk on the phone.

"Hey Charmayne, baby what are you doing?"

"Just sitting here talking to my sisters, what's going on?"

"I was just calling checking up on you, that's all. I wanted to know if I can come pick you up."

"I'll call you back. I don't know if my mom has anything planned."

"Okay, call me, and let me know."

"I will. I'll call you back in a minute."

Charmayne and Gram talked for a few minutes before hanging up.

Charmayne went and knocked on her mom's room door.

"Come on in."

"Ma, is it okay if Gram comes and picks me up?"

"Yes, he can come pick you up. I don't have anything planned at this moment. Call me and let me know where you're at."

"Yes, ma'am I'll call you."

Charmayne called Gram back to let him know that it was okay for him to come and picked her up. She went in her room and got dressed.

She played a game of Monopoly with her sisters while waiting for Gram.

"Where are you going Charmayne?" Ty'Meisha asked.

"I don't know. Gram is on his way to come pick me up. He didn't say where he was taking me. I have no idea where we're going."

Charmayne was ready when Gram came to pick her up.

Gram and Charmayne went to the mall. Gram bought Charmayne an outfit to wear after graduation.

"Gram, you really didn't have to buy me anything. My mom, sisters and brothers had already bought me an outfit to wear."

"I just wanted to do something special for you on your big day."

"Thank you Gram for the outfit. I love it."

"Make sure you take plenty of pictures in your cap and gown for me."

"I surely will."

"Where would you like to get something to eat from?"

"I don't know. I'll leave that up to you."

"We ended up at a soul food restaurant that we both liked."

Charmayne and Gram both ordered a rib dinner with macaroni and cheese, potato salad, collard greens with corn bread and a sprite soda.

"Let me call my mom and see if she needs me home."

Charmayne called home to check in with her mom. Her brother Rocky answered the phone.

"Hey Rocky where is ma?"

"Hold on while I get her."

"Hey, Charmayne is everything okay with you?"

"Yes ma'am. I was calling to see if you needed me."

"No, I'll see you when you get home. Have a good time. Don't be out too late."

"I won't ma. See you then."

"I know you're excited about your big day tomorrow. I hope you can spend some time with me."

"If it's not too late I will try."

Charmayne and Gram went to a park to eat their food. They enjoyed each other's company. After eating their food, Charmayne and Gram headed back to Charmayne's house.

"I don't want to have you out too late. I need you to get your beauty rest and be ready for tomorrow."

Charmayne thought that was sweet of Gram to be concerned about her needs.

Gram knew how important it was for Charmayne to get her rest for her big day.

I pray he don't have me out too late. I need to make sure I am prepared for my big day tomorrow.

Charmayne kissed Gram on his cheek and thanked him for everything he's done for her.

"Gram I just wanted to thank you for everything you've done for me. I appreciate it."

"You're welcome, Charmayne."

Gram made sure to have Charmayne home at a decent hour. They sat in her drive way talking. They talked about forty-five minutes.

As Charmayne was getting ready to get out of Gram's car, he turned me around and kissed Charmayne on her lips.

Charmayne leaned down and kissed Gram back.

Charmayne didn't want to stop tasting Gram's juicy lips and the sweetness that came with it.

"Dang Grams lips taste so delicious. Please don't stop kissing me."

Charmayne knew she had to stop before she regretted doing something she wasn't ready to do.

"Goodnight, Gram."

"Goodnight, baby."

When Charmayne got in the house, she had balloons, a fruit basket with all the fruits she likes, a card, and a teddy bear.

"Wow," what is this?"

"We wanted to show you how much we appreciate you and all the good things you've accomplished in life," her mom said. I know it's hard not having your dad here with you, but know every step you take your father will be with you. Your dad is looking and smiling down on you as we speak.

"Thanks everyone for your love. I know you all are proud of me, but I'm proud of myself."

"Oh momma, how I wish daddy was here to enjoy this special day with us."

Charmayne sisters ran out the room with a bag in their hands smiling at her.

"This is for you," Miracle said. "I made it myself."

Charmayne opened the card and began reading it.

"Miracle you drew this picture for me?"

"Yes, I did. Do you like it, Charmayne?"

"I love how you drew a picture of me with flowers in the background. You did a wonderful job."

Miracle drew a picture of me with flowers in the background. I thought this was the cutest picture of me. Miracle always puts a smile on my face. She always knows how to brighten up your day.

"You forgot to look in the bag."

Charmayne opened the bag and pulled out a black velvet box with a silver bow on it. Inside the box was a gold bracelet.

"I remember seeing this bracelet in the mall with mom."

"That's how we knew what to get you," Gracie said.

"When you saw the bracelet with your name engraved on it, you had such a beautiful smile on your face. I paid close attention."

"Thanks everyone, I truly appreciate it. You all have made my day. I love you all."

They all hugged each another. Charmayne was overwhelmed. They all sat in the living room.

"Are you ready for your graduation in the morning?" Rocky asked.

"Yes, I am Rocky." Not only if this day is special for me, but for my family as well. I know you all would be celebrating this day with me.

"Yes, we will, Charmayne," her mom said. "I know your dad is smiling down on you. If he were here, he would be helping us celebrate this day with you. After spending some quality time with her family, Charmayne went in the bathroom to take a shower. The water felt good running down Charmayne's body. Charmayne started thinking about her dad.

"Dad I wish you were here to see me walk across the stage." I know you're be there in spirit, but it won't feel right knowing you're not there physically. Seeing my friends with their dad is really going to put a damp in my heart.

After showering, Charmayne slipped into her pajamas and went in the den to play Monopoly with her siblings before retiring for bed. Charmayne then went into the kitchen to fix a snack for everyone to eat before bed.

"I'm going in the kitchen to fix us a snack before we go to bed."

"I want you all to know that every mistake you make in life is a cost. Never let anybody tell you to do something you're not comfortable doing. Get your education first and prepare for your future. School is very important. Don't let any of your friends try to influence you to skip school or do things you're not supposed to be doing. Charmayne and her siblings share a special bond. They also share a lot of secrets with one another.

"Your education is very important. Don't do things I used to do. If I was doing my homework like I was supposed to be doing in school, I wouldn't be where I am now. Make sure you choose positive friends to hang out with. Be a leader not a follower.

They said their prayers and went into mom's room to kiss her good night. Ty'Meisha usually slept with mom, but for some reason, on this night, she wanted to sleep with Charmayne.

My sister Ty'Meisha loves sleeping with me for what reason I don't know, but I love her company.

Ty'Meisha laid in Charmayne's arms all night.

Miracle and Gracie wanted to sleep with Charmayne too. They made a "sleep with big sister party." Charmayne enjoyed having her sisters sleeping in her room with her.

No More Being Abused

I'M NOBODY'S FOOL

BOOK 2

Chapter 17

Can I Maintain My Dignity

The day arrived for Charmayne to graduate. She worked hard for this day. Not just for herself but for her dad, and her family, as well. She was up early and ready to go to the auditorium to receive her diploma.

"You're up mighty early this morning," her mom said.

"I know, I couldn't sleep. I'm so excited."

"This is your day and you deserve it."

"I'm so excited to be graduating with my class. I know Dad will be walking with me and cheering me on when I walk across the stage."

"Yes he will baby girl." Your dad will be proud of you.

The phone rang. It was Charmayne's friend Sweet.

"Hey, Charmayne."

"Hello, Sweet." What's up?

"I was calling to see if you're ready to walk on stage to receive your diploma.

"I've been ready. I couldn't sleep at all. I guess I'm excited about graduating with my class. It has been a long journey for the both of us."

"Yes it has, Charmayne. I don't know about you, but sometimes I wish I could have done things differently in school."

"Yes me too, Sweet. I wish we can turn back the hand of time and start all over again. I regret some of the things I did in school and to my friends."

"Me too, Sweet. It hurts to know the things I've done to them. Thank God he changed me and made me a better person."

I tell you. Sweet and I was something else in high school. We did some terrible things to our friends and teachers. We didn't take no mess from no one. That's how bad we were in school.

"Girl it took this long for us to realize the things we've done to others and how we've hurt them down through the years. Now who would have thought we would be graduating with the same people. They still love us in spite of our wrong doing."

Charmayne and Sweet changed the subject about what they did in school. They were grateful for the things the Lord had done for them. They both became a better person. They were no longer the rowdy girls who caused a lot of drama to others. They've learned to respect themselves and others. They put others people feelings before their own.

"Girl, I couldn't sleep last night," Charmayne said. "It seems like I have a lot of energy in me."

"Girl, me too," Sweet said.

"Girl, we did that. Dang Sweet, who would have thought?"

"I don't know about you, but I never thought I'd be in the number. I thought I would be repeating the twelfth grade over again."

"I thank God for giving us this opportunity to be in the number. Nobody but God."

Charmayne and Sweet talked on the phone for about an hour or so. Both Charmayne and Sweet were glad to be graduating this morning with their class. They had it all planned out.

Charmayne and Sweet would take other students lunch money, have take their paper and pencils, and tell them they better not tell anybody. Charmayne and her friends were in a girl club. Whatever they wanted to do, they did it. Now, their lives were in jeopardy.

Dang as I look back at the things I've done in school and to others, my dad would not be proud of me or my behavior. "Lord, I thank you for your grace and mercy. Thank you for changing me and making me a better person not for myself, but to others as well."

Charmayne and several of her friends had to come to realization about their lives. They knew they had to change if they wanted to accomplish something out of life. Charmayne and her friends stayed in school, got good grades, maintained a certain GPA, and went to night school. They were determined to graduate with their other classmates.

I regret what I've done, but I can't take any of it back. Here I am getting ready to graduate with my classmates. It was nobody but God. I thank my mom too, because she kept me on the prayer list.

Charmayne's friend name Sweet was pregnant. A several of Charmayne's friends were either pregnant or already had a baby or babies. Some of Charmayne friends had problems as they were growing up. There were several of Charmayne friends whoswe parents were divorced or being raised by their grandparents.

"Well, I might not be there the way this baby is kicking me."

"At least he'll be walking with you."

Charmayne and Sweet both started laughed. Some of Charmayne's friends were very sexually active. They use to tell Charmayne, she's going to be an old lady with spider webs on her sweetness.

"I rather have webs on my sweetness than have different men in and out of me. I'm not like you all. You all started out young. I'm still fresh."

"Did Gram ever ask you to have sex with him?"

"No, why would you ask me that Sweet?

"I was just wondering?"

Why in the hell would my friend Sweet ask me a question like that? Had she heard something? Tell me so I can prepare myself for what he thinks he's going to get from me.

"Gram knows not to ask me that question. He knows I'm not ready to have sex."

"When will you be ready to have sex with him?"

"Listen if he wants to go and have sex with somebody else than he can. I don't want to be with him or anybody else who just wants to have sex with me. My life is more precious than giving a man my sweetness."

"Well, I hope he doesn't force you to have sex with him."

"Sweet, he can try all he wants too. I'm going to college to further my education. I don't want a baby to hold me down from achieving my goals. I'm not trying to be a mother at an early age."

"I hear you Charmayne. This is your life. Don't let nobody influence you to do anything you're not comfortable doing. I wish I would have listened to my mom. I wouldn't be in this predicament that I'm in."

"Sweet, there's nothing wrong with you being pregnant. You know I'm here for you no matter what."

"I know you're going to be here for me. I'm not worried about that. We've been friends for a long time and nothing will ever change the way I feel about you. You will always be my big sister."

"Sweet, I'm still growing up and I have a lot to learn. I'm not going to let anyone influence me to do something I'm not comfortable with. "I wish I could've waited." The damage has been done. I'm going to enjoy my bundle of joy.

"I know, but just think of it as a blessing to you and his dad."

"I'm grateful for my baby."

"Sweet, we both have to get dressed. Girl, I'll meet you at the auditorium."

"See you at the auditorium Charmayne."

They both hung the phone up. Charmayne went into the room to get her stuff together for graduation. There was a knock at the door. She peeped out the window to see who it was. To Charmayne's surprise it was Gram. Gram was standing there holding a card and balloons in his hands. As usual, Charmayne sisters and brothers were glad to see him.

Charmayne opened the door for Gram.

"Hey, Gram, what you doing here?"

"I came to drop off this card and balloons before you leave."

Charmayne gave Gram a kiss on the cheek. Her sisters and brother started chuckling.

"That's so nasty," Rocky said.

"Go in your room and stop being nosey, Rocky. Don't make me have to call momma and tell her you out here being grown."

Charmayne sisters and brother hurried up and went into their rooms. They made sure to close the door behind them. Neither one of them wanted to get in trouble.

"Charmayne call me when you get home. I'll be rooting for you when you receive your diploma."

"Thanks for the card and the balloons Gram. I really appreciate it."

Charmayne closed the front door behind her. She went into the room to get dressed. Charmayne didn't want to arrive at the auditorium late.

I want to arrive a little earlier so my family can get a good seat. I want them to be able to see me when I receive my diploma.

"Hurry up everyone, I don't want to be late."

Everyone came out of their room with bags in their hands to give to Charmayne. She had tears in her eyes. She couldn't believe that her mom, sisters and brothers had bought her something. Charmayne looked in the bag. She couldn't believe her mom, sisters, and brothers bought her a diamond necklace set she was looking at in the mall.

"Thank you all for buying me these gifts." How did you all know what to buy me?

"Every time we go in the store you always go in the jewelry department to look at certain pieces you like," Ty'Meisha said.

"Let's get in the car so you won't be late," Charmayne mom said.

When they arrived at the auditorium, some of Charmayne's friends were outside talking with their family members. Charmayne friends noticed them as they were walking toward the auditorium. They all ran toward Charmayne and her family and greeted them with a hug. Several of Charmayne's friends walked past her and spoke to her mom, sisters and brothers.

"Well, I guess I don't exist since nobody said anything to me."

"You know they love you Charmayne," Gracie said.

Everyone started laughing at what Gracie said.

Charmayne's sisters always had something sweet to say to make people laugh at them. They gave each other a hug and started walking toward the auditorium. Charmayne felt herself getting sick. She knew it was her nerves playing tricks on her. One of the staff informed the students it was time for them to line up and take their places.

"Congratulation girls on a job well done," some of their family and friends yelled out to them.

"They are so damn ghetto," Sweet said.

"I know I heard one of my cousin's voice in the midst," Fran said.

"Girl, they act like they are in the hood," Destiny said. I pray they don't act like that when we walk on stage to receive our diploma.

"I already told my family to act like somebody when I walk on stage, " Sweet said.

"Well, this is it," Charmayne said to her friends.

"Yes Lord," Marin said. Who would have thought we would be standing here getting ready to walk on stage and receive our diploma?

"Lord we made it by your grace," Camryn said.

Charmayne and her friends exchanged hugs and congratulated one another before going in the auditorium. The auditorium was filled with family and friends of the graduates.

"Lord, I'm so nervous. Please give me strength to be able to walk on stage to receive my diploma. I pray no one sees me crying, but who cares I'm a graduate. I can cry if I want to cry I deserve it."

When they called Charmayne's name, she stood up to walk on stage to receive her diploma.

"Oh Lord, here it goes. I'm about to walk on stage."

When Charmayne walked on stage, she noticed her family sitting in the audience waving their hands at her. Her sisters and brothers were blowing kisses toward her direction. She blew a kiss back at them.

"My family looks good sitting in the audience. My family and freinds took up two rows. They really love me. I wish my dad was here with us."

Charmayne saw one of her aunts crying.

Auntie, please stop crying before you have me crying. I need to try and calm myself down. I don't need my sisters or brothers see me crying. I definitely won't be able to do anything. I'm going to be no good on this stage.

Charmayne's family and friends stood up as she walked on stage. Not only did Charmayne's family and friend stand, but her entire class stood up as well. They all supported Charmayne in receiving her diploma. Her classmates knew her father had passed away. They all wanted to support Charmayne and help her celebrate this big day along with her.

Oh my God. I can't believe the entire class stood up for me as I walk on stage to receive my diploma. This is awesome. They really care about me.

When the ceremony was over, they announced the class. They all stood up and threw their hats up in the air.

Charmayne held on to her hat and tassel. She looked up toward Heaven and dedicated her diploma to her father. Some of Charmayne friends walked up to her and gave her a hug. They all felt Charmayne's pain.

"Daddy this is for you. I miss you so much."

Charmayne was crying uncontrollable. The only thing that could-soothe her pain was her father.

"I wish my dad was here to see me receive my diploma."

"Girl I know you wish your dad was here, but he's here in spirit," Fran sad. "I know he's looking down on you with a smile on his face."

A tear rolled down Charmayne's cheek. After their embrace they took pictures together. Charmayne and her friends met up with their families in the lobby of the auditorium. Charmayne sisters and brothers ran up to her. They all gave her the biggest hug anybody can give.

"We're so proud of you," they all said to Charmayne.

"Are you planning on hanging out with your friends tonight?" Charmayne mom asked her.

"Yes ma'am. We're supposed to meeting up, but I'm not sure if I'm going. I thought maybe you all wanted to go out to dinner."

"Yes, we are taking you out to dinner to celebrate your accomplishment. You deserve the world. One thing I can say, you never gave up. Even with the passing of your father, you stayed in the race. You can meet up with your friends after dinner. Charmayne and her mom both started crying. Next thing you know, the whole family was crying.

"Charmayne, if daddy was here with us he'd be happy for you," Rocky said.

"I really miss dad," Marc said. "He won't be able to see me and Rocky play football."

"Thank you Rocky for making me feel a little better," Charmayne said.

"Marc, no matter what you do in life, daddy will always be here with us."

"I know Charmayne, but it's hard watching my friends with their dads."

"It will get a little easier. Don't let that discourage you."

"Yeah, don't let that bother you," Miracle said. "One day their dad is going to pass away too. God has a better home for the ones who believes in him and follow his commands."

"Miracle?"

"Yes ma'am."

Nobody couldn't say nothing about what Miracle had said. Everybody was in shock of her remark.

"Ma, can we go just go and get something to eat? I'm starving."

Charmayne had to hurry up and talk about something else. Bad enough Rocky and Marc was feeling some type of way about their friends and their dad. Charmayne and her family went out to eat to one of Charmayne's favorite restaurant. They were greeted by the waitress.

"Hello everyone my name is Heaven, I'll be your waitress. Congratulation on your accomplishment!!!!

"Thank you Heaven," Charmayne said.

"Follow me and I'll take you to your table."

Everyone followed the waitress Heaven to their table.

"Can I get you all drinks while you're looking over the menu?"

When the customers saw Charmayne with her cap and gown on, they all stood up and being clapping their hands. Some of the guys were even whistling at her. That made Charmayne feel special.

I don't know these people and they don't know me, but they are showing me love. I think that was sweet of them to cheer me on.

Charmayne waved her hands at them and thanked them.

"Thanks everyone."

Charmayne and her family had a wonderful time talking and joking around with one another.

"I wish Uncle SB was here to see you walk on the stage to receive your diploma," my cousin Courtney said. "He would be sitting here at the table telling us stories about how he and his friends got drunk at

Auntie Joy birthday party. Uncle SB knew how to set an atmosphere on fire."

"My dad was there for me. He's still here in my presence."

"Charmayne you're scaring me," Courtney said.

"Courtney it's nothing to be scared of. The dead can't hurt you, it's the ones whose living you gotta watch out for."

Charmayne cousin Courtney was getting scared. She started trembling real bad

"Courtney I need for you to try and calm down," Auntie Pam said.

Charmayne didn't want to see her cousin Courtney get upset.

"Courtney, I'm not trying to upset you, but it's true. This is something I cannot forget. I'm sorry but it's true. When I walked on stage, I felt my dad's hand in mine. He let me know he was there with me."

Charmayne tried not to cry, but she had to let it out. Talking about her dad was difficult for her. It brought back a lot of memories. After listening to Charmayne talk about her father it brought tears to everyone at the table. They all felt Charmayne's pain. Charmayne's family knew she was hurting on the inside. She had to watch her friends with their dad and how they were taking pictures together. It was too hard for her not to talk about her dad.

"I feel what Rocky and Marc is going through." I know it hurts them to have sit and watch their friend's dad do things with them." It hurts me when I see all my friend's with their dad as well. Watching them have dinner together as a family brings back memories of my dad. I can remember times when we would go out to dinner, my dad would have everybody in the restaurant laughing at his jokes. I don't want anyone to have to go through what we are going through.

Charmayne's sisters and brothers all got up from where they were seated and wrapped their arms around her.

"Don't cry Charmayne," Marc said. "Rocky and I are going to be okay. Some of our friend dads take time up with us. I don't want to see you crying like this."

"Yes Charmayne," Gracie said. "This is your day. You supposed to be enjoying your special accomplishment you achieve in your goal."

Charmayne thought about all the good times they used to have with their father. She can remember when her brothers Rocky and Marc used to play Lil League Football. Her parents always attended their games and cheered them on.

The memories of my father will always remain in my heart.

Looks like everyone in the restaurant heard Charmayne crying. Even some of the customers in the restaurant walked over to their table and gave Charmayne a hug.

"Baby I don't know you, but my heart goes out to you, one of the customer said. I pray God gives you and your family strength."

One of Charmayne's friend's dad also walked over to where Charmayne and her family were sitting.

"Hello everyone."

"Hello Mr. Whaler" everyone replied.

"Charmayne I overheard you and your family talking. When I turned around, I noticed that you were crying. I want you and your family to know, my family is here for you all. Don't hesitate to stop by the house. We are only a few houses away from you all. I would love to spend some quality time with Rocky and Marc, Mrs. Dance if you don't mind. They love coming to the house playing with Gomez and Lance. I love having them over at the house."

"Ma, Mr. Whaler is always throwing the football to us," Marc said. "He always makes us feel welcome at his house."

"I don't have a problem with that Mr. Whaler I truly appreciate it.

"Thank you Mr. Whaler," Rocky said.

The manager overheard Charmayne and her family, he had his waitress to pick up their food ticket and bring it to him.

"I'm sorry, but I made a mistake on your ticket. I think I over charged you. Give me a minute and I'll be back with the correct amount."

"Again, I do apologize for my mistake."

The waitress finally came back with our ticket. This time she had the manager with her.

"How's everyone doing tonight?"

My mom looked at my Aunt Carrie daring her to say something.

"How was the food?" The manager asked us.

"The food was fantastic as always," my mom said. I believe we are your No.1 customers."

"Well, I'm glad you all enjoyed the food. The reason why I'm here is that some of the customers were concerned about you all. They overheard you all talking about the passing of her father. I am here to give you all my condolences. I will be paying for you all dinner. If there is anything I can do for you, please let your waitress know and I will accommodate you. Continue to enjoy your dinner.

"Oh Ma, that was so nice of him to do that."

"That goes to show you how God works in mysterious ways."

Everybody started crying again. When they got over the first episode of crying, here they are now crying again.

After dinner, Charmayne and her family handed their waitress Heaven a nice tip and a note saying "Thank You" and may God continue to bless you.

"Ma, I need to thank the manager for what he did."

"That will be wonderful Charmayne."

Charmayne Aunt Carrie asked to speak to the manager.

Everyone thanked the manager for what he did for them. They all gave him a hug.

There are still some nice people in the world who don't look at the color of your skin.

Chapter 18

His Warm Embrace

Having dinner with her family, was something Charmayne love doing. Charmayne noticed Gram left several messages on the phone for her to call him.

"Dang, Gram left me several messages on my phone for me to call him." Let me see what he wants." I guess he couldn't wait for me to get home.

Charmayne dialed Gram's number. They talked briefly on the phone. Before hanging up, Gram asked Charmayne if they could hangout.

"Charmayne if you don't mind I would like to stop by and see you."

"I'll have to make sure it's okay with my mom." I don't know how long we're going to be here, but I'll call you when I get home.

Charmayne and Gram both said their goodbyes.

"Ma, I really enjoyed myself with my family." They really showed me some love tonight.

"That's what family is for." We supposed to support one another. We are a closed knit family.

Everybody was exhausted and tired from Charmayne's graduation and hanging out with family.

"I'm going to take me a bath and go straight to bed," Miracle said.

"Me too," Ty'Meisha said. "I'm too tired to play with my dolls."

When Charmayne got home she called Gram.

"Hey I was just calling to let you know I was home."

"How was dinner?"

"Dinner was nice. We went to our favorite restaurant to eat."

"Did you ask your mom about me coming over?"

"No, I forgot. I'll ask her in a minute."

"I would like for us to hang out and talk. I see you already had dinner, but I would like to spend some time with you."

"Give me a minute to talk with my mom. I'll call you back."

"Okay."

"Gram must have something up his sleeves. I hope it's not sex, because he is going to get his feelings hurt. Just because you do things for me, does not mean my sweetness is giving to you in return. Hell, I told him to stop buying me things. If he wants to continue buying me things, then that's his business not mines. I'm not spending my money on him for nothing.

Charmayne and Gram both hung up the phone.

Charmayne went and knocked on her mom's room door.

"Who is it?'

"Mom it's me, Charmayne."

"Come in."

"Mom is it okay if Gram comes and pick me up?"

"Yes, he can come and pick you up as long as you're home at a decent time. I don't want you being out too late with him."

"Yes, ma'am. I won't be out too late."

Charmayne picked up the phone to call Gram back.

"Hey what are you doing? I was sitting here talking to my family waiting on you to call me."

"I was just calling to let you know my mom said it was okay for you to come pick me up. I just need to be home at a decent time."

"I promise not to have you out too late."

Charmayne went in her room to pick something nice to wear. She went in the bathroom to take a shower. Charmayne wore a pretty printed shirt with long sleeves and a pair of nice khaki pants.

"My parents know they made a beautiful daughter. I look good!"

While Charmayne waited for Gram, she went in her mom room.

Charmayne talked to her mom about a college she was looking into. There were several trades she wanted to take up as well.

Charmayne already had her plans in hand. She was going to work full time at a restaurant and attend college at night.

I'm going to make my mom proud. I'm going to help my mom out as much as I can. I don't want her to keep paying all the bills by herself. At least she'll be able to have extra money in her pocket just in case she wanted to buy her something.

Charmayne doesn't want her mom paying all the bills by herself and spending her money on her, her sisters and brothers.

"I'm so proud of you and the young lady you've become."

"Thanks mom, I appreciate you saying that to me."

"Charmayne your father would be very proud of you." I appreciate all the things you've done to help me out with your sisters and brothers. I know it wasn't easy especially not being able to hang out with your friends, but I do appreciate you for being very supportive to us. You don't know how much that means to me.

"Ma, my friends are not that important as my family are." Beside they know I have to take care of my sisters and brothers. My friends understand that I have to be there for them.

As Charmayne and her mom were in the room talking, there was a knock on the door.

"I'll get it," Miracle hollered.

Charmayne sister Miracle pushed past her and ran out the room to see who was knocking at the door. Charmayne was very proud of her sisters and brothers. They never opened the door until they looked out the blinds to see who it is. There's a way to open the blinds to peek out without the person outside seeing you looking at them.

"Charmayne, Gram is here."

Charmayne went in the living room to let Gram inside. Charmayne sisters and brothers was glad to see Gram.

Dang, I thought I was Gram's girlfriend. My sisters are crazy about Gram especially Ty'Meisha. My brothers always telling me that one day Gram and I are going to get married.

Gram gave each one of Charmayne's sisters a box with a balloon attached to it. "What is this for?" Gracie asked Gram.

"Where is my gift?" Asked Rocky.

Gram handed Rocky and Marc a blue bag with a card taped to it.

"You didn't have to buy them anything, Gram."

"I wanted to do something for them too. They never disrespect me in any way. I love hanging out with you and your family. My sisters be too busy."

Charmayne sisters and brothers all thanked Gram for buying them something. They all ran in their mom room to show her what Gram had bought for them.

"Ma look what Gram bought us," Ty'Meisha said.

"Oh that was very nice of him." Did you all tell him thanks for buying you all something?

"Yes ma'am," they all said.

Charmayne sisters and brothers loved the things Gram had bought them. Gram went back outside to his car and brought in more bags for Charmayne and her mom.

One of the gift bags was for Charmayne and the other bag for Charmayne's mom.

"Gram, I keep telling you to stop buying us things. I thank you for the gifts you brought us, but you really didn't have to buy us anything. You've already done enough for us my family and I."

"That's not all I have for you."

Charmayne went in her mom's room to give her the gift bag Gram had bought her.

"What is this Charmayne?"

"I don't know, Gram just told me to give this to you."

Her mom walked out her room with rollers still rolled in her hair.

"How are you doing, Gram?"

"I'm doing fine ma'am."

"Thank you for the gift. I truly love what you bought me. You didn't have to buy us anything, but I thank you anyway."

"You're welcome ma'am."

"I keep telling him that, but he doesn't listen."

"It was something I wanted to do for you all."

"I would like to know if I can take Charmayne out to dinner. We won't be out too late."

"Yes, Gram, you may take her out to dinner. Just make sure you have her home at a decent time."

"Yes ma'am I will. Thank you."

"No, thank you."

Charmayne kissed her mom, sisters and brothers on their cheeks.

"I'll see you all later."

"Have fun you two," Rocky said.

Charmayne's mom walked back in her room and closed the door behind her.

"Lord, Gram is such a nice young man, I pray he's not trying to take advantage of Charmayne. Give her strength to open her eyes to see the things he's doing for her. I don't want her to get caught up in a situation she's not able to handle."

Charmayne brothers and sisters were in their room playing with the things Gram had bought them.

"I like Gram," Miracle said.

"He's just trying to win some brownie points because he's dating our sister," Rocky said.

Charmayne brothers and sisters walked them to the door.

"Have fun," they shouted to Gram and Charmayne.

Rocky locked the door behind them.

I hope Gram is not trying to buy us so he can have Charmayne all to himself. I'll kick his ass if he hurts my sister. Since my dad is not here with us I have to protect my mom, sisters and my brother Marc. I'm not going to let no one hurt either one of them.

"Lord, look after Charmayne. Cover her in your blood. Amen."

Gram opened the car door for Charmayne.

"Oh, you're such a gentleman. Opening doors for me, how sweet."

When Charmayne got ready to get in the car, she noticed several bags in the front seat of Gram's car.

"What is this Gram? Another one of your gifts. You really have to stop what you're doing. For real now."

"I just wanted to show you how much I love you."

He loves me? He don't even know me that well to say he loves me. I really think we need to slow things down quick fast and in a hurry. Gram is really scaring me. I don't know if he's trying to buy me to keep me all for himself or he's trying to prove a point. I don't know what's going on, but I'm going to stop it before it goes any further between us.

Charmayne was puzzled at what Gram had said to her. She had forgot what she was about to say to him.

I wish Gram would stop buying me things. I don't want to hurt his feelings, but he needs to stop pushing himself on me. He's only going to make me push away from him. Don't get me wrong, I like the vibe we have between us, but he's doing too much. Buying me things doesn't make you win my heart.

Gram gave Charmayne a box wrapped in pink and yellow paper with a dark blue bow on it. The card on the box read "Congratulations."

Charmayne tore the paper off the box. When she opened it, she noticed a gold bracelet with a heart pendant on it.

"Thank you Gram. I appreciate all the things you have done for me and my family."

"No problem Charmayne. That goes to show you how important you are to me."

Gram reached in the back seat and handed Charmayne a vase with red, pink, and white roses with balloons attached to the vase.

"The flowers smells nice."

I guess he's trying to prove his point to me that he's my man. The roses looks good in this unique vase he bought me that was wrapped in silver foil paper.

Chapter 19

He Keep Surprising Me

"You really didn't have to do this, Gram." You keep surprising me with all these gifts.

"I know, but I wanted to do something nice for you."

"Why you keep buying me all these gifts?"

"Like I said, you deserve it."

"Thanks," but you don't have to keep doing this for me. Please stop buying me things. I'm satisfied with the things you have already given me.

"Baby, let me make you happy."

Baby, let me make you happy? What the hell? I'm nobody's baby. I wish he would stop calling me his baby.

"The things you do for me and my family means a lot to me. Everything you do makes me happy."

Gram had bought Charmayne a gold necklace with her initials engraved in a pendant heart. He also had a teddy bear and one of her favorite perfumes in between the teddy bear hands.

"Baby, you deserve the world. If I can give you the sun, moon and the stars I would. You mean a lot to me. I really love the way you make me smile. You mean everything to me.

"Gram, you really didn't have to do this." I really appreciate what you've given me, but I don't want to lead you on to something I'm not ready to make happen.

"I'm not trying to make you do something you're not comfortable doing." I just want to be with you. Just let me prove to you that I am a good guy.

"Gram, you're scaring me."

"Baby, I'm not trying to scare you or anything. I just want to show you my love."

"How can you keep saying you love me?" We really don't know each other. I don't know if you're an abusive person or if you're a criminal. I don't even know if you sell drugs or you do drugs. So, I really don't know a lot about you or anybody in your family.

"I understand, but I'm not like that." I am a good guy who does well in school and gets good grades. I don't get into any trouble in school or in the street. I'm just a cool guy. I mind my own business and stay out of other people's business.

"Yeah, that's what they all say." I definitely don't want a man who's going to put his hands on me, cheat on me or lie to me. You can say anything to me. I take everything you say into consideration. I'm nobody's fool.

"Baby, I didn't say you were anybody's fool." I'm just trying to get to know you if you let me.

"If you think you're going to be mistreating me, then you have the wrong female." Love don't live here under false pretenses. I think we need to take our time and get to know one another before we go any further.

"I agree with you on that." We need to take things slow with one another. I'm not trying to rush into this relationship or anything else. I just love hanging out with you and your family.

"Now you're speaking my language. I think I'm going to enjoy your friendship."

Gram and Charmayne both started laughing.

"Well, I think we better go to your favorite restaurant and have dinner." I have to make sure I have you home at a decent time. If not, your mom is going to stop us from seeing one another.

"Yes, my mom is very strict when it comes to her kids." I don't blame her for that. She's the one who takes care of us and makes sure we don't go without. I respect my mom to the upmost.

"Yes, baby I understand."

Gram took Charmayne to one of her favorite restaurant she loves eating at.

Charmayne and Gram waited for a waitress to escort them to their table.

As the waitress was walking Charmayne and Gram to their table, Charmayne heard someone call out her name. When she turned around, Charmayne noticed her friend Fran and her boyfriend sitting at a table next to a window looking over the ocean.

"Hey Charmayne, would you like to join us for dinner?" Fran's boyfriend Jordan asked.

Charmayne and Gram walked over to where her friend Fran and Jordan were sitting.

Hello Fran and Jordan."

"Hello Charmayne."

"Fran and Jordan, this is my boyfriend Gram."

"How are you doing?" Both Fran and Jordan asked Gram.

"I'm doing well. Nice meeting you both."

"Thanks for the invite, but Gram and I need to spend a little time together. If you both are still here after we eat dinner, we'll come over and chill with the both of you.

"No problem Charmayne and Gram. Have a nice dinner."

"Charmayne, we'll catch up later."

"Okay, Fran." Talk to you later.

The waiter walked Charmayne and Gram to their table.

The waitress introduced herself to Charmayne and Gram.

"Hello my name is Kelley, I would be your waitress for tonight. Can I start off by getting your drinks?

Charmayne and Gram both ordered a sprite soda to drink.

"Do you want me to give you a few minutes to look over the menu?"

"No, we know what we want," Gram said.

Gram and Charmayne ordered a half rack of ribs with French fries and baked beans with garlic bread.

"I'll be back with your drinks."

"Thank you," Charmayne said.

The waiter took up the menus from Charmayne and Gram. While they were waiting for the waitress to return with their drinks, Gram asked Charmayne about College.

"Is there a specific college you are looking into?"

"No, not really. But, I am planning on going to college. My friend Julie was telling me about this college she attends."

The waitress brought Charmayne and Gram their drinks.

"I'll be back in a minute with your food."

"Thank you," both Charmayne and Gram said.

"Do you know how to get there?"

"Yes, she told me where it was located."

"Do you want me to take you there?"

"If you're not doing anything tomorrow, I would appreciate it."

"What time do you want me to come and pick you up?"

"You can come around nine o'clock am. That's when they open."

Charmayne and Gram were glad the waitress brought their food out to them. Charmayne's stomach was growling.

On the way to Charmayne's house, Gram reached over and turned his radio on. One of Charmayne's favorite artists came on.

Oh, this song is the bomb. I love it when this song comes on the radio.

The song that was playing over the radio was one of Charmayne's favorite songs.

Charmayne looked up at Gram and grabbed his hand.

"Thank you for all the things you've done for me."

"No problem baby. Come over and sit next to me."

Charmayne unbuckled her seatbelt and sat next to Gram.

Gram wrapped his arms around Charmayne's shoulder.

It felt good sitting up under him with his arms around my shoulder. It was a feeling I've never felt before.

Charmayne didn't know if it was a good idea or a bad idea for her to sit up under him while he was driving.

I hope this boy doesn't think he's going to have sex with me. I don't think this was a good idea for me to sit next to him. I think I better buckle myself back in the seatbelt. Gram better not ask me to have sex with him, because that is out of the question. No panties of mines would be coming down or let alone coming off. Panties stay on at all times. Maybe I might just give Gram some of my sweetness, boy lying. One minute my mind is telling me to have sex with him, then the next minute it's telling me not to do it. And guess what? I'm not doing it.

Charmayne was always listening to how her friends talk about their first time having sex and how painful it was.

Charmayne had to come back to reality and erased that from her mind. She knew she wasn't about to have sex with Gram or anybody else.

Well, I'm listening to what my friends were telling me about their first experiences of having sex. It won't happen TONIGHT, not in my BOOK.

When they arrived at Charmayne's house, she had to hurry up and sit back on the passenger side.

"Gram, I appreciate what you did for me. You really didn't have to."

"I know Charmayne, but you're my girl. You deserve it."

"Dinner was nice Gram. I really enjoyed myself tonight."

Gram reached over and kissed Charmayne on her lips.

I don't believe Gram just kissed me. He really got some nerves. I don't remember giving him permission to kiss me, but I did enjoy it.

Charmayne's knees buckled. She didn't know what was next. She couldn't believe Gram kissed her in a romantic way.

"Dang his lips tasted like gummy bears."

Charmayne did not want Gram to stop kissing her, but she knew she had to stop before something happened.

Charmayne was a virgin and she planned on keeping it that way.

"I know you want to have sex with me, but I'm not ready to have sex."

"Listen baby, I'm not trying to pressure you into having sex with me or doing anything you're not comfortable doing. I told you that already. I'm not the type of guy to force a female to have sex with me."

"I know, but one day you might get the urge to want to have sex with me. If I keep turning you down, eventually you're going to get it from somewhere else. Let's take it slow before I regret having sex with you."

"I want to enjoy our friendship, that's all Charmayne."

"Me too, but….."

Gram interrupted Charmayne's conversation.

"There's no one else. I want to be with you and no one else."

Charmayne thought what Gram said to her was sweet.

Charmayne still had her mind made up. She wasn't about to have sex with Gram. Even though she wanted to, she had to stick to her word.

"I care about Gram, but I want to see how things go between us."

Before Charmayne got out of Gram's car, she reached over and kissed Gram on his lips.

I want to have sex with Gram, but I'm not ready to. If we keep kissing like this I'm going to end up giving him all of me. Before you know it, both my pants and panties will be pulled down.

Charmayne pushed Gram away from her.

"Look Gram, I think we need to stop. Yes, I want to have sex with you, but I'm not ready."

"Baby, I'll stop if you want me too."

"Yeah, we need to stop. I'm not ready to have sex with you right now. I have to stick to my goals."

"Baby, your lips taste good to me. I don't want to stop tasting your lips."

"Me either, but we have too."

I don't want to stop kissing Gram, but I need to stop before I do something I'm not ready to do.

Charmayne looked down and noticed Gram was getting aroused. Not only that, Charmayne felt a tingle between her legs as well. She straightened up her clothes before getting out of Gram's car.

Let me get myself together before getting out of Gram's car. I don't need them looking at me funny.

Charmayne grabbed all the gifts Gram had bought her.

"Goodnight Gram. I'll call you when I get in the house."

"Okay baby, goodnight."

Charmayne closed the car door when she got out.

Before going in the house, Charmayne looked back and waved her hand at Gram.

When Charmayne walked in the house her mom, sisters and brothers was sitting in the living room playing a game call Family Trivia.

"Hey Charmayne we need you to play on our team, Marc said.

"Yeah because we're beating you," Gracie said.

"No you're not. We're only down by three points."

"So, that mean we're beating you.

"Look you have momma on your team. That's why you all are winning." Rocky said.

"Rocky stop being a cry baby," Miracle said. I can play you with my eyes closed.

Charmayne sat down with her family and played with them.

"I love when I can sit down with my family and how we enjoy each other's love." We have so much fun when we play a game called, "Family Trivia."

"Charmayne where did you get all those bags from?" Asked Ty'Meisha.

"Gram bought me these gifts."

"Let us see what he bought you."

"Ty'Meisha you need to stop being so noisy, Gracie said." If Charmayne wanted you to know what he bought her, she would have showed you.

Charmayne showed everyone what Gram had bought her.

"The gifts are nice Charmayne," everyone said.

"Thanks everyone."

"Charmayne remember what I have told you."

"Yes ma'am, I remember what you said to me."

"Come on and let's finish this game, Marc said.

"Why so we can beat you," Ty'Meisha said.

After playing Family Trivia, everybody said their prayers and went to bed.

Chapter 20

A Bright Light

It was around nine-thirty am when Charmayne got up. Charmayne got up and went to the bathroom to brush her teeth. She overheard her mom on the phone talking.

"Good morning ma."

"Good morning sunshine. Breakfast would be ready in a minute. I have homemade biscuit in the oven."

"Thanks ma." I was hoping you would have made some homemade biscuit. My mouth was watering for them.

"I'm still celebrating your accomplishment. I just want you to know how proud I am of you. You never gave up on achieving your dream."

Charmayne went to the bathroom to brush her teeth and wash her face. After, she went in her room to make up her bed. She overheard her mom talking to Ty'Meisha.

"You all just don't know how overwhelmed I am. My baby, your sister just graduated from high school. I'm so proud of her."

"We're proud of her too ma." Ty'Meisha said.

"Oh, how I wish your father was here to see Charmayne walked on stage and receive her diploma. He would have been proud of her."

"Momma, Daddy was there," Gracie said.

Charmayne overheard Gracie talking to their mom.

Charmayne walked out of her room.

"What do you mean Daddy was there?" Charmayne asked Gracie.

"I saw a bright light over your head when you walked on stage. It was Daddy letting you know he's proud of you."

Charmayne started crying. She couldn't believe what Gracie said. She knew Gracie was telling the truth. Not only did Gracie see the light, but Miracle saw it too. They were both telling the truth about a light shining over Charmayne's head.

"Charmayne, Gracie is telling you the truth. I also saw the light over your head when you walked on stage."

When Charmayne walked on stage, she noticed a bright light shining over her head as well. She didn't pay it any attention. She thought it was someone taking a picture of her.

I hope my family is taking plenty of pictures of me, but at the same time I wish the camera lighting is blinding my eyes.

"Momma, Gracie is telling you the truth. I saw the bright light too. I thought it was somebody taking a picture. As I was walking on stage, I felt daddy hand in mines. It felt like he was walking right next to me."

"Charmayne are you telling me the truth? Did you see a bright light as you walked on stage?"

"Yes ma'am. I'm telling you the truth. When I walked on stage, it was like a shining bright light just over my head. I really thought it was light flashing from some of the people cameras in the audience."

"We all saw the light momma," Ty'Meisha said.

"Momma daddy talks to us all the time," Miracle said. "Do you remember when you would come in the room and tell us to stop laughing so loud?"

"Yes, I remember that. How does this have anything to do with what we're talking about?"

"It was daddy who was making us laugh," both Marc and Rocky said. "He was telling us things he used to do when he was our age."

Knowing what her children had experienced at a young age. Charmayne's mom never thought their father would pay them a visit like that. Their mom couldn't believe what her children were telling her.

"I didn't know my husband went to our children and had conversations with them. I thought I was the only one who was experiencing his presence. He shocked me in doing that. At least I know they're not afraid of him when he comes to them."

"Mom dad talks to me all the time," Miracle said. "He lets me know that I shouldn't be afraid of him when he comes and talk to me."

Charmayne's mom was totally shocked at what she was hearing from each one of her children. She didn't know if she should cry or be angry at their dad. Charmayne, her sisters and brothers stopped talking about the experience they each had with their dad. Their mom begin to tell them about the visit she had with their dad as well.

"Momma it scared me at first," Gracie said. "I almost ran into the wall trying to get out of my room."

"Me too momma." Rocky said. "I didn't know what it was. I was in the bathroom taking a shower and then I felt a cool breeze brush against my shoulder. I thought somebody had opened the bathroom door. When I pulled the curtain back I didn't see anyone."

"Where you scared when that happened to you?" Asked Gracie.

"I was scared a little. I didn't think nothing else of it until I felt the cool breeze brushed past me again. This time is was daddy telling me not to be afraid. I started crying.

"What happened next Rocky?" Asked Ty'Meisha.

"I felt his hands wipe away my tears. He told me since I'm the oldest son I have to protect you all. He also apologize for scaring me."

"Well your father is everywhere in this house. He comes to me when I'm in the room on my knees crying."

"Why are you on your knees crying ma?" Asked Rocky.

"There are days I which your father was here so I can talk to him. I miss your father dearly."

"Momma, God can help you in whatever you're going through," Miracle said. "All you have to do is have faith the side of a mustard seed. He will bring us out."

Everybody couldn't believe what Miracle had said.

"Momma God is our protector. He want leave you or forsake you. All you have to do is believe and put all your trust in him and not man."

"Miracle, I know what you're saying is true. God did it before and I know he'll do it again."

The things Miracle was saying to their mom was powerful. Everybody started crying.

Charmayne's mom knew there was something special about Miracle.

Miracle walked over to her mom and put her hands on her forehead. She started praying asking God to protect her mom and keep her from harm and danger.

Miracle begin to pray for each one of her sisters and brothers.

"Don't be afraid everyone, God is going to protect us."

"Momma, daddy loves you. He told me to tell you that he will always love you no matter what. He said when you close your eyes at night he will be lying right next to you. He's going to comfort you when you're going through."

Everybody started looking puzzled in the face.

Oh my God, I couldn't believe Miracle and what she was saying to our mom. A lot of things Miracle or my other sisters and brothers don't know. Only my mom and I knows what my dad had said to us. Out of nowhere she just start telling my mom what our dad had said to her. My dad always said to us, "Miracle is the little preacher in the house. Her prayers is what's going to keep us together and keeping us strong."

"Momma, daddy also told me to tell you not to worry about the things he left behind because they don't mean him no good. He also said, stop going down on your knees asking God to give you strength. He's already given you what you need."

Charmayne mom couldn't do nothing but look at Miracle in a strange way.

"Miracle thank you for your conformation, God has already reveal to me what I was going through. He let me know that he is God and God alone."

Charmayne and her family almost had church in their house. The spirit was so high in the living room. Everybody was giving God the praises.

"Lord I thank you for the conformation. Thank you for blessing my daughter to reveal what you're already had reveal to me. Lord I praise you, I lift you up."

As they got ready for bed, they got on their knees and began to pray.

"Lord, I ask that you protect us throughout the night. Give us strength where we are torn down. Lord, I ask that you bless my children one by one and name by name. In your precious name I pray, Amen."

"Amen," everybody said.

"Goodnight." they all said in unison.

Chapter 21

Reaching My Goal

Charmayne got up around seven thirty a.m. She went in the bathroom and took a shower. She wanted to be dressed when Gram came to pick her up. She didn't want Gram to have sit and wait on her. She was excited about going to visit the college her friend Julie told her about.

I'm so excited about visiting this college my friend Julie was telling me about. This is a fresh start of a new chapter in my life.

"Mom I'll see you later. Gram is here to take me for my tour at the college. I'm kind of scared. I never been to a college before."

"Charmayne you are a smart young lady. You have come a mighty long way. There's nothing for you have to be scared of."

"Good luck," Ty'Meisha said.

"Thank you," Ty'Meisha.

When Charmayne and Gram arrived at the college they were greeted by the receptionist at the front desk.

"Hello, my name is Ms. Paris. How may I help you today?"

Charmayne gave the receptionist her name and what time her appointment was.

"My name is Charmayne Dance. I have a nine thirty am appointment with Ms. May."

The receptionist looked in her up in the appointment book.

"Okay Ms. Dance have a seat and Ms. May will be with you shortly."

"Thank you."

Charmayne and Gram sat in the waiting area for Ms. May.

Ms. May finally walked in where Charmayne and Gram were seated.

"Hello, Charmayne Dance. My name is Ms. May. How are you doing today?"

"I'm doing well, thanks for asking. This is my boyfriend Gram."

"Hello Gram, how are you doing this afternoon?"

"I'm well, thanks for asking."

Ms. May extended her hand out to shake their hands.

"I'm glad you decided to come in today. Are you ready to take a tour?"

"Yes, I'm ready. I'm excited to have a tour of this college. My friend Julie goes here. She told me about the classes I can take. She loves it here."

"I know Julie. She's also in my typing class. You'll get a chance to see her in class."

Ms. May introduced Charmayne and Gram to several of the staff who were seated at their desks."

"Charmayne this is where you'll come when you commence your night class. Let's go inside so I can introduce you to your teacher."

Charmayne was introduced to her teacher and to some of the students in the class.

"Look at my friend Julie, sitting over there typing like she knows what she's doing. Well, I guess she do. Julie is typing fast, but sometimes I'll catch her looking at her fingers."

After touring the college Ms. May, Charmayne and Gram went in her office to discuss some brochures she had on her desk for Charmayne.

"Have a seat Charmayne and Gram."

Charmayne and Gram sat across from Ms. May's desk.

Ms. May congratulated Charmayne for taking the first step to attend college.

"Charmayne, I just want to say "Thank You" for making the right choice in going to college. I know you're just getting out of high school, but you did the right thing. It's good to continue your education while everything is still fresh on your mind."

"I pray I'm doing the right thing. I want to better myself in life. I want to be able to show what I've accomplished."

"Well Charmayne, you did accomplish something. You graduated with your class and now you're on your way to college. You will accomplish another goal in your life. So, you have a lot to be thankful for. Ms. May gave Charmayne several brochures and financial aid forms to look over and sign.Charmayne looked at several brochures, but only one caught her eye. She was interested in taking up Office Specialist. Charmayne would earn her degree in two years.

Wow, I would earn a degree as an Office Specialist in two years. This is wonderful.

"Ms. May before I sign these forms, I would like for my mom to look over them if you don't mind."

"Sure that's fine with me, Charmayne. I rather for you to have your parents look over the paper work before signing anything. I recommend that to all students. I tell the students who come here to make sure that they sit down with their parents and read over the forms before signing them. I tell my students if you don't understand anything in these brochures feel free to call me. Don't sign anything you don't understand."

"Thank you Ms. May."

On the way home, Gram asked Charmayne what degree was she interested in taking up.

"I don't know. There were several of them in the brochure that caught my eyes. The one that stood out the most to me was Office Specialist."

"Do you want something to eat, Charmayne?"

"Yes, I'm hungry. I'm just so excited about going to college."

"I understand how you feel Charmayne. I'm proud of you. I am going to support you in whatever you want to do in order to better yourself."

On the way to Charmayne's house, Gram told her to think about what degree she wanted to take up.

"Yes, I know. I'm not going to pick just anything. I'm going to pick something that is going to benefit not just me, but my family as well. I want to be able to get a job with my degree."

"Baby, you know I'm here for you."

"Yes, I know you are. I appreciate everything you do for me."

Gram didn't stay long when he dropped Charmayne off.

"Baby, I'm not going to stay."

"What do you mean you're not going to stay?"

Gram wanted to give Charmayne and her mom some time to discuss the forms she received from Ms. May.

"I think you and your mom need to talk about the college and the forms Ms. May gave you to give to her. Charmayne thought Gram was going to spend a little time with her.

"I thought we were going to spend a little time together."

"We will baby. I just want you and your mom to sit down and go over these forms. I can't tell you what to do, but I will back you up one hundred percent."

Charmayne kissed Gram on his lips.

"I'll call you after me and my mom talk."

"Okay, baby I'll be waiting on your call."

"I'll let you know what she said."

Charmayne got out of the car and waved her hand bye to Gram.

When Charmayne got in the house her mom, sisters and brothers were seated in the living room waiting for her to tell them the good news.

"Tell us what they said," Marc said.

"Yes, Charmayne tell us what they said."

"We all want to know what they said."

"Well if you all stop asking her all these questions maybe she'll tell us." Miracle said.

"Thank you, Miracle, because Marc, Rocky and Ty'Meisha must think they're my dad and mom."

"I don't think neither one of you are the parent." Gracie said.

"Well, I have good news if you all just let me tell it."

Charmayne handed her mom the paperwork from Ms. May.

Charmayne and her mom looked over the paperwork and forms. Charmayne mom wanted to look over the paperwork before signing them. She didn't want to sign anything that would put Charmayne in jeopardy or that was going to have her paying out of pocket.

Charmayne's mom was very pleased with the college and what they had to offer.

"Mom, what do you think about me going to college?"

"As long as you're making the right decisions in your life I'll stand behind you one hundred percent. Your father and I always want the best for our children. We want our children to be successful."

"I made one good choice by graduating with my class. I'm making another good choice in going to college."

"Yes, you did, baby. I am so proud of the young lady you've become. You didn't give up on getting your diploma and graduating with your class. You stayed in the race. That's what makes me so proud of you Charmayne. You could've gave up, but you didn't."

Charmayne and her mom fought back tears.

Charmayne sisters and brothers all ran up to her and gave her a hug.

"In two years I'll receive a degree in Office Specialist."

"Charmayne, only you can decide what you want to do in life. Nobody else can tell you what to do or how to do it. You'll have friends who are going to be against you attending college. Don't let that hinder you from furthering your education."

"Yes ma'am I know. Nobody can tell me what to do. I wish anyone of my friends would say something like that to me. If they do say that to me, they were never my friend. Daddy always told me to choose my friends wisely. I can remember him saying to me, "Charmayne, you don't have friends, you have associates."

"Your father always said that to you all. He doesn't want his children to be hurt by anyone."

"Man, I miss dad." Marc said.

"We all miss him." Gracie said.

"I wish daddy was still here with us." Miracle said. "He would be so proud of you Charmayne and us too."

Talking about their father brought back a lot of memories and tears. Neither one of them could control their emotions. They had a family moment.

Man, I truly wish my dad was here for us. I hate not having my dad around.

The house was silent for about an hour. No one said a word.

"Okay I think we need to change the subject," Charmayne said. "I know we all miss dad, but we have to stay strong for each other."

Charmayne loved her mom. Her mom never mislead her.

I love my mom and I know she wants the best for me. She's always telling me to "Stay strong and finish the race."

Charmayne's mom stood by her side through the toughest time in her life.

"Mom, I wish daddy was here to help us celebrate my graduation." I know he'll be proud of me in making the first step in going to college. I miss daddy so much. Charmayne's father's absence has become increasingly difficult. Sometimes she'd sit in her room and cry herself to sleep.

Daddy, I just need to know you hear my voice crying out for you. Please show me a sign that you're here with me.

Charmayne felt a cool breeze brushed against her face. It was her dad letting her know he sees her tears.

Thanks dad, I knew you would come through for me.

Charmayne father was a good father to his children. He made sure they never went hungry or needed for anything. He would starve before he would let them starve. One thing Charmayne can say is her parents took good care of them. There's nothing her parents wouldn't do for them.

I'm so glad to be blessed with such good parents in my life. Yes, my dad is not here with us, but he was the best father a child would want to have. My dad will always be honor "Father of the Year."

Charmayne started thinking about her father and how he would tell them jokes about his friends. He used to tell them the things he used to do when he was young. Charmayne hated seeing her friends or anybody else she knows with their dads. It made her sick to her stomach. Sometimes she would stay home and lock herself in her room. What she really wished was for her father to see Marc and Rocky play football.

Dad only if you can see how big Rocky and Marc has gotten. You would be proud of the both of them. They missed playing football with you or you going to their football game. Only if you were here.

"I wish my dad was here to see how Marc and Rocky play football. He would be yelling, **"Those are my boys there"** whenever they made a touchdown. That was my dad favorite word whenever Marc or Rocky score a touchdown.

Charmayne's brother Marc and Rocky would talk about their friend's fathers doing things with them. Rocky and Marc hate when their friends tells them how their dad be throwing the ball to them and how they be doing father and son stuff. That really put a hole in Charmayne's heart.

Charmayne hated seeing her brothers in pain. She wished there was a way to make the pain go away for Rocky and Marc let alone her sisters.

I can't tell my mom things I'd tell my dad. My dad is more understanding than my mom. My mom don't play with us. What my mom says, "goes."

Sometime Charmayne will be in her room crying thinking about the good times she shared with her father. Charmayne would start talking to her father telling him things she wanted him to know about what she did in school that day or what she did with her friends.

Why am I telling my dad about my day at work or what I did today? My dad sees it all.

As Charmayne was talking to her father, she felt a cool breeze brush up against her face. She felt her father's presence in the room with her. She looked up toward heaven and closed her eyes. After feeling the presence of her father, she felt much better.

Sometimes Charmayne heard her mom in the room crying.

I know my mom is lonely without my dad. I wish I can erase everything and make her feel better, but God knew what was best for us. He didn't want my father to suffer any more. He didn't want to put that burden on us.

Charmayne thanked God for giving them a good father like their dad.

"Lord, I thank you for blessing us with a good father. Dad, if only you were here to see how much we've grown up. We miss you dearly.

The tears flowed heavy from Charmayne eyes. She tried to console herself, but it didn't do any good. Charmayne really missed her father.

Charmayne decided she would share the good news with some of her friends about going to college. She and several of her friends were on a four-way telephone conversation.

"Guess, what I did everyone."

"What did you do Charmayne?" Asked Sweet.

"Girl I hope you're not about to tell us you're pregnant."

"We all know Charmayne is not having sex," Charisma said.

I was calling to let you all know that I'm taking college courses."

"I'm very proud of you," Charisma said. "I wish you the best."

"I can't do college," Destiny said. "I've had enough of homework in school. I don't need another headache."

"Girl, you stupid for real," Fran said. "When you were in school, you didn't do nothing anyway."

"Well I did enough to graduate. I can't say that much about you. All you wanted was to beat people up and take their lunch money."

"Both of you all need to be quiet," Sweet said. "Charmayne called us to share her good news and you two are acting like jack asses."

"Charmayne, finished telling the good news. I dare either of you to say another word. I promise I'll be knocking at your door."

Neither Destiny nor Fran said anything else while on the phone.

What the hell. I know Destiny and Fran are actually being quiet on the phone. Neither one of them said a word. They must have known Sweet wasn't playing with them. That don't sound like my friends. They would have cursed you out with all the letters in the alphabet.

Each one of her friends wished her the best. After talking to her friends for a while, Charmayne laid across her bed and dozed off.

Charmayne had it all planned out. She was going to achieve all the goals she's set forth to do for herself. She did not want anyone or anything to hinder her from making her dreams come true.

Charmayne wanted to work full time and go to school at night. She couldn't believe she'll be graduating in two years with a degree in Office Specialist.

"Lord, I thank you for giving me this opportunity to achieve another goal in my life. Couldn't have done it without you. Dad you are going to be proud of me. I achieve another goal in my life."

Charmayne knows her father is looking down on her. She knows her dad and sister are having a family reunion in heaven. I know they are looking down on me with a smile on their faces. Charmayne missed them both.

If my dad was here he would say, "Baby girl, I'm so proud of you." *My oldest sister Amy would say,* "Big head you make me sick or you gets on her nerves."

Charmayne sent a kiss toward heaven to her father and sister.

Chapter 22

Missing My Father

Friday was Charmayne's first night in class. She was excited to attend college and meet some of the other students in her class. Charmayne really didn't know anyone in her class, not even the teacher.

I pray I like this class. I hope nobody starts asking me a lot of questions. If they do, their feelings will be hurt. I'm not here to make friends, but to do what I have to do in order to graduate.

Gram dropped Charmayne off at school.

"Have a good time in class."

"Thanks, Gram, I appreciate it."

When Charmayne walked in the building she was greeted by the receptionist name Kira.

Charmayne walked in class and was greeted by her teacher.

"Hello, Charmayne, my name is Mrs. Green. I am your computer teacher.

"Hello, Mrs. Green.

"Everyone, this is Charmayne."

"Hello, Charmayne," they all greeted her.

"Hello, everyone."

Everybody made Charmayne feel comfortable. They all introduced themselves to Charmayne. She was nervous trying to fit in. She didn't have a clue in what to do next.

I don't have a clue how to work a computer. I don't think I want to continue this class. This looks too hard for me.

She sat down next to a young lady who gave her a thumbs up.

"Hi, my name is Leslie."

"Hi Leslie, my name is Charmayne. Nice to meet you."

"Nice to meet you too, Charmayne."

"It's okay to be nervous. I was just like you when I first started here."

"Was it hard for you to adjust?"

"No. Not really. I know a little about computers. I can type a little without looking at the keys, but not that much."

"I don't know anything about computers or the keys on the computer. Let alone, I don't know how to type."

After Charmayne and Leslie talked for a while she started asking Charmayne a lot of questions. Leslie wanted to know what high school Charmayne attended, what are her goals, and other little things Charmayne wasn't interested in telling her.

This girl don't even know me and she's asking me a lot of questions. This female is nosy as hell. I'm trying not to hurt her feelings or stop talking to her, but she needs to slow it down a notch. I'm trying to stay calm because this is my first night. I don't want no one to see the bad side of me.

Charmayne responded to Leslie's questions.

"Well, you tell me a little about yourself."

Leslie started telling Charmayne all her business. She was telling Charmayne about her relationship and how she caught her baby daddy cheating on her.

One thing I can say, I'll tell you what I want you to know. You'll never know my business and that's for sure. When you start telling people your business, everybody knows your business. My parents always told us, "You don't have friends, you have associates." I'm not here to make friends, but to learn and get my degree.

Charmayne didn't want to hurt Leslie feelings, so she changed the subject. Leslie was trying to get a little too personal with Charmayne. Charmayne had to stop her before it went any further.

This chick will never know my business or anything else I have going on. Yes, Leslie seems to be a nice young lady, but I don't know her like that. If she's telling you her business, than she'll tell someone yours.

However, Leslie did help Charmayne out with the computer when she got confused.

Well I am thankful for Leslie showing me how to work the computer, but that's how far it will go.

Mrs. Green asked everyone to pay close attention to her as she demonstrated how to work the computer.

"I need everyone to look at the screen and watch it carefully. I will show you only twice, but after that you're on your own. That's why it is important for you to pay close attention."

If you don't watch Mrs. Green carefully, you will get confused. I'm glad she takes her time in teaching you.

Sometimes Charmayne fingers would get caught between the keys. Charmayne finally was getting the hang of it, or so she thought. Mrs. Green saw Charmayne was struggling on the computer. She walked over to where Charmayne was seated and helped her out.

I'm glad she came over to help me because I was sure was struggling.

Mrs. Green was patient and took her time with Charmayne. She wanted to make sure Charmayne had the hang of it.

"I'm here to help you Charmayne. I know it's your first time typing and yes it can be challenging to type without looking at the keys. So far you're doing well."

"I'm letting my nervous get the best of me.

"It's okay to be a little nervous, but I'm here to help you."

Mrs. Green showed Charmayne the best way to not getting her fingers caught between the keys on the computer.

"Thanks Mrs. Green. I appreciate you taking the time out to show me how to type without getting my fingers stuck between the keys."

"Don't get discouraged. Each one of these students had the same problem as you did when they first started out. I took my time to show each student the proper way to type. I want my students to learn how to type without looking at the keys. Charmayne really didn't know anything about computer or the keys on the computer.

After Mrs. Green worked with Charmayne for a while she was able to type a little better. Charmayne was also progressed to type without looking at the keys on the computer.

I'm so glad Mrs. Green came over to work with me. Trying to type without looking at the keys was hard, but she showed me the proper way in typing. I think I got the hang of it.

Some of the students started a week or two before Charmayne did. Half of the students were still learning how to operate the computer as well as learning the keys.

There was a young lady sitting across from Charmayne, she was typing without looking at her fingers. The young lady typed so fast Charmayne lost track of what she was supposed to be doing.

Hell she's typing so fast, let me see if I can type like her. Yeah right, who am I fooling? Mess around and get it wrong. I think I better take my time in learning how to type. One day, I'm going to be just like her or even better than her.

Charmayne thought she did a pretty god job. She made a few mistakes, but not that much. Mrs. Green asked Charmayne if she was ready to take a test on what she's learned today in class.

"I believe I'm ready, Mrs. Green."

The girl sitting next to Charmayne said, "Give it a try, I have confidence in you."

"Charmayne, you can do it," all the students encouraged her.

Charmayne felt good knowing the other students thought she could do it.

"Alright, I'm ready."

Everybody stopped doing what they were doing and focused on Charmayne. It made her nervous having the other students watching her type, but that didn't matter to her. She wanted to show everybody that she has confidence in herself.

Dang, do they have to look at me while I'm typing? They're making me nervous. I have confidence in myself. I know I can do it, just have to stay focused and forget about whose watching me.

Charmayne had to look straight ahead. She had to type without looking at the keys or her fingers while typing. After taking the test, Charmayne noticed she made a couple of mistakes. That didn't discourage her, instead it gave her a lot of confidence in herself. Charmayne typed about twenty five wpm.

I think I did well for my first time in typing class. I'm proud of myself. I was still able to see my fingers as I was typing on the computer. I just didn't have my head down as I was typing.

Mrs. Green thought Charmayne grade was good considering it was her first time typing without looking at the keys on the computer.

Mrs. Green gave each of the student homework to do before they left.

When Charmayne walked outside, Gram was sitting in the lobby waiting for her.

Look at my boo sitting in the lobby waiting for me. That's so sweet of him.

Gram made sure to be on time when picking Charmayne up. One thing Charmayne can say, Gram was never late when picking her up or taking her to work or school.

Charmayne was glad to have Gram in her life. She don't know what she'd do without him.

I'm so glad to have a man like Gram. He makes sure I'm on time for work and school. To set it off, he's never late in picking me up. I guess he earning his brownie points.

Gram never pressured Charmayne into having sex with him or staying out late with him. He was a gentleman true to his word.

I'm going to try him and see what he's going to do. To my surprise he might take me up on my offer. I better be prepared of what his answer might be. Everybody knows, Charmayne is not about to have sex with anyone. I don't care what you do for me or how much money you spend on me, I'm not giving up my sweetness.

After Charmayne and Gram left the school, they went to a fast food restaurant to get something to eat. Charmayne asked Gram to take her to the park.

"Gram let's take a walk in the park if you don't mind."

"I can't take you to the park tonight, Charmayne. Maybe we can go tomorrow. I promised your mom I'll have you home at a decent time. I don't want to disrespect her in any kind of way."

Charmayne kept on pressuring Gram in taking her to the park. Gram wouldn't budge or attempt in taking Charmayne to the park. He didn't want to disrespect Charmayne's mother.

"If I wanted to go straight home I would have told you to take me home."

"Baby, I'm not going to disrespect your mom. You can get mad at me all you want too, but I'm taking you home. I don't want your mom to think any less of me."

Charmayne was dying laughing on the inside at Gram.

Gram actually passed the test. No matter how I kept pressuring him in taking me to the park, he wouldn't take me. I respect Gram in what he did. Now, he really earned his brownie points in my book.

Gram didn't know Charmayne was testing his faith.

"If Gram knew I was testing him, he'd be mad at me."

Charmayne wanted to see just how much Gram love her.

If Gram takes me to the park instead of taking me home, I know he wants to have sex with me. That let me know, he doesn't respect me or my mom. There's no way I'm going to have sex with him. I don't care how bad he wants to have sex with me, I'm not having sex with him.

Charmayne felt at ease knowing Gram respected her and her mom.

"Thanks for nothing, Gram."

"I'll take you to the park another day. Right now is not the time."

She was glad when Gram pulled in her driveway. She couldn't wait to get in the house and laugh at Gram.

Boy, I can't wait to get in the house. I'm going to have a good time laughing at Gram. If I never laugh at anything before, I sure am now.

Before going in the house, Charmayne and Gram sat in the car talking. Gram explained to Charmayne the reason they didn't go to the park.

Only if Gram knew how I was testing him. I just wanted to see if he was going to disrespect my mom and what she had told him. I wouldn't want to be with someone who disrespect my mom let alone disrespect me. If he disrespect me or my mom, there's no way I was going to continue being in a relationship with him. If Gram would have did that, that goes to show me he don't give a damn about me or my mom.

Charmayne reached over and kissed Gram on the cheek.

"I'll call you when I get home."

'Okay, talk to you then."

They exchanged goodnights. When Charmayne walked in the house everybody was sitting in the living room talking.

"What's going in here? Why is everybody sitting in the living room looking sad in the face?"

"Ty'Meisha had a bad dream," Rocky said.

"She was screaming so loud it woke all of us up," Gracie said.

"She had a bad dream, that's all," my mom said.

"She started crying for daddy," Miracle said.

Charmayne's sister Ty'Meisha was four years old when their dad died. She really didn't understand why he was not there with them.

We all missed our dad. Not being able to see him around the house is really taking a toll in our lives. It gets harder by the day knowing we can't see him or talk to him. Our dad always made us laugh. He did things with us. He made sure to be at every football games my brothers had. He never let us go without anything. I can understand why my sister Ty'Meisha is crying. Sometimes I find myself crying, wishing he was here with us too.

Charmayne's sister Ty'Meisha reached for her. She wanted Charmayne to pick her up. Charmayne walked over to where they were sitting at and reached for Miracle.

"How you're feeling Miracle?"

"I want Daddy to come home."

"I do too Miracle, but dad is in a better place." We all wish dad was here with us.

We all had tears in our eyes. We tried to compose ourselves, but we just couldn't.

I sang one of Ty'Meisha's favorite songs to her. When I sing to Miracle it calms her down. Lord, please give us strength to hold on and stay strong. We need you right now, father.

Charmayne made a promise that no matter what happens, she's going to protect her mom, sisters and brothers.

"Ty'Meisha don't never think Daddy doesn't love you or misses you, because he does. Remember every step you take, Daddy is taking one with you. I'm going to protect each and every one of you all. That's the promise I made to daddy. It's okay to cry Miracle. Can you feel daddy's presence in the room? I can feel him touching your hand. Daddy is letting you know he's here for you."

Charmayne felt a cool breeze brush up against her shoulder.

"It feels kind of cool in here," Rocky said.

"What was that, Charmayne?" Miracle asked.

"Daddy is letting us know he's here with us," Gracie said.

"Did anybody else feel the cool breeze pass by them?"

"Charmayne, we all felt the cool breeze. Your dad is letting you know he's in here with us. You all don't need to be afraid of him. Your father will never hurt you in any kind of way."

"I miss Daddy, Charmayne," Miracle said.

"We all miss dad," Rocky said." I miss him playing football with me and Marc. I hate seeing my friends with their dad."

Miracle was so upset she ran in her room and closed the door behind her. Marc and Miracle are very close. They are twins. They can feel each other's paisn.

"Momma, let me go in her room and talk to her," Marc said.

Not having our dad around was tough for all of us. I hate seeing my family in so much pain. Yes, we all miss our dad. He was the joy of all of our hearts. He always made sure to take care of his family. Now, it's up to my mom to do all of the providing. Dang daddy, you left us too soon. I know you are in a better place.

"Listen everyone, we are going to be alright. Yes your dad left us too soon, but God knew what was best for him. I don't want any one of you to feel like we can't make it. I don't want you to give up because your dad is not here with us. I want each and every one of you to cry and let it all out. You all will feel much better knowing you cried your last tear. God is going to continue providing for us."

Charmayne, her mom, sisters, and brothers let it all out. They cried until they couldn't cry no more.

Marc went in the room to talk to Miracle.

"Hey Miracle."

"Hey Marc."

"Listen Miracle, go ahead and cry. You'll feel better when you let it all out. Remember dad may not be present with us, but he's still with us."

"I know Marc, but it hurts when I can't see or touch him."

Marc and Miracle went back in the living room where everyone gathered at.

"Are you okay, Miracle?"

"Yes, Charmayne, I feel much better after me and Marc talked about dad. I just wish he was still with us."

How can I protect my sisters and brothers now? Let alone my mom. That's my Dad's job. He promised he'll never leave us and he's not here to protect us.

Charmayne loves her family. She had to be the one to protect them as well as her mom. That's a promise Charmayne was going to keep.

Chapter 23

I Gave It Up

It was a nice Saturday morning the sun was shining bright, people were mowing their lawn and children were playing with their friends. The sun shone brightly through Charmayne's window as she slept soundly in her bed.

Charmayne was still in bed sleep when Gracie woke her up.

"Charmayne wake up, you have a phone call."

Charmayne reached under the bed and pulled out her bedroom slippers. Not paying attention while walking out the room, she hit her ankle on the dresser and screamed out in pain.

"Dang I hit my ankle on the dresser."

Charmayne;s mom, brothers and sister all ran in her room.

"Charmayne what's wrong with you?" Asked Gracie.

"I hit my ankle on the dresser."

"How did you manage to hit your ankle on the dresser?"

"Gracie woke me up out of my sleep and told me I had a phone call." I wasn't paying any attention as I was walking out the room. It feels like a throbbing pain. Dang, that jive hurt bad."

"Gracie, please go in my room and get the alcohol and cotton balls so I can rub some on Charmayne's ankle."

"Yes, ma'am."

The pain Charmayne felt in her ankle felt like somebody hit it with a rock.

"Rocky, could you please tell Gram to hold on?"

"Okay sis, I will."

"Thank you."

"Gram asked me what happened to you, because he heard you screaming out."

After Charmayne's mom rubbed the alcohol on her ankle, she was able to get up and limp over to the phone.

"Hello."

"I heard you screaming. Are you okay?"

"Yes, I hit my ankle on the dresser. I'll be okay. Just in a lot of pain."

"Do you have any plans for today?"

"No. I was going to relax and hang out with my family."

"I would like to come and pick you up if you want me too."

"I'll call you later. Right now I want to stay off my feet for a while."

"Okay, I have to take my cousin to work. His car broke down."

"Okay, I'll call you later."

As she hung up the phone, her mom handed her an ice pack.

"Here put this on your ankle to stop the swelling. You need to stay off of it for a while."

"Thanks ma. You always know what to do to make us feel better."

Charmayne's gave her mom a big bear hug. She tried her best not to put pressure on it, but it was painful for her to walk on it. She managed to walk to her room and grab some clothes to take a shower.

Charmayne was in so much pain, she wanted to cry. She knew she had to suck it up and be a big girl. She didn't want her sisters and brothers to see her in pain. After taking a shower Charmayne sat in the living room with her foot propped on a pillow that Miracle had given her. Even with her foot propped up, Charmayne was still able to play with Ty'Meisha and Miracle. They played dress up with their baby dolls, had a tea party and colored in their coloring book. Charmayne and her sisters had a good time playing and doing fun things together. It was around twelve-thirty p.m. Charmayne and her sister were still in the living room playing.

I love it when I can still play with my sisters and brothers. Some of my friends can't stand having their sisters or brothers around them. I thank God I'm not like that. I need my sisters and brothers in my life. They keep me on my toes laughing at the things to be doing and saying.

Charmayne's sisters pretended that she was a patient at the hospital and waiting to be seen by the doctor. Miracle came out of the room wearing her mom's white smock, her white gloves she used for communion at church, and a white hat. Charmayne and Ty'Meisha started laughing at Miracle.

My sister Miracle keeps me on my toes at the silliest things she does." It won't be silly if my mom catches her wearing her white gloves she uses for communion.

"Miracle you better go and take Momma stuff off before she catches you and beat you."

"I'm not going to let momma catch me."

"Alright now, when momma comes in the house and catch you with her stuff on you know she's going to beat you."

"Don't tell her nothing Ty'Meisha. I tried warning you Miracle."

"Okay, keep playing with momma white gloves, Ty'Meisha said. Your butt is going to be burning. I'm going to sit right here and watch you get a whooping.

It was a good thing their mom was outside hanging out clothes on the clothes line.

"I'm the doctor and I have to give you a shot to make you feel better."

"Miracle go in the room and take off momma gloves. You know she uses them for communion on First Sunday."

"Be quiet, Ty'Meisha."

The back door opened. Charmayne and her sisters eyes got big.

I know my mom is going to beat the brakes off of Miracle for wearing her white gloves she uses for communion.

Charmayne's mom caught Miracle with her white gloves on. She couldn't do nothing but laugh at Miracle.

"Girl, I know you're not playing with my white gloves I use for communion."

"Sorry, momma. I was pretending to be Charmayne's doctor."

"What did you do with the old pair of white gloves I gave you?"

"Momma, I'm the doctor. I have to give Charmayne a shot so she can feel better."

"Didn't you just hear me ask you a question? I don't care about you being a doctor and who you had to give a shot too. I asked you about the old pair of white gloves I gave you."

"I can't find them."

"You better go and find them. If I catch you with my stuff on again, I'm going to burn your butt."

Charmayne and Ty'Meisha couldn't believe their mom didn't beat Miracle.

Mom always told us not to mess with her stuff in her room, especially her white gloves. Whatever we wanted out of her room, we had to get permission. Our mom did not allow us to go in her room for nothing unless she tells you too.

Later that day, Charmayne was feeling a little better.

The swelling on Charmayne's ankle went down a little but not that much. It wasn't as painful as it was earlier.

Charmayne asked her mom if it was okay for Gram to come pick her up.

"Yes you can go, but stay off your feet."

"Yes, ma'am. I will."

"Make sure you let me know how you're feeling and where you're at."

"Yes, ma'am."

Charmayne picked up the phone to dial Gram's number.

"Hey, what's up?"

"Hey, how are you feeling?"

"It feels a little better. Just got to stay off of it. My mom told me not to put too much pressure on it."

"Your mom is right. We don't want nothing to happen to you."

"I was calling to see if you were still coming to pick me up?"

"I thought you needed to stay home and prop your feet up."

"I do, but I feel a little better. It's okay as long as I stay off of it."

"Okay, I'll be there in about thirty minutes."

"Okay, I'll be ready when you get here."

She went in the bathroom to freshen up before Gram arrived. After getting dressed, Charmayne and her sisters played a game called "Mother May I."

If you wanted to do something, you had to ask the other person whose the mother, "Mother May I." The mother may say, "Charmayne take four steps backward" and then you would say "Mother May I." The mother might say, "No you may not." The person who gets to the finish line wins the game. It's a fun game that every child plays in the neighborhood.

It's a fun game and everybody plays it. It kind of boring, but we have fun playing it. See, we know how to make you have fun when playing "Mother May I?

Charmayne was ready when Gram came and picked her up. She kissed her mom, Miracle, Gracie and Ty'Meisha on their cheeks. As Charmayne prepared to walk out the door, Rocky and Marc were coming in the house.

"Where are you going, Charmayne?" Rocky asked.

"Boy, mind your business. I'll see you and Marc later."

"Charmayne, you need to call me when you get where you're going."

"Yes, ma'am. I will."

Miracle had a frown on her face as Charmayne walked out door.

"Charmayne, please stay home with us. You need to stay off of your ankle. I promise to take good care of you."

"Miracle, I promise to stay off my ankle. I'm not going to put a lot of pressure on it. If my ankle starts bothering me, I'll have Gram bring me home. I know you'll like that."

"I'll like it if you stay home. If you stay home, I promise not to bother you."

"Charmayne go ahead, Miracle will be alright."

"Alright ma, I'll see you all later."

"Miracle, I'll bring you something back if you're good."

"What about me Charmayne?" Asked Ty'Meisha.

"You too! I'll see you all later."

Charmayne walked out the house and closed the door behind her. When Charmayne got in Gram's car she noticed a box wrapped in paper with a white envelope that had her name on it.

"What is this Gram? I thought I told you not to keep buying me things."

"I wanted to do something nice for you. You mean a lot to me."

"You didn't have to do this."

"I know, but I wanted to."

Charmayne took the envelope off the box and open it. In the corner of her eyes, she could see a smile on Gram's face.

Why does Gram keep buying me things? The more I keep telling him to stop buying me things, the more he keeps doing it. I wish he would stop.

Charmayne read the card. The words were nice and sweet.

"The card is nice Gram" You mean a lot to me as well, but I keep telling you to stop buying me all this stuff. You don't have to do this. I know you care about me, but you don't have to keep doing this."

Charmayne picked up the box and begin ripping the paper off. Charmayne couldn't believe what she was looking at. In the box was a gold ring with diamonds around the band.

"Charmayne, I want to spend the rest of my life with you."

It took a minute for Charmayne to say anything. She just kept her hands over her mouth still in shock. She couldn't believe Gram had bought her a diamond ring.

What is wrong with this boy? Now, he's really scaring me. He keeps buying me stuff as if he owns me. I don't know if I should accept it or give it back to him. Well, it does looks good.

"Gram you bought me a gold ring with diamonds around the band. Why did you buy me a ring?"

"Charmayne, I can't see myself without. I need you in my life."

"Well, I appreciate what you did, but I can't take this ring. I have a lot of things I need to accomplish before I can say or do anything. I like being around you and doing things with you, but this is too fast for the both of us."

"Charmayne, I don't care how long it takes for you to do what you have to do, I just want to be with you."

"Gram I would love to spend the rest of my life with you too, but we need to take it one day at a time. I don't need you to keep buying me things. This is too much for me to swallow."

They pulled in the parking lot at one of Charmayne's favorite chicken and ribs diner. Charmayne and Gram sat in the car talking about the ring he had given her.

Gram is really doing too much for me. He says he want to spend the rest of his life with me. Whose to say if we're going to be together forever?

After talking for a while they went inside and ordered two rib dinners to go.

Charmayne and Gram went to his house to eat their food. Charmayne's ankle was still giving her problems. She was trying not to let Gram see her in pain.

"Charmayne, I noticed you limping earlier, are you okay?"

"Yes, Gram. I'm okay. The swelling went down a little, but my ankle is still bothering me."

"Let me look at it. If you need to go to the hospital I'll take you."

Gram looked at Charmayne's ankle.

"Well, the swelling did go down a little but not much. You still can see a little swelling around the ankle."

Gram went in the kitchen and grabbed a plastic bag from out of the cabinet. He put ice cubes in it to put on Charmayne's ankle so the swelling can go down.

"Thanks for getting some ice to put on my ankle."

"That's what I'm here for to make sure you're okay."

Gram turned the television on to a comedy show they both loved to watch. Charmayne laid her head on Gram's shoulder. She started rubbing her hands up and down his legs.

Here I am about to start something sexual with Gram. I know I shouldn't be putting any pressure on my ankle, but I thank I can handle the pain.

Charmayne could feel Gram's manhood was aroused. She also felt a tingle between her legs.

Charmayne didn't know what came over her, she was ready for Gram to make love to her.

Boy am I glad no one is home but us. I want Gram to make love to me.

Charmayne and Gram started kissing and feeling on each other.

"Baby, make love to me."

Gram refused to make love to Charmayne.

I know good and well Gram didn't turn me down about having sex with me. Are you kidding me? Gram is refusing to have sex with me. I don't believe this shit.

Charmayne asked Gram to make love to her again, but he said no.

"Gram how come you don't want to have sex with me?"

"Charmayne it's not that I don't want to have sex with you."

"Then you need to tell me what the problem is."

"It's not a problem Charmayne. Your ankle is swollen and I don't want you to put a lot of pressure on it.

"My ankle doesn't have anything to do with us having sex."

"Are you sure you want to have sex?"

"Yes, I'm sure. Please make love to me."

Gram laid Charmayne down on the sofa and started undressing her.

Charmayne was getting a little scared. She never had sex with anybody before. Charmayne didn't know what to expect or what was going to happen next.

Gram better make love to me before I change my mind. I can't believe I'm about to have sex with Gram. I hope it don't hurt me like all my friends said it will. I don't think I'm ready. Gram might get mad at me for teasing him.

Charmayne's mind started playing tricks on her. She was nervous and scared at the same time.

Dang, what if he's too big for me. What will he do if I tell him to stop? I'm nervous as hell. I don't think I'm ready to have sex right now.

Charmayne began to close her legs real tight. She didn't want Gram to go any further with her. Charmayne could hear Destiny in her ear saying, *"Girl, it's going to hurt when you use the bathroom."* By that time Charmayne's heart was beating fast.

I came this far, so why not go on with the plan. I rather take the chance in having sex with Gram than having sex with him later.

"Charmayne, I'll take my time with you I promise. When you want me to stop just let me know and I'll stop."

"Gram when I tell you to stop you better stop. This is my first time having sex and I never had this experience before. I'm really scared in having sex with you."

"Baby, I know you are. I don't want to make you feel uncomfortable. I think we need to wait a little longer before we start having sex."

"No. Go ahead, before I change my mind."

After Gram got undressed, he laid down next to her on the sofa. He began to climb on top of Charmayne.

Wow, I'm actually about to have sex for the first time. I hope Gram takes his time with me.

Charmayne spread her legs open for Gram to enter inside of her.

"Now if I tell you to stop, you better stop."

"I promise you I will."

During their sexual intercourse, Charmayne experienced intense pain between her legs.

"Dang, I see what my friends were talking about. They never lied about how painful it would be when you start having sex."

Charmayne wished she could take it all back, but the damage had been done and it started feeling good to Charmayne. Charmayne and Gram had a rhythm of their own.

I don't want Gram to stop. It feels a little better, even though it was painful going in.

Charmayne heard Gram say, "He was about to come."

Did Gram just say he about to come? Hell no, I don't want him to put that nasty stuff in me. He better pull out.

Charmayne knew it was wrong for not using protection, but she was ready for Gram to make love to her. When Gram said he was about to come, Charmayne hurried up and pushed him off of her. She wasn't trying to get pregnant.

If I let Gram shoot his sperm inside of me, I might end up getting pregnant? Now, how would I explain that to my mom?

Gram didn't get mad when Charmayne pushed him off of her. He understood why she pushed him off. He apologized for not using any protection.

Charmayne and Gram both went in the bathroom to wash off and put back on their clothes. They didn't want anyone coming in and catching them in the act. When Charmayne sat on the toilet to use the bathroom she let out a loud scream. It was too painful for her to use the bathroom.

"Aww, shit."

"What's wrong, baby?"

Charmayne couldn't say a word. She just put her hands down on her sweetness, trying not to cry.

Oh Lord, my sweetness is on fire. Lord, please let this pain go away. I promise I'll never do this again. If I had a knife, I would cut my sweetness off. That's how bad it was hurting me when I tried to urinate.

Gram poured a cup of cold water on Charmayne sweetness, but that didn't help. He was being very gentle and protective of her.

"Oh that's so sweet of Gram for pouring water down on my sweetness to ease the pain away. Now, that's what I'm talking about a real true gentleman looking out for his woman."

Gram did not want to see Charmayne in pain. He kept on apologizing for what happened.

"It's not your fault Gram. I wanted it just as bad as you did."

Charmayne sat on the stool until the pain eased away. After the pain eased, she was able to wash off and put on her clothes back on.

"I hope it doesn't show that I just had sex. I better get myself together before going home. My walk has to be on point and normal."

Chapter 24

The Burning Sensations

Now I see what my friends were talking about. They warned me when you have sex for the first time it will hurt. Boy, they wasn't lying. Every time I try to use the bathroom it was painful. It feels like a bee had stung me on my sweetness. That's how painful it was. Never again. He won't get a taste of my sweetness until we're married.

Charmayne's sweetness was burning so bad she thought somebody had lit it on fire. That's how bad it was burning. It was stingy like a bee had stun it. Charmayne was ready for Gram to take her home.

"I'm ready to go home. I need to soak my sweetness in some warm water."

"Charmayne are you okay?"

"Yes, I'm okay."

Charmayne lied to Gram. She did not want Gram to know she was in pain.

"Baby, I'm so sorry." I never meant to hurt you.

As Charmayne got ready to sit down in Gram's car, she felt pressure between her legs.

Gram knew something was wrong with Charmayne. He hurried and ran to her rescue.

"Baby, what's wrong with you? I know something is wrong. Is anything hurting on you?"

"Gram, I'm okay just a little sore, that's all."

"Baby, I'm so sorry. I tried not to hurt you. You should have told me to stop and I would've stopped. Now, I feel bad for putting you through this."

"Gram, stop blaming yourself for something I wanted to do too. It's not your fault. Just take me home so I can take a bathe. I feel nasty."

Dang, my sweetness is in a lot of pain. Lord, knows I should have waited to have sex, but no I wanted Gram to make love to me. That's just what I get for being stupid and dumb in wanting to see what it felt like when having sex. Now, I see that it's no joke.

When Charmayne got home she went in her mom's room to let her know she was home.

I hope I don't smell like sex. Would my mom noticed something different about me?

Charmayne didn't see Rocky, Gracie, or Ty'Meisha in the house. Miracle was glad to see Charmayne. Charmayne was no fun for Miracle. Her body ached all over and her sweetness was more than sore.

 "I'm going to take a shower and we can play dress up with your dolls."

Miracle loved it when Charmayne played dress up with her and Gracie.

"Charmayne why are you walking like that?" Asked Miracle. "Is your ankle still bothering you?"

"Yes, it's still hurting me. Gram put an ice pack on it to keep the swelling down."

"Well you need to try and stay off of it. If you don't, then you will have to go to the hospital and get a shot."

"Thanks Miracle. I'll stay off of it because I definitely don't want to get a shot."

Really, Miracle. If Miracle noticed I'm walking funny then my mom, sisters, and brothers would notice too. Let me go soak.

Charmayne went in the room gathered her clothes and went in the bathroom to take a shower. She decided to take a bubble bath instead of a shower. She wanted to sit in the tub and soak to help ease the pain she was enduring. The water felt good, but Charmayne was still in pain.

I'm glad I decided to shake a bubble bath instead of a shower. Soaking my sweetness was very relaxing. It eased some of the pain away.

Charmayne made sure to sit in the tub with her legs spread apart so the water can hit the right spot. Sitting in the tub brought back memories of their first sexual encounter.

Having sex with Gram was nice and sweet, but it was painful. I should have listen to what my friends were saying to me. They all told me the same thing. Each one of my friends had familiar stories about their first time in having sex with their partner.

Charmayne had to come back to reality when Miracle knocked on the door.

"Charmayne, Gram is on the phone."

"Tell him I'll call them back."

Charmayne let the water out of the tub, dried her body off and put on her clothes. She made sure to clean the tub out. She didn't want to leave it dirty knowing her sisters and brothers had to take a shower or a bath.

Let me call him back before he keep blowing up my phone. I know he cares about me and he don't want to see me in pain, but don't keep bothering me. I'm already paying for what we did. I know what I did was wrong and I can't take it back.

Charmayne picked up the phone to dial Gram's number.

Gram picked up the phone on the first ring.

"Hello, Charmayne."

"Hey, Gram."

"I was calling to make sure you were okay."

"Yes just a little sore, but I'll make it."

"Well I just want to apologize for what happened to you."

Charmayne had to make sure her room door was closed. She didn't want anyone to hear her conversation with Gram.

"You don't have to keep apologizing for something I agreed to do.nIt's not your fault. I'll appreciate it if you stop blaming yourself for what we did. Nothing we did today will ever change the way I feel about you and our relationship."

"I know, but I feel bad. I just wanted to make sure you're doing okay. I know you said you were in a lot of pain when use the bathroom."

"Well, the pain is still there. I guess it'll ease away slowly."

"Charmayne, are you still going to play with us?" Asked Gracie.

"Yes, give me a minute, Gracie. I'm putting on my clothes."

"Gram, let me call you back later. My sisters and I are about to play doll house."

"Okay, baby call me back."

Charmayne and Gram said their goodbyes.

As they was hung up, she couldn't believe they had just had sex.

I just had sex with Gram. I don't know what I was thinking about. I said I wasn't going to give it up until I'm married. I was trying to save myself for my husband, but that didn't happen. I just gave my womanhood away. I should have listen to what my friends were saying about having sex. They wasn't lying about the burning.

Charmayne knew her mom would kill her if she found out.

If my mom finds out I had sex with Gram, she will kill me. My parents always taught us about safe sex. There wasn't nothing safe about our sex. We didn't use no condoms. Another reason why my mom would kill me.

Charmayne was glad to play dress up with Ty'Meisha. They dressed them, did their hair and put make up on them.

"I want to play too," Gracie said.

"Come on we got enough dolls to play with," Miracle said.

Charmayne's sister Ty'Meisha wanted to pretend they were at a Michael Jackson concert. They all dressed up in Michael Jackson outfits. Each one of them put a white glove on their right hand. Charmayne and her sisters made sparkling tennis shoes. They used the diamonds their mom had given them when they were creating a T-Shirt of diamonds and pearls. Charmayne and her sisters had a good time playing with one another. You would have thought it was a room full of children.

Playing with my sisters helped ease the pain.

Charmayne's mom walked in the room.

"I could have sworn I heard other children voices in here."

"No, ma. It's just us pretending to be at a Michael Jackson Concert."

"Charmayne the way you and your sisters are carrying on, you would have thought I had a house full of kids."

Charmayne and her sisters started laughing.

"Charmayne I love to see you and your sisters playing together. You all bring so much joy to my heart. You and your sisters gets along well.

"Yes ma'am. I try my best to spend quality time with them. My sisters and brothers means a lot to me."

"Some children wish their big brothers and sisters would play with them and do things with them like you do with your sister and brothers."

"Well ma unfortunately, they don't. Some of my friends don't even won't to be bothered with their sisters or brothers."

"What do you tell them Charmayne?"

"I talk to my friends and I be straight up with them. I explained to them how important it is for me to be a role model for my sisters. Yes, there are days when I just want to hang out with my friends, but I know my sisters want to spend time with me as well. Family is everything.

"Charmayne, you are a very intelligent young lady. I know half of your friends look up to you and ask you for advice."

"Yes ma'am they do. They love to come to me for advice. I told them the next time they come to me for advice, they are going to have to pay me for my services. They know I'm going to keep it real with them."

"That's what I admire about you. You are a true person to your word. You never put yourself on a high pedestal or have people think you're better than them."

"Why I should be fake to people? You and dad never taught us to be like that. You and dad taught us to treat people with respect and don't pretend that you got it going on because you don't. Trust me ma, I stored everything you and dad taught us. I have a file cabinet stored in my brain. I can pull out everything you both have told us and taught us."

Charmayne's friends knew her parents brought them up in the right way. Charmayne promised her mom that she was going to be there for her sisters and brothers no matter what.

"Ma, I need my sisters and brothers just as much as they need me. You may not know this, but they are the ones who keep me going. They all keep a smile on my face."

I love spending time with my sisters and brothers. I love doing things with them. Without my sisters and brothers in my life, I would be lost. My sisters and brothers are my world and pride of joy.

Charmayne tries her best to be there for her sisters and brothers whenever they need her. Charmayne vowed to take care of her mother, sisters and brothers. She wanted to help her mom out with the bills. She did not want to see her mom struggling to take care of them and paying all the bills by herself.

I can't stand seeing my mom taking on the load by herself. I have to help my mom out as much as I can.

Chapter 25

Honoring My Mom

Another year passed and Charmayne and Gram were still in a relationship. Their relationship still going smooth. They truly enjoyed each other's company. Gram did everything he could do to keep Charmayne happy and satisfied. No matter what Charmayne needed or wanted Gram made sure she had it. Gram never took Charmayne for granted. He made sure not to step on her toes. He knew how fiesty she could get sometimes. He'd seen her in action.

Just three months left to graduate with a degree as Office Specialist.

Gram made sure Charmayne had a ride to school, work, had money in her pocket, and food to eat. One night while Charmayne sat at her computer desk in class, she decided to get a second job.

I think I want to get a second job to help my mom out around the house and help buy things for my sisters and brothers.

Charmayne wanted to work at a fast food restaurant in her neighborhood full time and work at a retail store on the weekend. She had it all figured out. She made sure to calculate her hours and that included spending time with her sisters and brothers.

If I don't do anything else, I need to make sure I spend time with my sisters and brothers. They need me in their lives. I promised my dad that I would play a big role in their lives.

Charmayne knew how she wanted her life to be and what she wanted to do. She would work fulltime. She would start saving money to help her mom out with the bills, do things with her sisters and brothers and buy a few things for herself as well. She knew her mom always put their needs before her own.

I no longer want my mom to pay all the bills by herself. Since I'm working, I can at least help her out.

Charmayne couldn't wait to tell Gram her plan. She had it all figured out. Gram waited for her outside of her school. She had a big smile on her face when she saw Gram. She wanted to pamper her mom. She thought her mom deserved the world with all the things she did for her kids and anyone else who needed help.

My mom would not just go out the way for her kids, but other people as well. She loves to give to the needy. She never wanted people to think she was better than them. My mom always said, "I don't mind giving to people who are in need, because one day it might be me." You never know when you might need somebody help.

Charmayne's mom made sure her children never went hungry, made sure their clothes were clean, and they had plenty of lights and water. She was going to make sure that her mom gets treated like a queen. Nothing or nobody was going to stand in her way

"Gram, if you don't mind can you take me by a store? I need to buy my mom a nice card. She's been struggling trying to make sure we have everything we need. I owe her that much."

Before Charmayne can say anything else, Gram interrupted her.

"Charmayne, your mom is a very strong woman. I watch how she is with you, your sisters and brothers. It takes a real woman to do the things she does. Your mom never shows her pain.

"Gram, my mom is strong. There are days she may have her time, but she's incredible. I appreciate the things she does for us.

Charmayne and Gram went to a drug store. They both browsed through the cards. Charmayne read the card to Gram. It almost had both of them in tears.

"Baby, you picked the perfect card for your mom. I know your mom will love this."

Charmayne was getting ready to hand the cashier her money, but Gram handed the cashier his money.

"Thanks Gram. You didn't have to buy it, but I do appreciate it."

The cashier put the card in a plastic bag and handed Gram his change.

"You all have a nice day," the cashier said

"You as well."

Charmayne and Gram walked out the store hand in hand.

"Gram thanks again for buying my mom this card."

"No problem, by now she's like a mother to me too."

As Charmayne got ready to seal the envelope, Gram reached in his pocket and handed her a hundred dollar bill to give to her mom. This surprised her.

"You don't have to do this, Gram."

"I know, but I want to. Your mom deserves the best. This is something I've been wanting to do from all of us.

Charmayne kissed Gram on his cheek. Before Gram took Charmayne home they went to a convenience store closer by Charmayne's house to get some snacks for her sisters and brothers. Gram pulled in Charmayne's driveway.

Before getting out of Gram's car, Charmayne reached over and gave Gram a kiss on his lips. Charmayne felt herself getting aroused. Not only was she getting aroused, but so was Gram. She began to caress his manhood. She kissed on Gram's earlobes teasing it with her tongue.

"I appreciate everything you do for us, Gram."

"Baby, you deserve the best and so does your family. There's nothing

I wouldn't do for you all."

Charmayne and Gram started kissing passionately. She wanted Gram to take her right then and there. She didn't care who came out and saw them having sex. The window were all steamed up and the music was playing softly in their ears. Charmayne didn't want Gram to stop.

"Baby, please don't stop."

They rocked to their own rhythm. Charmayne felt herself about ready to explode. She held on a little longer. They reached climax at the same time.

"It felt better than the first time."

"Baby, I just want to make you feel good that's all."

After Charmayne and Gram finished making love, Charmayne reached in her purse and grabbed a rag to wipe off.

"I think we need to get dressed before someone catches us."

Charmayne and Gram both got dressed and started wiping the moist off the windows. She reached over and kissed Gram on his forehead.

"I'll call you when I get home baby."

"I'll be waiting on your call."

"I love you," they both said in unison.

Charmayne picked up the envelope Gram had given her to give to her mom.

"Thanks again for the money and card. Baby, I wish you stop thanking me for something I wanted to do. I love your mom as well."

Before Charmayne got out of Gram's car, she made sure her clothes were neat and her hair was in place. She did not want her mom, sister and brothers to see her looking like a hot mess.

"You look good baby."

"Thanks. I got to make sure I don't look like I just had sex."

Charmayne closed the door behind her. She made sure to wave bye to Gram. As, Gram was backing out of Charmayne's yard he tooted his horn goodnight. Charmayne turned around and gave Gram a smile.

When Charmayne got in the house her sister Miracle was sleep, her brothers were playing their Nintendo game, and Gracie and Ty'Meisha were pretending to be models.

Charmayne went in her mom's room to let her know she was home.

"How was class tonight?"

"Everything went well ma. The teacher is overwhelmed of how much I've learned since I've been there. Also ma, I've decided to take another job to help you around the house with the bills. You work too hard to make sure we have this and that. You don't have to do it all by yourself anymore."

Charmayne handed her mom the card Gram bought for her.

"Here mom, this is for you."

"What is this Charmayne?"

"Ma, can you just open the envelope, please?"

"Charmayne, what is this I asked you?"

"It's something me and Gram wanted to give you. You deserve to be honored for all the hard work you do around here for us."

Charmayne's mom sat up in her bed with a smile on her face. She opened the envelope and begin reading the card. She started to cry.

"Ma, why are you crying?"

"The words in the card are so beautiful. Charmayne, I love the card. Make sure you tell Gram I said thanks when you talk to him. Better yet, I'll tell him myself."

Charmayne's mom didn't notice the money in the card. When she finished reading the first page, she turned to the second page.

Her eyes opened wide.

"Oh my God, what is this?"

"Mom, you deserve to be honored."

"Charmayne you and Gram didn't have to do this."

"Gram wants you to know how much he appreciates the love you have for him." He also said "You're like a mother to him."

"Oh how sweet of him to say that about me."

"Ma, we appreciate the sacrifices you've done for us. Since Daddy been dead, you've taking on a lot more responsibilities. I see the pain and hurt in your eyes each and every day. You still get up in the morning and go to work without complaining about this and that."

Charmayne bent down and gave her mom a kiss on her cheek.

"Ma, you don't have to cry. You deserve to be praised with all the things you do for us. I love you ma."

Her mom couldn't stop crying. She was overwhelmed at what Charmayne and Gram had done.

"Thank you again Charmayne. I wasn't expecting anything from you or Gram. You two have touched my heart. Make sure you tell Gram I said thanks."

"Goodnight, ma."

"Goodnight, Charmayne."

Charmayne went in her sisters and brothers room to make sure they all were in bed.

"Marc and Rocky you need to turn that game off and get in bed. Don't make me have to come back in here and tell you again."

"Okay, Charmayne, just let us finish this last play." Rocky said.

"Okay, but I'll be back in later to cut the game off."

Charmayne closed their room door behind her. She could hear Marc and Rocky talking about who was going to win the game. She was so exhausted she didn't feel like bathing. She just wanted to lie down and reminisce on what had just happened between her and Gram.

Charmayne could smell Gram's sex scent all over her. If Charmayne could smell Gram's scent on her, then her mom smelled it too. She quickly grabbed her pajamas out of her drawer and headed in the bathroom to shower.

The water felt good against Charmayne's body. As, Charmayne was about to close her eyes, she remembered they didn't use protection. She knew she wasn't being careful with Gram. All Charmayne wanted to do was to make love to Gram. She wasn't thinking about no protection. Charmayne wanted Gram to take her right then and there.

It never crossed Charmayne's mind about getting pregnant or catching any type of disease.

Dang, we didn't use any protection. What was I thinking? All I wanted was to have sex with him.

To Charmayne's knowledge, she was the only girl Gram was seeing. Her heart raced so fast she didn't know what to do. Soon as she opened the bathroom door, the phone rang. She hurried up and answered it before it woke up her mom and sisters.

"Hello."

"Hey baby, I was calling to let you know I made it home safe."

"Gram, give me a few minutes and I'll call you back. I'm just getting out of the shower."

"Okay baby. Wish I was getting out the shower with you".

Charmayne and Gram both laughed. She went back in the bathroom to dry herself off. She had dripped water from the bathroom floor to the living room. She got the mop and dried the water off the floor before anyone slipped and fell. Charmayne finally called Gram back.

"Charmayne, can we talk for a minute?"

"What do we need to talk about, Gram?"

"Charmayne, we didn't use any protection."

"Yes, I know. I was too busy trying to make love before anyone caught us. I wasn't thinking at all about any protection."

Gram assured Charmayne he was disease free and he wasn't having sex with anyone else but her.

"I hope you're telling me the truth Gram. Even though you say you're disease free I need to make sure for myself. I'm going to call my doctor in the morning and make an appointment to get checked out. Charmayne didn't want to have a disease or be pregnant.

I have goals and I'm determined to reach them. Nothing will stand in my way or stop me from achieving what I want to accomplish.

"I understand, Charmayne. Just let me know when you want to go and I'll take you."

Charmayne and Gram talked for a while before saying goodnight.

Chapter 26

Caught In the Act

Charmayne's alarm clock went off exactly at four-thirty a.m. She had to be at work by five a.m. It was a good thing her job was only five minutes away from her house. She got up went in the bathroom, brushed her teeth, took a shower, and put on her work uniform. She went in her mom's room to let her know she was leaving for work.

"I'll see you when you get home. Have a good day at work."

"Yes ma'am."

"Have fun at work," Gracie said.

What in the hell Gracie doing up at five am? She should be sound asleep this time of morning.

Charmayne's friend Marin waited outside for her.

It's a good thing to have a friends who lives down the street from you and have the same hours as you do at work.

Charmayne always made sure to give Marin gas money. She was glad Marin was friendly enough to give her a ride to and from work. On this particular day Charmayne got off from work early, so she decided to surprise Gram.

As Charmayne walked toward Gram's house, she noticed a girl sitting in the passenger seat in Gram's car as they rode passed her. Gram and the girl didn't see Charmayne when they passed her.

What the fuck? Who in the hell is this girl in Gram's car? Are you fucking kidding me?

Charmayne's mind started playing tricks on her. She felt flames coming out both of her ears. She tried to reach Gram's house before they both got out the car. It felt like her legs couldn't move any faster. The harder Charmayne walked the slower her pace seemed to get. Charmayne could see Gram looking around to see if anybody was watching them as they both got out of his car.

Look at his ass looking around to see if anybody is watching them. His ass is up to no damn good.

By the time Charmayne reached his house they were already inside.

Damn, I tried to get here before they both got out the car.

Charmayne looked inside Gram's car and noticed a girl's book bag sitting in the front seat. She opened his car door and looked through the book bag. She recognized the name on the inside of the book bag. She couldn't believe he was messing around on her with someone else.

Charmayne went to thinking.

How can he so easily lie about being faithful to me?

Charmayne knocked on Gram's front door. She could see the curtains in the living room move just a little. She knocked on the door a couple more times, but this time a little harder.

"If I were you I'd open this door."

There were silence in the Gram's house. She could no longer hear them talking or hear movements in the house.

"Either you open the door or I'm coming through the window. It's your choice. I know you have another female in there. I saw the both of you pass right by me."

Charmayne knew who the girl was that Gram had in his mom's house. She heard them in the house talking and moving around.

"If I was you, I'd open this door. I promise you, neither one of you is going to like what I'm going to do next."

Charmayne heard their footsteps racing towards the back door. She ran in the back to see if the girl was going to come out the back door.

Their asses think they're slick. They're going to run to the back like I'm not going to run back there and catch them coming out the door.

Neither Gram nor the girl came out the back door. Charmayne ran back to the front. She was trying to catch them coming out the front door. She got tired playing their silly games.

Damn, I'm tired. I don't have time trying to chase them all around.

To Charmayne their relationship didn't matter anymore. She was done with Gram and his lies.

He can have whomever he wants to.

Gram finally opened the door.

"Charmayne what are you doing here?"

"I know you're not asking me what I'm doing here. You're the one who's cheating on me. You can see and fuck whoever you want to, because I'm done with you. I trusted you with my life, my body and my family.

Gram couldn't say anything to Charmayne. He was silent.

"If you think I'm cheating on you, then you can come in the house and see for yourself."

"Boy, you really think I'm stupid."

"I never said you were stupid, Charmayne."

"Do it look like I have Dumb Ass written on my forehead? If you're going to cheat, you need to leave me alone. You will not play with my feelings or emotions. I've been faithful to you throughout our relationship and not one time have I ever cheated on you. I've been faithful to you from day one. I don't deserve this from you. I deserve better. Charmayne never entered Gram's house to see who was in there. As Charmayne was walking away, Duke called out Charmayne's name.

Charmayne turned around.

Oh hell no. What is Duke doing here at Gram's house? What is really going on here? Oh boy, I can't wait to see his girlfriend Amber. I'm going to tell her everything. I'm not going to leave anything out. Hell, I can't wait to tell all of their girlfriends about their little festivity.

"Duke, what do you want?"

Charmayne couldn't believe Duke was at Gram's house. He was supposed to be at work.

"What the hell are you doing here at Gram's house?"

All of Gram's friends came outside when they heard Charmayne's voice. They all were inside Gram's house.

"Wow, you got all your homeboys here with you. I see what's going on here now. You all are up to no good. You all are in Gram's house and there is only one female. Yes, something is going on here."

"What are you talking about, Charmayne?" Asked Scotty.

"Gram, you need to lose my name, address, and number."

"Charmayne, what are you talking about?

"I know what I saw. You had another female in your car."

"Charmayne, there was nobody else in his car but me," Duke said.

"Duke, don't you say anything else to me. You just wait until I see Amber. I'm going to tell her everything I know."

"Charmayne, there is nothing to say," Scotty said.

"So I guess you all think I have dumb ass on my forehead too. All of you can go to hell along with your no good ass friend."

"Charmayne, what do you mean about lose your name and number?"

"You heard what said. Go be with the bitch who was in your car."

"Charmayne don't fucking play with me."

"You go your way and I'll go mine. It's better for the both of us. You can cheat with whomever you want to. I'm not going through this."

"Baby, I know you don't believe me."

"And why should I believe anything that comes out of your mouth?"

As Charmayne talked to Gram, Treasure and Amber pulled up.

"Girl what are you doing here?" Amber asked Charmayne.

"Girl, I got off from work earlier. I came by here to surprise him, but he had another female in his car."

"Girl, he had a who in his car?" Asked Treasure.

"You heard what I said. I found her book bag in the front seat of his car."

"Gram, please tell me this is not true." Treasure asked Gram.

"Treasure, listen I'm telling you the truth."

Charmayne walked up to Gram's car. She stopped in front of his car.

"Gram, I'm not about to do this with you."

"Duke! What the hell are you doing here?" Amber asked Duke. "You told me you had business to take care of."

"Girl, don't start with me. I told you what I had to do. I'm not going to keep explaining myself to you."

"Well, being here at Gram's house is not taking care of business or doing what you said you had to do. So, it's must be true."

"If you don't believe me Amber, then you can take a look in his car and see for yourself."

The expression Gram and his friends had on their faces knew they were about to get caught. Duke was praying Amber didn't go to Gram's car. They all knew Charmayne wasn't lying. If looks could kill they all would be dead. Gram nor his friends were about to say that it was a girl in his car.

"Duke, if I find out you've been lying to me, there will be consequences to pay."

"Man go head on with the bullshit. Amber, you know not to keep trying me."

"Trying you like what? Duke, you don't scare me. I'm not one of your flouncy females who bows down to you. Try me if you want to."

"Charmayne, let me talk to you for a minute."

"You can talk to my ass as I walk away from you. Now, that's what you can do."

'Treasure just take me home. Evidentially they're not going to tell you why another female was in Gram's car."

"I don't understand." Treasure said. "You all know Gram was cheating on Charmayne. Neither one of you said a word to her about his cheating."

"Treasure be quiet, because you don't know what you're talking about." Gram said. "I'm not cheating on Charmayne."

"Well explain to me why another female book bag is in Gram's car. Better yet, what are you all doing here with him and her anyway? Duke, Trey, and Scotty you all supposed to be at work."

Neither one of the boys could say anything. Just as Scotty was about to say something Treasure interrupted him.

'Inquiring minds want to know the answer to that too, Duke."

"Amber, I just got here. I know for sure there's nobody in his house but us."

"Why in the hell you're not at work then?"

"I just came here to drop off this paperwork to Gram. He supposed to be getting me a job where he works at.

"Duke don't fucking lie to me. You know I'll drop your ass in a heartbeat."

"There you go lying for your no good ass friend."

"Charmayne, I'm not lying. I would tell you if he's cheating on you."

"Yeah right. You, Gram and the rest of you all can all go to hell and kiss where the sun don't shine."

Charmayne, Amber, and Treasure walked away.

"Charmayne, call me when you get home."

"No, thank you. I'm good."

Charmayne, Amber and Treasure drove away.

"Charmayne, I'm so sorry this had to happen to you. You don't deserve to be treated like this." Treasure said.

"I'm still trying to figure out what made you come over to his house." Amber said.

"He's my man. I don't need an open invitation to come to his house."

"No, I'm not talking about that. I was asking you what made you come to his house that's all. I know you be working round about this time. I'm sorry if I offended you in any kind of way."

"Let's all breathe. We don't need to get upset with each other."

"No. I'm not getting upset with Amber. You didn't offended me."

"Charmayne, I just want you to know I'm here for you that's all."

"Thank you for being concerned about me."

"No problem. That's what I'm here for. We supposed to look out for each other."

"I had got off early and wanted to spend some alone time with him. As I was walking to his house they rode right pass me. Neither one of them saw me. I was trying to hurry up and get to his house before they both got out of the car. My legs wasn't moving fast enough."

"Girl, I'm not going to tell you what to do, but you need to leave him. I know he had a girl in his car because you can see her book bag sitting in his front seat."

"Amber, I'm nobody's fool. He can have her and anybody else he wants to. He's not going to bring me no diseases. I'm good."

Charmayne's feelings were hurt. She never thought Gram would do her like this. Let alone his friends stood by his side knowing he was cheating on her.

They probably were going to run a train on her. Charmayne thought to herself.

"I'll call you all later. Thanks for bringing me home."

"That's what friends are for," Treasure said. "Go in the house and take it easy. We'll be checking up on you."

"I'm here for you if and when you need me," Amber said.

Charmayne waved her hand at Treasure and Amber. Charmayne had to get herself together before going in the house. She put on that happy smile. She didn't want her mom, sisters and brothers to see the hurt in her eyes.

Let me get myself together before going in the house. I don't want nobody to notice that I was crying.

Charmayne knew she had to take matters into her own hands. She wanted to break off their relationship.

I think it's best we both go our separate ways. He will not play me like a fool. I'm done with him and this relationship.

Later on that night Charmayne pretended she was enjoying her family, but on the inside she was hurting. Charmayne's mom cooked a nice dinner. She made macaroni and cheese, string beans, cornbread, barbeque chicken and yellow rice. And to top it off her mom made a peach cobbler for dessert.

Charmayne didn't eat much for dinner. She nibbled from her food. Her mom noticed she hadn't eaten much of her food.

"Charmayne, what's wrong with you? Are you feeling okay?"

"Yes, I'm okay mom. I ate at work. I'm just going to go and lie down for a while."

"Okay I'll be in there to check up on you."

"Thanks, mom. I appreciate it."

Charmayne got up from the table and ran into the bathroom. She was vomiting all over the floor. She was really feeling the hurt Gram caused her.

"Charmayne are you okay?" Asked Miracle.

"Yes, I'm okay Miracle. It was something I ate at work."

Charmayne was scaring her mom, sisters, and brothers. They never seen Charmayne this way before.

"Mom, I think you need to call the doctor," Miracle said.

"Oh baby, your sister will be alright. It was something she ate that didn't agree with her stomach."

Charmayne overheard her mom and Miracle talking.

Only if they knew what was going on with me. How can I tell my mom what Gram did to me today? Let alone, if I tell my mom I got off work early she would definitely be mad at me. She probably would have put me on punishment. The first thing that would have come out of her mouth is, 'You should've came straight home instead of going to his house. That's what happen when you lie to your parents.' I didn't want my mom to criticize me for my wrong doing.

Charmayne cleaned up the bathroom and gathered herself together.

"If anyone call me, please take a message. I don't feel like talking to anyone."

"Charmayne, do you want me to call the doctor?"

"No ma'am. It's just probably something I ate at work that don't agree with my stomach."

"Okay, we'll make sure not to disturb you."

"Pray you feel better Charmayne."

"Thanks everyone. Goodnight."

"Goodnight, Charmayne."

Charmayne hated lying to her family especially her mom.

I hate lying to my mom about anything. I know this is not right of what I'm doing to her. How would my mom ever forgive me for lying to her?

Charmayne didn't sleep peacefully. She tossed and turned all night, in her sleep.

Chapter 27

His Apology

Charmayne woke up the next morning still thinking about what Gram did to her and their relationship. Gram caused a gaping hole in Charmayne's heart. She no longer wanted to be in a relationship with him. She couldn't comprehend how one minute he wants to spend the rest of his life with her, then he's getting caught cheating on her.

I can't believe Gram cheated on me with another female. I don't think I can ever be with him again.

At this point, Charmayne was completely confused. She was in love with Gram, but she couldn't trust him anymore. How was Charmayne going to explain this to her mom, sisters and brothers? They all had shared special moments with Gram.

"Good morning, Charmayne." Marc said.

"Good morning, Marc."

Marc was in the living room drawing on his sketch board. Charmayne sisters and Rocky was still in their rooms. Her mom was in the kitchen cooking breakfast.

"Good morning, ma."

"Good morning, Charmayne. How are you feeling this morning?"

"I feel much better mom. Thanks for asking. I just had a stomach virus that's all. I had to get all that poison food out of my stomach."

"Your sisters and brothers were all worried about you, especially Miracle."

"I know ma. I heard her talking to you about calling the doctor."

Charmayne and her mom both started laughing.

"Since you have the weekend off what are you going to do?"

"I want to take them to the mall. I'm going to buy each one of them a pair of shoes and an outfit."

"That would be nice. They will love and appreciate that."

Charmayne went back in her room and grabbed some money to give to her mom.

"Here mom this is for you. You can pay some bills or buy you a church suit."

"Charmayne, you don't have to give me no money. You keep your money."

"No ma, this is for you. I told you that whenever I start working I was going to help you pay the bills and take care of my sisters and brothers."

Charmayne's mom was thankful for what Charmayne had done. Charmayne went in her brothers and sisters room to tell them to get dressed.

"Where are we going Charmayne?" Asked Rocky. "I'm taking you all to the mall".

"We're going to mall, we're going to the mall." Gracie kept repeating.

As Charmayne was in the room getting dressed, the phone rang.

Gracie went in the living room to answer the phone.

"Charmayne, Gram is on the phone.

"I'll get it in my room. You can hang it up Gracie."

"What the hell are you doing calling me? I thought I told you to leave me the hell alone."

"Charmayne, listen I need to talk to you."

"What the fuck you have to say to me now? You've already proven to me that you're not trustworthy. I've never cheated on you not one time, so what is it that you need to talk to me about?"

"I'm calling to see how you're doing."

"Again why are you calling me? I've made it perfectly clear to you not to call me. You need to lose my name and number."

"I know I hurt you and I'm sorry."

"What are you sorry for Gram? Are you sorry for getting caught?"

"Charmayne, I didn't do anything wrong."

"Gram you had a girl in your car. You really take me for a fool. Both of you passed right by me as I walked to your house. I can tell you exactly what the both of you had on."

Gram became silent on the phone.

"Hello… don't be silent now."

"No, I thought my boss was calling my name."

"Boy who do you think you're fooling. You're quiet because I'm telling the truth."

"Charmayne, I'm sorry for putting you through this."

"Are you sorry for getting caught or are you sorry that I'm breaking up with you?"

"Yes I took your love for granted, but I never meant for any of this to happen."

"*News flash!* It happened. I don't think we need to be together anymore. We both need to go our separate ways."

"Charmayne, what are you saying?"

"Exactly what I just said. We need to go our separate ways. I can't continue being in a relationship with someone who cheats and lies."

"Charmayne, please don't do this to us."

"You've done this to us, not me."

"Charmayne, please listen to me. Don't leave me baby. Let's try and work this out."

"What is there to work out? You're the one who cheated on me and now you want to work things out? How does that sound?"

"Baby, what I did to you hurts me just as much as it hurts you. All I ask is that you forgive me for hurting you like this."

"Gram, I've never cheated on you or lied to you. I've been faithful to you throughout our entire relationship. Not only did you hurt me, but you hurt my family as well."

"Charmayne I love you. You and your family mean a lot to me."

"One thing, I do want you to know, I'm not going to tell my mom what you did to me. I will let her know that we're not together. I don't want to cause any conflict between you and my family."

"Thank you Charmayne. I appreciate you not telling your mom about what happened or what I've done to you. Your mom will never forgive me."

"Because of what you did to me we can never be together. I'll always love and care for you, but that's all it will ever be. I truly appreciate everything you did for me and my family, but I can do better."

"Charmayne, I understand. I can't see myself with anyone else."

"Gram, you don't care anything about me. If you did, you would have never cheated on me."

"I know what I did to you was wrong. I do apologize for my mistake. I wish I can take it back, but the damage has been done. Baby, you mean a lot to me."

"Evidentially, I don't mean that much to you if you cheated on me."

"Charmayne, I really don't want to lose you or the love we have."

"How can you say you love me and you don't won't to lose what we have? What you're saying is going in one ear and coming out the other."

"Baby, just let me explain. I never meant for any of this to happen."

"Gram, let me ask you something."

"Baby, you can ask me anything."

"How many other women have you cheated on me with while being in a relationship with me? How many times have you had unprotected sex with them? I just keep it real with me and tell me the truth."

The phone was silent on the other end.

"Hello. Don't get silent on me now. I need for you to answer my questions. Every time I ask you a question, you get silent on the phone. Now is not to be quiet."

"The thing is, I never cheated on you. We were about to run a train on her and that's it."

"So I guess you want me to believe your lies" I wasn't born yesterday. I'm nobody's fool. You may try that shit on somebody who doesn't give a fuck about their life, but I care about mines. You hurt me in every way you know how too."

"Baby I know I hurt you, but I never meant for any of this to happen. If you hadn't come to the house we would have ran a train on her."

"I can't believe your homeboys were going to have sex with her too. I see they don't care about their girlfriends either. Just like you didn't care about me."

"Charmayne, you need to know the truth. You asked me a question and I'm trying to tell you what happened."

"You should have told me the truth when I was at your house. Don't wait to get behind closed doors to pour your heart out to me."

"Charmayne, if you shut up for a minute and listen to me. I'm trying to be honest with you."

"The pain and damage you caused me will never go away. I love you and trusted you, but can I say that about you? I guess this is the thanks I get from you."

"Charmayne, what can I do to make things right between us?"

"Gram, there's nothing you can do. You showed me exactly what you wanted to do."

"Charmayne, please let me come over so we can talk."

"There's nothing we need to talk about. You did this not me."

"Baby, I know I just want you to forgive me."

Charmayne and Gram talked for a couple more hours before Rocky knocked on her room door.

"Rocky, give me a few more minutes I'm still talking to Gram."

"I just want to tell you we're dressed and ready to go to the mall."

"Okay, I'll be out in a minute."

"Rocky get away from your sister's door."

"Yes ma'am."

Charmayne resumed her conversation.

Charmayne was angry at Gram and what he'd done to her and their relationship.

"Once again Gram, you need to lose my number. I don't want anything to do with you anymore."

"Baby, please don't leave me."

"How dare you call me your baby. You lost your baby when you cheated. I will never be your baby again. From now on when you see me in the street or where ever you see me, you can address me by my first name and my first name only."

Charmayne heard the hurt in Gram's voice.

"Charmayne, you already know what I've told you about your mouth."

Who do he think he's scaring? Yes, Gram told me that he would knock my ass out for running my mouth. He don't scare me. I want him to hit me. If he put his hands on me, Gram will regret it.

"Gram that shit don't scare me. You will never put your fucking hands on me. My dad never beat me and neither would you. This is my mouth, I can say what the hell I want to say."

He might as well stop putting on a show thinking I'm going to forgive him. I will never forgive him or forget what he's done to me.

Charmayne didn't care if Gram's feelings were hurt. She wasn't trying to hear nothing he had to say and it was time for her to get off the phone.

Don't get me wrong, Gram was the first boy who I fell in love with. Gram took my virginity. I let him have sex with me. I gave my body to him. I promised I wouldn't have sex with anyone until we are married. Boy, did I make a fool of myself.

"Gram I still love you, but it will never be the same between us."

"Baby, please don't give up on us or our relationship."

"I don't want to give up on you or our relationship, but it's a little too late for that."

Charmayne knew she had to get off the phone with Gram before things got out of hand. She had promised her sisters and brothers that she would take them to the mall.

"Listen I have plans with my family. I think we need to end this conversation."

"Ba"

Before Gram could finish saying "baby," Charmayne cut him off.

"What did you just called me?"

"I'm sorry, Charmayne."

"You better be sorry. That name should no longer come out of your mouth. I am not your baby anymore. What else do you want to tell me before I hang up on you?"

Charmayne decided to let Gram tell her what was on his mind.

Gram apologized again to Charmayne for the mistakes he'd made.

"Charmayne, I'm sorry for all the things I've put you through. I never meant for any of this to happen to you."

Gram begged Charmayne not to give up on him or their relationship.

"I'll call you later. I have to get off the phone."

"Okay, I'll wait for your call."

Charmayne and Gram hung the phone up.

"I thought you were not ever getting off the phone with Gram." Charmayne's mom teased her.

"Me either, ma."

"What's going on between you two?"

"He did something I wasn't pleased with."

"We'll talk about this when we return from the mall."

"Yes ma'am."

Charmayne, her sisters, brothers, and mom all went to the mall.

Charmayne brought each one of her siblings a pair of shoes and an outfit to match their shoes.

"Thank you Charmayne for buying us something." Her sisters and brothers said thankfully.

"You all are welcome. There's nothing I wouldn't do for my sisters and brothers."

"That's what I'm here for. There's nothing I wouldn't do for you all."

When they returned home from the mall, Charmayne asked her mom if she could talk.

"Ma, can we go outside so I can talk to you?'

"I need for you all to stay in the house while Charmayne and I sit on the porch to talk"

"Yes, ma'am."

Charmayne told her mom what happen between her and Gram.

"Charmayne, I need you to be honest with me."

"Yes ma'am."

Charmayne didn't know what her mom was about to ask her.

"Are you having sex?"

She began biting her fingernails.

"Yes ma'am. It was my first time with Gram."

Charmayne didn't know what was coming next after telling her mom she was having sex.

"I hope you had enough sense to use protection. Please tell me you used protection."

"No, ma'am. We didn't use protection."

"Charmayne what were you thinking? Bad enough you had sex with someone who didn't use protection. Don't you know you can catch a disease without protecting yourself, let alone get pregnant?"

"Yes ma'am. It was in the heat of the moment."

"I don't care anything about being in the heat of the moment. A disease you can get in the heat of the moment. A baby you can get in the heat of the moment. I don't want to hear that come out of your mouth again about in the heat of the moment."

"Yes ma'am. I'm sorry ma."

"No need to be sorry. I thought I taught you about all these warning signs. You never let a person talk you into doing something you're not ready to do. I'm surprised at you. When you get up in the morning you need to call your doctor."

"Yes ma'am. I was planning on doing that."

"You need to make an appointment as soon as you can. See if he has anything available for this week. I need to make sure you're neither pregnant nor have a disease."

Charmayne and her mom had a long conversation about pregnancy and diseases. Charmayne knew she hurt her mom feelings.

"How can I be so stupid?" I never meant to hurt my mom. I know she's mad at me. What was I thinking?

Charmayne picked the phone to call Gram. She had to let him know she told her mom about what he did to her.

"Hello, Gram. We need to talk."

"Hello, Charmayne. What's going on?"

"Well, I told my mom about what you did to me."

"What do you mean you had to tell your mom what I did to you?"

"Listen it was bothering me and I had to tell her. I don't ever want to think I cannot come to my mom and talk to her about anything. I love my mom and I know she loves me. So if anything is bothering me, I'm going to have a talk with my mom about what is bothering me."

"Oh my God, I know your mom is going to be angry with me. I don't blame you Charmayne, I knew you had to do what was best for you. I'm not mad at you, but I wish we could've did this together. It's my fault for what I've done to you."

Charmayne and Gram talked for a few more minutes. Again, Gram apologized.

"Goodnight, Gram."

"Goodnight, Charmayne."

Chapter 28

How Could He

When Charmayne got up the next morning her mom was in the kitchen cooking breakfast. Her brothers and sisters were setting the dinette table waiting to eat.

"Good morning Charmayne."

"Good morning momma."

"How did you sleep?"

"I kept tossing and turning. I was taking in everything you were saying to me on last night. I know you want the best for me. I made a big mistake."

"I just want you to understand what I was saying. You have to be the responsible one. Don't never let a man talk you out of not doing the right thing. You are a LEADER and not a FOLLOWER."

"Yes ma'am I understand."

"Momma, what happen to Charmayne?" Asked Marc.

"Marc, I'm not talking to you." I am talking to your sister.

"Sorry momma."

Charmayne's nerves raced non-stop. She went in her room to call her doctor. She was hoping her sisters and brothers didn't come in her room.

"I need you all to listen to me."

"Yes ma'am."

"Whenever I'm talking to someone, I don't never want to hear neither one of you asking me what happen to that person. It is none of your business in what we are talking about. Do I make myself clear?"

"Yes ma'am we understand," they all said.

"I don't want to have to keep repeating myself over again about this situation."

"Momma, I'm so hungry I can eat a cow," said Ty'Meisha.

"I'm with you on that, Ty'Meisha," Charmayne said.

Charmayne's mom fixed everybody plates with grits, bacon, sausage, eggs and toast.

After eating breakfast Charmayne and Rocky cleaned up the kitchen.

"Charmayne, don't forget what I've asked you to do."

"Yes, ma'am. I won't."

Charmayne mom told her sisters and brothers not to bother her.

"Listen everyone, Charmayne has a very important phone call she needs to make. I better not catch neither one of you knocking on her door or calling her name."

"Yes ma'am," they all said.

"If I see either one of you doing the opposite, I will tear your behind up. I mean what I say. You can try me if you want to. Her sisters and brothers knew not to try their mom.

Charmayne went in her room and locked her door behind her. She dialed the clinic number. She was so scared her hands were trembling. The phone rung about three times before the operator answered.

"*Dang, I wish someone would answer the phone.*" *I'm already nervous as a fox chasing a squarrel.*

The operator transfered Charmayne's call to the nurse station. Charmayne gave the nurse her name and date of birth.

The nurse gave Charmayne an appointment to come in and see her doctor in the morning. Usually you had to wait about two weeks to get a doctor's appointment, but she was glad to get an early appointment.

When Charmayne hung up with the nurse she told her mom about her doctor's appointment in the morning.

"I pray everything comes back negative with your tests."

"I'm praying too momma. This is a lesson learned."

"I pray you've learned from this mistake. Don't never let this happen again. Charmayne you know better. If your father was living, he'd be disappointed in you."

"Yes ma'am. I know. I don't want you to be disappointed with me. I want you to be able to trust me when I'm with Gram or just hanging out with my friends."

"Charmayne, don't never think you can't come to me and talk. You should be able to come to me and talk about anything. That's what I'm here for. I am your mother."

"I know mom. I was too scared to come and tell you."

"I rather for you to come to me than going to your friends and telling them. They cannot give you a mother's advice. Only thing your friends would say to you 'You better not tell your mom.'"

She looked at her mom as if she had heard their conversations.

"How did my mom knew my friends had said that to me?"

Charmayne knew her mom was telling the truth about what her friends had said to her. She felt comfortable knowing she could talk to her about anything. Charmayne vowed to never keep a secret from her mom.

I'm glad my mom understood what I was saying to her. I really thought my mom would actually be mad at me, but she was very supportive.

Charmayne and her mom had a good relationship. She did not want to ruin that with her mother. Charmayne knew she had a lot on her plate. She didn't know if she was pregnant or if Gram has given her a disease.

"What if I'm pregnant? I'm too young to raise a baby. What if Gram gave me a disease? I'll kill him. What am I going to do? How can I handle being picked on? Lord knows I won't be able to handle the stress. How would my friends treat me if they knew I had a disease?

Charmayne really didn't know how to handle either being pregnant or having a disease. Mixed emotions consumed her and intrusive thoughts clouded her mind.

"Momma, I'm scared."

"Charmayne, there's nothing for you to be scared of. You just have to learn from your mistakes that's all."

How would my mom treat me if I'm pregnant or have a disease?"

"Ma, how would you treat me if I'm pregnant or have a disease?"

"Charmayne, you will always be loved by me. I will never stop loving you or caring for you. You are my child. Don't never think I would think of you any differently. We are going to handle this situation together. You will not go in this alone."

"I know momma, but I disappointed you in a way I've never thought I would do. It hurts me knowing I've hurt you. I'm ashamed in what I've done. I know God is not pleased in what I've done either."

Charmayne started crying.

"Stop crying Charmayne. Everybody makes mistakes. This is a mistake you definitely have to learn from."

"Christians don't go out and makes mistakes like I've done."

"Stop beating up on yourself." Everybody is not perfect. You are going to make mistakes. I made plenty of mistakes when I was young."

"Did grandma beat you when you made mistakes?"

"Yes and No." Your grandmother would talk to me instead of beating me. She thought by beating me was only going to make me keep doing the things I've been doing. She rather talk to me. I could never understand why she would tell me about certain little things, but now I know. She was only telling me for my good.

"I wish daddy was here. He would help ease the pain away."

"Yes, you and your daddy had a special bond no one could come between. Your daddy truly loved you. You could do no wrong in his eyes."

Charmayne was glad she had this talk with her mom. She knew that every mistakes she made would come with a heavy price.

Later on that day, Charmayne decided to give Gram a call.

"Hello, Gram."

Hello, Charmayne."

"Well, I called to let you know I have a doctor's appointment in the morning."

"Charmayne, I'm glad you decided to call your doctor. I don't want you to think I'm not going to stand behind you one hundred percent. I want to make sure you're okay."

"Gram, what you did to me will never make it right between us."

"Charmayne I know I've made a mistake in our relationship. I know you don't want to be in a relationship with me, but I love you."

"Gram, please don't say you love me. If you love me you would have never did what you did to me. Your love don't live here anymore."

"Baby, please don't say that. You know how much I care about you."

"Yes Gram, I know you care about me, but it's over between us. You've hurt me in a way I never thought you would. You stabbed me in the heart like it was a piece of steak. That pain will never go away."

"I love you so much it hurts me knowing what I've done to you."

Charmayne and Gram talked for about another forty-five hours before hanging up the phone. Charmayne really did love Gram. She wished things could go back the way it was when they first met.

I wish things could go back to how it was when we first met. Now here I am worrying if I'm pregnant or have a disease. He had to really messed things up between us. I hate what he did to me and our relationship.

Gram knew he made a huge mistake by cheating on Charmayne. He had to come up with a solution to win Charmayne's heart back.

I really love this boy. I can't believe he did this to me. How can a person who say they love you and then turn around and cheat on you? Is that what you call love? Now, I don't know if I'm pregnant or if I have a disease. I am so scared of what my doctor might tell me. Lord, I pray my test results comes back negative. I need to keep calm. I don't want to think nothing positive about what's going on. I can't believe Gram did this to me. How dumb and stupid he was. I can't believe his homeboys was going to participate in a sexual encounter with this female. They are dumb and stupid just like him. They don't know if this girl is disease free or if she has a boyfriend as well. None of them were thinking about their significant others. They damn sure wasn't thinking about her boyfriend if she had one.

Charmayne couldn't seem to shake the feelings she was feeling inside. She was scared on not knowing what her doctor might say to her.

She finally made up in her mind to accept whatever the doctor had to say to her.

Whatever the results is, I have to be ready to accept the consequences. Now I know what I have to do.

Charmayne knew she had to pay the consequences of her actions. Even though she was nervous about going to the doctor this is something she had to do.

Charmayne started biting her nails. That's how nervous she was.

Chapter 29

The Results

When Charmayne got to the doctor's office she had to sign her name on the clipboard. She was hoping she didn't see anyone she knew. Her heart was raced. She was nervous as hell. She sat in the waiting area for about fifteen minutes until the nurse called her name.

Thank God the nurse called my name. I was about to find out what was taking them so long to call my name.

Charmayne immediately jumped up and walked in the back with the nurse.

Charmayne did her normal routine physical examination. She was then escorted to the back in a waiting room.

"The doctor will be in soon to see you," the nurse said.

Dang I know I have to take this test, but my stomach is hurting bad. I know it's my nerves that's bothering me.

When the doctor came in, he sat down and started looking at Charmayne chart.

The doctor checked Charmayne's blood pressure to make sure everything was good. He checked her eyes, listened to her heart, checked her ears, and her throat.

"What can I do for you today young lady?" The doctor then proceeded to ask Charmayne.

"Well Doctor, I'm here because my boyfriend had unprotected sex with another woman. I need to be tested to make sure I don't have a disease."

"Do you know how many sex partners he may have?"

"No, I don't know how many sex partners he have. I thought I was the only girl he was messing with until he got caught. I asked him if there were any other females he was involved with."

"And what did he tell you?"

"He told me there were no other females he was messing around with."

"To be honest with you doctor, I don't know how many other females he's been having unprotected sex with. That's why I'm here to make sure I don't have a disease."

"Well, I'm glad you decided to come in and get checked out. I can understand how important this is to you. I know this is weighing you down."

The doctor called the nurse in so she could get a blood and urine sample from Charmayne.

"I'll make sure I put a rush on your blood work."

"Thanks Doctor, I appreciate it."

How could he do me like this? He's always telling me how much he love me and how he want us to be a couple. Some kind of love he have for me. I can choke the shit out of him. Got me looking stupid in the face.

The nurse told Charmayne to squeeze the ball so she could find a vein.

Charmayne squeezed the ball tight as she could so the nurse can draw blood from her vein.

"You have several good veins for me to draw blood from."

Lady just pick a vein so I can get the hell out of here. Now is not the time for you to choose which vein you want to draw blood from. This nurse is really getting on my damn nerve. I don't want to hear about what vein looks good, just pick a vein and draw the blood from it.

"I don't like needles like that. They hurt too much."

"You're not alone. A lot of people don't like to get stuck by needles."

"It's not so much about getting stuck, but that some of the nurses handle you rough. They act like they don't know what they're doing."

"See, it's all over and you didn't feel a thing."

"Now that's what I'm talking about. Thank you."

"No problem."

The doctor walked back in the room and started educating Charmayne on practicing safe sex.

"In the meantime, I'm going to give you some condoms to protect yourself. This doesn't mean to go out there and have unprotected sex. I'm trying to protect you from catching any type of diseases or getting pregnant."

"Thanks Doctor, I understand. I wish we would've use these when we were having unprotected sex. I wouldn't be here getting stuck with these needles."

"Don't get yourself caught up with the wrong people Charmayne. You need to be careful when having sex with your partner."

"I sure will. I don't need this scare anymore. I'm going to make sure if and when I do decide to have sex, we are going to use these condoms."

"That's the best way to go if you don't want to get pregnant or catch a disease. We give you condoms to protect yourself."

"Well, I'm going to use mine. You don't have to worry about that."

Charmayne's doctor kept it real with her.

Charmayne appreciated word her doctor spoke to her. Most doctors wouldn't be honest with their patients about certain things. He showed genuine concern.

"If you want too, you can have him come in and get checked out as well. Do you know if he's been tested?"

"I don't know the answer to that, but I will find out."

When Charmayne left the doctor's office, she couldn't wait to call Gram.

Charmayne picked up the phone to call Gram.

Gram picked up the phone on the third ring.

"Hey Gram, what are you doing?"

"Nothing but sitting at the house. What's going on? I was waiting for you to call me."

"Well, that's why I'm calling you now. I should get my results in about a week or so. The nurse said she'll have the doctor try and put a rush on it."

"That's how long it takes?"

"I guess, I'm not a doctor. You better pray to God that I don't have a disease. If my test comes back positive I feel for you."

"Please, don't talk like that baby. I've been praying all day and all night asking God to forgive me for hurting you. I prayed that he keep you in perfect peace and health."

"That's what you better had been doing! This is all your fault. You wanted to go and have unprotected sex with another female. You just don't know what's in store for you. I promise things between us will get ugly.

"I know it's my fault." I truly regret what I've done to you.

"Everything you've done to me, is your fault. You're the one who put me in this predicament."

"Charmayne, you never done anything but make me happy."

"I don't think we need to see each other until I get my results back."

"I can't live without you Charmayne." I need you in my life.

"Well, you should have thought about that when you decided to go out there and mess around with someone else.

Charmayne hung the phone up on Gram. She did not want to hear anything else he had to say to her.

Charmayne mind was already made up.

Nothing Gram says or does is going to make me change my mind about him or our relationship. He really has messed things up between us. I guess I wasn't giving it to him the way he wanted me to, so he decided to get it from somewhere else.

Charmayne and Gram's relationship was over with. She told herself she could never be with Gram again let alone trust him.

When Charmayne got home, her mom and sisters were sitting on the porch talking.

"Hey Charmayne." Gracie said.

"Where you been at?" Asked Ty'Meisha.

"Ty'Meisha, didn't I tell you about your mouth?"

"Yes ma'am. I was just missing her that's all."

"Momma, it's okay. She's just being protective of me. I had some important business I had to take care of. Now, that I'm home we can do whatever you want to do."

"Charmayne how did everything go?"

"Everything went well." I have to wait about a week or so for everything to come back.

"I've been on my knees praying asking God to cover you."

"Thanks ma." I've been praying too.

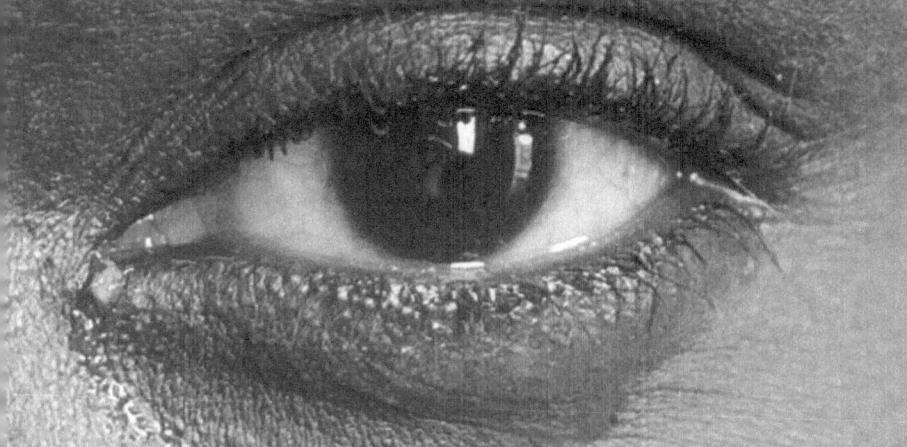

BOOK 3

No More Being Abused

I'M TAKING MY LIFE BACK

Chapter 30

God Is Good To Me

It was around six a.m. in the morning. Charmayne couldn't sleep. She tossed and turned all through the night. She even tried taking some supplements to help her sleep, but that wasn't working.

Charmayne was worried. She didn't know if the tests would come back positive or if she had a disease.

Lord, I pray that my test results don't come back positive. I have a lot to explain to my mom. How would I tell her my test results came back positive? My mom is going to flip the hell out.

Charmayne kept telling herself she was fine and that it was just her mind playing tricks. This was a true wakeup call for Charmayne.

God said, "I won't put no more on you than you can bear." I kept repeating that scripture in my head. I know my God got me covered. Lord, I thank you for your healing. My healing is already done.

Charmayne knew God wasn't pleased with her and the things she'd been doing lately.

How could I be so lame? I have let this man manipulate me all through our relationship. One thing I can say, Gram never stopped me from going to church or giving God my time.

God has been good to Charmayne. He's been there for her through her toughest times.

Lord, you've been good to me through all my mess. You never turned your back on me or gave up on me.

Charmayne sat on the edge of her bed as tears filled her eyes. She started feeling sick to her stomach.

Charmayne knew it was her nerves making her feel this way.

I thought he really loved me, I guess I was wrong. Some kind of love Gram had for me. If Gram loved me like he said he did, I wouldn't be in the predicament I'm now in.

Charmayne was finally able to calm herself down and fall asleep.

Charmayne woke up to Miracle tapping her on her shoulder.

"You have a phone call, Charmayne."

"Dang, I just closed my eyes."

Charmayne was too tired to get up and talk on the phone.

"Tell whoever it is, that I'll call them back."

Before walking out of the room, Charmayne requested Miracle write down their name and phone number on a piece of paper.

"Leave it on my dresser and I'll get it when I wake up."

"Okay, Charmayne."

"I love you, Miracle."

"I love you too, Charmayne."

Miracle closed the door behind her.

When Charmayne awoke it was around ten thirty am.

Charmayne's body was tired and drained.

"*Lord, I'm so tired, but I know I have to get up and gather my thoughts. Yes, this is weighing me down heavily. This is a mistake I've made having unprotected sex with Gram."*

When Charmayne finally got out of bed, she noticed the piece of paper on her dresser.

Charmayne looked at the paper and laid it back down on her dresser. She then headed to the bathroom to take a shower. She had to be at work at one p.m.

Charmayne was already running behind schedule.

I hate being late to work. I pray they don't fire me for being late.

Charmayne was always a dedicated worker and she intended to keep it that way. She never wanted to be late for work.

Charmayne gave Miracle five dollars for being her little secretary.

Miracle had a big smile on her face when Charmayne gave her five dollars.

After Charmayne got dressed for work, she picked up the piece of paper that was on her dresser.

When Charmayne looked at the piece of paper she recognized the number. It was from her doctor's office.

I pray my results came back negative.

Charmayne immediately called the doctor's office back.

Charmayne gave the receptionist her name.

The nurse put Charmayne on hold.

"Hello Charmayne, how are you?"

"I'm doing well. How are you doing this morning? Sorry I missed your call."

"No problem, I was calling to let you know we have your results."

"Can you give me the results over the phone?"

"I'm sorry, but we're not allowed to give patients their results over the phone."

"Okay, I understand. I'll be there in a minute."

Charmayne knocked on her mom's room door.

"Come in."

"Good morning ma. Well, the nurse just called and they have my results. I'm going to go there before I go to work."

"The Lord has already worked it out for your good."

"Yes ma'am I know he has. I've been praying too."

"I'll see you all when I get home."

"Don't let them work you too hard Charmayne." Rocky said.

"Rocky, you know your sister doesn't work hard."

"See you later, Charmayne." Gracie said.

"See you later, Gracie."

Charmayne arrived at the doctor's office at exactly ten forty-five am.

I better call my manager to let her know what's going on.

Charmayne signed her name on the clipboard. She waited in the waiting area for her name to be called. She then called her job to inform them that she might be a little late for work.

Charmayne's heart was racing fast. It felt like it was about to explode.

The nurse finally called Charmayne's name.

It's about time she called my name. It felt like I was waiting for hours for them to call my name.

Charmayne jumped up so fast, she forgot her purse.

Charmayne hurried over to where the nurse was standing.

"Excuse me ma'am, you forgot your purse."

Charmayne turned around and thanked the young lady.

"Thank you." Can't afford to leave this behind.

Charmayne's purse was the least thing on her mind. All she could do was think about the result of her test.

The doctor walked in the room Charmayne was in.

"Good morning, Charmayne."

"Good morning, doctor."

"How are you doing this morning?"

"I could be doing better if I knew the results of my test."

The doctor glanced over Charmayne's chart.

Damn, the test came back positive, Charmayne said to herself.

Charmayne tried swallowing her saliva, but it wouldn't go down.

"Your test result came back negative. You're in good health."

Charmayne started giving God the praises for working it out in her favor.

"Even though your test result came back negative, that doesn't mean you can go and have unprotected sex. It could've been worse on your end."

"Thank you for pushing me to get my results quickly. I appreciate it."

Before Charmayne left the doctor's office, her doctor gave her several pamphlets about safe sex and the type of diseases you can catch from having unprotected sex.

When Charmayne got in her car she started crying. She had a lot to be thankful for. She also only had about thirty minutes to get to work. When Charmayne arrived at work, tears were still falling from her eyes.

She quickly dried her tears before walking in. She did not want anyone to know she was crying. She had a good day at work. Every chance she got, Charmayne gave God the praise.

Charmayne couldn't stop praising his name.

Lord, I thank you for your miracle work. Thank you father for keeping me and watching over me.

When Charmayne got home from work, she couldn't wait to tell her mom the good news. Her brothers Rocky and Marc and sisters Ty'Meisha and Miracle were in all the yard playing Monkey in the Middle.

"Come on Charmayne and play with us," Marc said.

"I'll be out in a minute. I have to talk to momma. Where is Gracie?"

"She's in her room playing with her friend Kayla," TyMeisha said.

"Alright, I'll be out when I change my clothes."

When Charmayne walked in the house, her mom was on the phone talking.

Charmayne went into the room to speak to Gracie and Kayla.

"Hi, Charmayne." Gracie and Kayla said in unison.

"Hey Gracie and Kayla. What's going on?"

"Nothing, just playing with our dolls," Gracie replied.

"Do you want to play with us, Charmayne?" Asked Kayla.

"Not right now, I told Rocky that I'd go play with them."

Charmayne closed Gracie's room door.

"Charmayne, you can come back to the living room. I'm off the phone now," her mother called out to her.

Charmayne walked back to the living room where her mom was seated.

"Hey ma, how are you doing?"

"You look cheerful today. What's going on with you?"

"Thank you ma, for praying for me. My results came back negative. I'm in good health."

"God was in the midst of all your problems. He worked it out for your good. He already knew your results were going to come back negative."

"Mom, all I could do at work was give him praise. I know people were looking at me like I was crazy, but I didn't care. I just had to give God the praises."

After talking with her mother for a while, Charmayne went outside to play with Rocky, Marc, Miracle and TyMeisha.

Charmayne remembered she hadn't called Gram.

"I'll be back out to play, I have to make a phone call."

Charmayne went into the house to call Gram.

Gram picked up the phone on the second ring.

"Hey Gram, how are you?"

"Hey Charmayne, what's up?"

"I just called to let you know my result came back negative."

"Can I see you tonight?"

"Hell no. I don't think we need to see each other until I'm ready. Right now I'm not ready. You did enough damage to me already. Now is not the time for you to try and make up for what you did to me."

"If you need me, I'm here for you. I'm not going anywhere. You can try and push me away, but I'm going to keep coming back."

"Every time you keep coming back, I'm going to keep ignoring you. You're wasting your time trying to make things work between us."

"Charmayne, I hate what I've done to you. I wish I could take it back, but I can't. I hope one day you'll find it in your heart to forgive me."

"I don't hate you Gram, I hate what you did to me."

"Charmayne, I know you don't hate me, but I hate me. I hate what I've done to you and our relationship. I can understand why you're mad at me."

"Yes you're right, I am mad at you. Gram, you are a good person don't get me wrong, but you do stupid stuff."

"Baby, I'm so sorry for all the things I've done to you. One day I hope you can forgive me."

"I'll call you after I come from outside playing with my sisters and brothers. They're waiting for me to play 'Monkey in the Middle' with them."

"I remember that game. My nephews always wanted me to play that game with them. They always wanted me to be the monkey."

Charmayne and Gram both laughed at what Gram said.

"Just call me when you can. I'll be waiting for your call."

Charmayne and Gram both hung the phone up.

Charmayne went back outside to play Monkey in the middle with her sisters and brothers.

After playing outside for a while, everyone grew tired.

"Man, I'm tired." Rocky said.

"Me too," TyMeisha added.

"Let's all go inside and get something to drink," Charmayne said to her sisters and brothers. "We all need a break."

Charmayne, her sisters, and her brothers all went into the house to cool off.

Charmayne's mom walked out of her room and told everyone to get washed up for dinner.

"You all need to go get washed up for dinner. I don't want to see any dirty hands at my dinner table."

"Momma can Kayla stay and have dinner with us?"

"Kayla, would you like to stay and have dinner with us?"

"No thanks. I have to go somewhere with my mom. I appreciate the invitation. Maybe next time I can have dinner with you all."

"We would love that Kayla," Gracie said.

"Momma can Kayla use the phone to call her mom?"

"Sure, Kayla you may use the phone to call your mom. I don't mind."

"Momma, I'll walk her home," Charmayne said. Come on Kayla so I can walk you home.

"Goodnight everyone."

"Goodnight, Kayla," they all replied.

Charmayne walked Kayla home. While walking Kayla home, Charmayne noticed Gram's car at a female's house who she works with.

Charmayne couldn't believe Gram's was back to his old ways.

Charmayne didn't want to jump to any conclusion about his car being at another female's house.

Okay, I guess he's back at his old tricks. How dare he be at another female house down the street from where I live? He's going to make me bust out all his windows and flat his tires.

Charmayne was getting upset, but she didn't want Kayla to notice.

"Thanks, Charmayne, for walking me home."

"No problem, Kayla." See you tomorrow.

Charmayne waited until Kayla got in the house.

Charmayne walked slowly to see if Gram was going to come out of the girl's house.

Bump it, I'm not going to keep going through this with him. If he's in her house, he might as well stay there with her. Charmayne said to herself.

Charmayne went into the house and dialed Gram's number.

Gram didn't pick up.

So that is his car at her house. Wow, here we are once again with the same bullshit.

"Charmayne, is everything okay with you?"

"Yes ma, everything is okay. I'm just hungry. What did you cook for dinner?"

"I made a special meal just for you. You just don't know how hard I was praying for you. I need you to do the right thing and protect yourself."

"Yes, ma'am."

Charmayne wasn't about to tell her mom Gram's car was at another female's house down the street.

Charmayne went to the bathroom to take a shower.

I'm not going to keep worrying about what he's doing and who he's with. I'm going to enjoy having dinner with my family. I don't want to hear any of his lies. I know he's going to try to talk his way out of this, but not this time. I see it with my own eyes. Everybody in my neighborhood knows we are in a relationship and they know what kind of car he drives. I'm quite sure people will wonder about his car is at another female's house.

Charmayne and her family enjoyed the dinner their mom prepared for them.

"Ma, the dinner was delicious," Gracie said.

"Mom, you're the best," Miracle added.

"Momma, I think you put your foot and all your toes in this dinner," TyMeisha chuckled.

They all laughed at what TyMeisha said.

"Can I have some more, momma?" Asked Gracie.

"Yes you may Gracie. Does anyone else want more before I put the food away?"

"No ma'am. I'm full," Rocky said.

After eating dinner and cleaning up the house, they all played family trivia.

Marc and TyMeisha won family trivia.

"Goodnight everyone," Charmayne said.

"Looks like someone is already knocked out, " Marc said.

"Gracie pick your sister up and lay her down on the bed."

"Yes Ma'am."

Gracie did exactly what her mom had asked her to do.

"Goodnight everyone, Rocky said."

"Goodnight Rocky," Charmayne and her mom said.

Charmayne's mom made sure the doors were locked and all the windows had the security lock on them.

Charmayne's mom kissed each and every one of her children's goodnight.

Chapter 31

My First Slap

Charmayne arose the next morning and rearranged her room. She was trying to avoid calling Gram. She was so mad at him, but she was so weak for him too.

"Charmayne you have a phone call," Miracle yelled out.

Charmayne walked out the room and picked up the phone.

"Hello, who is this?"

"Hey baby, I was calling to see if we can hang out for a while."

"I'll call you back, I have a lot to do around the house."

Charmayne knew she was telling Gram a lie. She didn't want Gram to know she saw his car at another female's house down the street from her house.

How dare he ride on my street and park at another female house? I can't wait to see his punk ass. I know he's going to tell me one of his homeboys had his car. I don't want to hear his lies.

"Okay baby, don't forget to call me."

Charmayne hung the phone up without saying another word to Gram.

Who in the hell is he trying to play? Boy, you don't deserve my love let alone my heart.

After rearranging her room, Charmayne decided to cook breakfast while everyone was still asleep.

Charmayne's mom walked in the kitchen.

"Good morning, Charmayne."

"Good morning, ma."

"I see someone is in a good mood."

"Yes, momma, I am in a good mood. I'm thanking God for allowing me to see another blessed morning. I owe all this to him."

"Yes Lord, he's been better to us than we've been to ourselves" to which Charmayne continued, "God won't put no more on you than you can bear."

"Ma, I decided to cook breakfast and give you a break. You're always doing for us. I just want you to know how much I appreciate you."

Charmayne walked into her sisters and brothers room to wake them.

"Get up and go wash your face. Breakfast is ready."

"Momma thanks for cooking breakfast for us," Gracie said.

"The thanks goes to your sister Charmayne. She did this for us."

"This breakfast is fantastic Charmayne," Rocky said.

"Thanks Rocky."

After eating breakfast, Rocky and Gracie decided to clean up the kitchen.

Charmayne decided to call Gram back. She picked up the phone and dialed his number.

Gram picked up the phone on the second ring.

"Hey baby, I was waiting for you to call me."

"I should have waited longer than that. Don't be sitting here waiting for me to call you. You never know if I'm going to call you back or not."

"Baby, what's wrong?"

"I'll tell you later, now is not the time."

"Charmayne, your attitude is changing."

"I wonder why my attitude has changed. I'll call you when I get out of the shower. If you don't hear from me then I'm busy."

Charmayne and Gram both hung up.

Charmayne and her mom had a long conversation about her future.

Charmayne had it all planned out. She wanted to take care of her mom, sisters and brothers. She did not want her mom to suffer any more in paying all the bills and taking care of them. She wanted to help support her mom.

"Ma is it okay if Gram comes and picks me up?"

"Yes Charmayne, you can hang out with Gram for a while. Just be careful and be home at a decent hour. I don't want you hanging out with him too late. I don't need to get another scare from you."

"Yes ma'am. I'll be home at a decent time. I'm not planning on staying out late with him. I told him we need to be friends and friends only. I'm not trying to be put back in a predicament with him. The damage has been done. He will never get that opportunity to do that to me again."

Charmayne waited about an hour to call Gram. She wanted him to suffer for the things he'd done to her.

Charmayne picked up the phone to dialed Gram's number, but the phone started ringing.

"Hello."

"Hey baby, are you busy?"

"I was just about to call you. What's up?"

"I was wondering if I can come and pick you up. I miss you baby."

"What time are you planning on coming to pick me up?"

"If you're ready now, I can come and pick you up."

"I'll be ready by the time you get here."

"Okay baby, I'm on my way."

Charmayne couldn't wait to see Gram. She was ready to see what his excuse was going to be when she tells him she saw his car last night.

Charmayne, her mom, and Mr. Home were seated on the porch talking when Gram pulled up.

"Momma, look at your nosy neighbors Mrs. Fashion and Ms. Lovett peeping through the curtains. You sure have some nosy neighbors."

"Yes they are" Mr. Home said. "They are watching and seeing who is coming and going out of your house. I had to tell Ms. Lovett about herself one day."

"Are you serious, Home?" My mom asked Mr. Home.

"Yes, I'm serious. They started telling me who was coming to my house and stuff like that. I told her she needs to mind her own damn busy and stay out of mine. That lady is so damn nosy. I can't stand people like that."

"I don't either, Home. They get on my nerves. I stopped them from telling me anything. I don't need you to tell me what my children be doing. I know what my children are capable of doing and what they're not capable of doing.

Gram got out his car and spoke to everyone.

"Good afternoon everyone."

"Good afternoon Gram. How are you doing?"

"I'm doing great."

"Hey Gram, I haven't seen you in a while."

"I heard you were sick Mr. Home. How are you feeling?"

"I could be doing better just got to take it easy."

"Glad to know you're doing better."

"Okay ma, I'll see you later."

"Don't be out too late. Remember what I told you."

"Yes ma'am I won't be out too late."

"I'll have her home at a decent time."

"Have fun."

Gram was pleased that Charmayne went on a date with him. He really didn't know what Charmayne was going to do or say to him.

"I'm glad you decided to meet up with me."

"Listen Gram, this is not a date for either one of us. I just agreed to meet up with you and nothing else."

"Have you had anything to eat yet?"

"I'm not hungry. Why did you want to meet up with me? I hope you're not trying to apologize for what you did to me."

"Charmayne, can we just have a good time hanging out? I am sorry for what I've done, but I can't take it back. I just want to spend a little time with you, that's all.

Charmayne and Gram went to a city park to talk. She was still upset for having seen Gram's car at another female's house. She wanted to let him know what she saw.

"Come on baby, let's get out and walk around the park."

Charmayne told Gram she didn't feel like walking around the park.

"I don't feel like walking around the park."

"What's wrong baby?"

"Can we just sit in the car and talk?"

"Sure, whatever you want to do."

"Listen, I think we need to be friends and friends only."

"What do you mean by be "friends?" Where is all of this coming from? One minute we're in a relationship and now you want us to just be friends."

"Gram, what was your car doing at another female house? You could have at least parked your car somewhere else and then walk to her house. You know I live on the same street she stays on."

"If you let me explain."

"Explain what Gram? One of your homeboy's had your car."

"Yeah, one of my homeboys had my car."

"I knew you were going to say that. I was waiting on you to come up with an excuse about your car being there. Which one of your homeboy had your car?"

Gram couldn't say nothing. He knew Charmayne was going to be angry if he told her the truth.

"Yes I was over there, but I was there for her brother, Keith."

"Well you and Keith must have a good relationship, because you were over there for two fucking hours."

"So what are you trying to say Charmayne?"

"Just as I said. You and Keith must have a good relationship. I don't bite my tongue and you of all people should know that."

"Charmayne I'm telling you the truth. I am not cheating on you with anyone. I would never cheat on you with someone on the same street you live on. Come on now, you know me better than that."

"Man whatever. No. I don't know you like that. Maybe you should refresh my memory."

"Don't man me whatever."

"Evidentially I don't know you too well. I had to go to the clinic to make sure you didn't give me a disease, so no I don't know you like that."

Charmayne never cheated on Gram. She was too afraid.

I don't believe in going out of my relationship and cheating on the person I'm with. Cheating causes lots of problems. I guess Gram is too blind to see what his lying and cheating put me through.

"Gram, not one time have I ever cheated on you. Yes, I had plenty of guys who wanted to take me out, but I turned them down. I take my relationship seriously with whomever I'm with. I don't believe going out and cheating on the person I'm with. Right now, I don't think we can be in a relationship. You hurt me so bad, nothing you do is ever going to make it right between us."

Charmayne saw anger flickering in Gram's eyes.

Charmayne looked through the corner of her left eye and she noticed Gram had his fist balled up as if he was about to hit her.

I pray this boy does not hit me. If he hits me, I promise you, he won't hit anybody else! His ass will be behind bars.

Charmayne knew she better change the subject before things escalated to something worse.

"Charmayne, if I was you, I'd be quiet. Now I have let you do all the talking, but it's my turn. I hope you don't think I'm going to let you continue running your mouth to me."

"What do you mean running my mouth to you? This is my mouth and I can say what the hell I want to say. The thing is, you're mad because you got caught again in your own lies. So, I guess you want to get mad at me for being real with you."

"It's not about you being real with me, it's about your flip ass mouth. I apologized to you for what I've done, but you seem not to forgive me."

"Why in the hell should I forgive you when you put my life in jeopardy? No, I'm not going to forgive you."

At that moment Charmayne didn't care what came out of her mouth.

Charmayne wanted Gram to know what he did to her hurt and that he could never ease the pain.

Does he actually think I'm going to forgive him for what he's done to me? He's the one who did this, not me. I deserve better. He better be glad I decided to let him come pick me up. The hell with Gram. I don't need this kind of mess in my life.

"Charmayne keep running at the mouth, it's only going to make me knock your ass out. I'm trying my best not to hit you, but you're not going to keep trying me."

"Gram, you tell me how am I making you want to hit me? I promise you, if you hit me there will be consequences. I'm not going to sit here and let you beat up on me. Now, that I will not let you do."

Gram was scaring Charmayne. She felt that something was about to happen to her.

"Gram just take me home. I'm ready to go."

"So, now you're ready to go. When I'm fucking done talking to you, then I'll take your ugly ass home."

Charmayne felt her heart leave her chest. She couldn't believe Gram was talking to her like she was a piece of shit to him.

Are you serious? He is talking to me like I don't mean anything. This is the man who says he loves me unconditionally. How could he love me and put his hands on me? Yes, the best thing he can do is to take me home.

Charmayne tried to calm him down, but he wasn't trying to hear anything she said.

"Gram, you're scaring me. You really need to calm down. Can you please just take me home?"

"What did I just say to you? When I'm fucking ready I'll take your ugly ass home. What part did you not understand?"

"You're mad at me because you know I'm speaking the truth. You're the one who got caught and now you're taking it out on me. Before she said anything else Gram reached over and slapped her face.

Charmayne's face hit against the door. That's how hard Gram hit her.

Still feeling the sting, Charmayne grabbed the left side of her face.

"What in the hell did you do that for? I never put my hands on you."

"Bitch and you never will. I have told you about getting slick out at the mouth with me."

Charmayne got ready to say something to Gram, but he punched her in the head.

"Gram stop it, you're hurting me."

"I know, that'll teach you from running off at the mouth. The next time you get slick at the mouth, you'll think about my fist going upside your head."

Charmayne started crying.

"Your tears don't mean shit to me."

Charmayne's only hope was to get out of the car and run or keep her mouth closed.

Charmayne noticed several people walking the trail. She didn't know if she should run for it or just take his abuse.

Gram noticed Charmayne looking at the people who were walking the trail.

"I wish you would try and open my door. I'll beat your ass silly."

Charmayne started crying even harder.

Gram's pager went off.

"If you open your mouth and tell anyone about what I did, bitch I'll kill you. Do you understand what I just said?"

Charmayne didn't know if she should answer that question.

"Bitch, I asked you a question. Don't let me have to repeat myself."

By that time, Gram had grabbed Charmayne by her arm.

"Gram, I heard what you said. I'm not going to tell nobody."

"If you do, your ass will be dead. Do you understand?"

"Gram I heard what you said. Can you please take me home?"

Gram pointed his fingers as if it were a gun at Charmayne.

"Try me if you want too, your ass will be dead."

On the way home Charmayne was quiet. She was afraid to say anything else to Gram.

When Gram pulled up in Charmayne's yard, they both noticed Charmayne's mom car wasn't in the driveway.

Gram turned the car off and beckoned her to sit closer to him.

Charmayne did just as Gram asked her.

"Give me a kiss baby."

He just beat my ass and now he wants me to give him a kiss. This boy is really stupid. I better do it before he punches me again.

Charmayne kissed Gram on his lips.

"Damn baby you taste good. I'm sorry for what I just did to you. I never meant to hurt you. I don't know what came over me. Baby, let me taste those lips again."

Charmayne kissed Gram again, but this time she began teasing him with her tongue. She then moved her hand up and down Gram's thighs making him want her.

Charmayne knew exactly what she was doing. She was giving Gram a taste of his own medicine.

I hope he isn't thinking I'm going to have sex with him. How can I have sex with someone who just beat my ass? I'm not going to be that stupid and sleep with him. I'll make him think I'm going to have sex with him, but little do he know.

Charmayne felt herself getting aroused. She knew she had to take control of it before she gave herself to Gram. She wasn't about to let her feelings take control over her. She wanted Gram to feel her pain and what he put her through.

I know I shouldn't be teasing Gram, but he deserves it. All what Gram put me through, I wish I would have sex with him. Gram doesn't deserve my love or my heart. Let alone, he doesn't deserve me. I can't be with a person who beats me up. My father would NEVER approve of Gram putting his hands on me. If my dad was here, he would kill Gram. He doesn't play about any man putting their hands on his daughters. Boy, I wish my dad was still here with us. I have no one to protect me from Gram. I have two younger brothers, but they are too young to fight Gram. Daddy, I miss you dearly.

Charmayne continued rubbing her hands up and down Gram's leg. Charmayne knew exactly what she was doing. She was having fun teasing Gram in every way she could.

Gram started calling out Charmayne's name to make love to him.

"Baby, please make love to me."

Charmayne wouldn't say a word. She kept on teasing Gram.

Gram started unzipping his pants.

Charmayne started stroking him in a seductive way.

"Well, I think I better go inside before my mom pulls up and catches us in the act."

Charmayne could tell Gram didn't like that. She could care less what Gram was thinking.

"Goodnight, Gram."

Charmayne got out of Gram's car and closed the door behind her.

Gram rolled down the window and called out Charmayne's name.

As usual the nosy neighbors, Mrs. Fashion and Ms. Lovett were sitting on their porch watching Charmayne's every move.

Charmayne didn't look back. She went into the house and closed the door behind her. She refused to have sex with Gram. She knew Gram was cheating on her and messing around with God knows who. At this point, Charmayne really didn't give a damn. She was used to all his dirty little secrets and lies.

However, Charmayne couldn't believe Gram had hit her. Her face was swollen. She did not want her mom, sisters, or brothers to see her face all swollen up. Charmayne knew she had to get it together. She took a nice warm shower and let the hot water hit against her face.

After taking a shower, Charmayne went in the kitchen to get some ice to put in a rag.

I know this ice will help keep the swelling down. I pray to God nobody catches me with this ice-filled rag against my face.

Charmayne started crying.

Dang what have I done for Gram to do this to me? He don't like to hear the truth. I have to keep this a secret. If I tell anyone and he finds out, he's going to kill me. The look he had in his eyes when he told me that, let me know he meant business. As bad as I want to tell my mom, I know I couldn't.

Charmayne heard her mom's car pull in the driveway.

Charmayne hurried up and went to the bathroom. She flushed the ice down the toilet and hung the rag on the shower rod.

"Hey Charmayne we're home," yelled out TyMeisha.

"I'll be out in a minute," TyMeisha.

Before leaving the bathroom, Charmayne made sure the swelling on her face was unnoticeable. She walked out of the bathroom with a smile on her face.

"Hey ma. I didn't see your car when I came home. Where did you all go?"

"I went to the store. I had to buy a little grocery to put in the house."

Charmayne went outside to help them bring the grocery bags in the house.

"Oh Okay. I was wondering where you all were. Don't you know when I came home, your nosy friends were sitting on their porch staring at me when I got out of Gram's car."

"Well Charmayne, they are still sitting on the porch looking like they lost their best friend."

Everybody started laughing.

"Momma, why do you and Charmayne say that Mrs. Fashion and Ms. Lovett is nosy?" Asked Gracie.

"Because they are," Rocky and Marc said.

"They told Jarvis mom that he be having girls at her house when she's not home."

"Are you serious Rocky?" Asked Gracie.

"Yeah, I'm serious. Jarvis told them one day, to mind their business and stay out of his."

The phone started ringing.

"I'll get it momma," Miracle said.

Miracle went in the house to answer the phone.

"Hello."

"Hello Miracle, can I speak to Charmayne."

Charmayne and her mom wondered who Miracle was on the phone with.

"Hold on. Charmayne, Gram wants to talk to you."

Charmayne went in the house to talk to Gram.

"Hello."

"Hey, what are you doing?"

"Talking with my family. I'll call you back later."

"Charmayne, you better not tell your momma or anybody else what I did to you. I promise you, don't try me, your momma won't be able to identify your body."

"Goodnight, Gram."

Charmayne hung the phone up. She was hoping no one saw how nervous she was.

Before going back outside, Charmayne had to act normal. She was really scared of Gram.

Gram had the upper hand on Charmayne. Whether Gram knew it or not, he had Charmayne scared of him.

Charmayne was so terrified in hearing the name Gram. Hearing Gram's name brought fear to Charmayne's heart.

I hope my mom, sisters and brothers don't noticed my hands shaking." Dang, I thought he loves me. How a person can loves someone so dearly and then jumps on them? I don't get it, what went wrong between us?

Charmayne was contemplating the reason Gram became so violent with her.

All I did was ask him about being at another female house. I didn't cursed at him, put my hands on him or caused a scene between our con-

versations. I don't recall any of this happening between us. So, why did he slap me?

Later on that night Charmayne couldn't stop thinking about what Gram had said to her.

Charmayne wanted to tell her mom, but she knew she couldn't.

I want to tell my mom, but I can't.

Charmayne tried going to sleep, but it was too hard for her to close her eyes. All she can see was Gram's fist against her face.

Charmayne was glad the swelling went down.

Gram already made it plain and clear that he'll kill me if I tell my mom or anyone else. Thank you Jesus for your healing hands and taking the swelling away. If the swelling doesn't go down, I don't know how I'm going to explain this to my mom.

Charmayne face was still sore. She had a lot of pain on the left side of her face.

All Charmayne can feel is Gram's hands slapping her hard against her face and his fist punching her in the head.

Charmayne wanted to tell her mom, but she knew that would become a problem between her and Gram.

Charmayne cried so much, she cried herself to sleep.

Chapter 32

You Heard What I Said

It was around twelve thirty-two pm when Charmayne woke up. All through the night Charmayne was having bad dreams about what Gram had did to her.

Dang my face is still sore from the slap of Gram's hand. I'm still trying to figure out what I've done wrong for him to slap me.

"Good morning, Charmayne."

"Good morning, ma."

"Charmayne, I've been noticing a change in your behavior lately around the house. Is everything alright with you and Gram?"

"Yes, ma'am. Everything is alright between us. I just be tired when I get off from work."

Charmayne was lying to her mom. She knew she couldn't tell her mom what Gram did to her if she wanted to live.

I hated lying to my mom about my relationship. I have to keep his dirty little secret about what he did to me. If I tell anyone, he will kill me. The words that he said, I know he meant well. I wish I could tell my mom, maybe she can save me.

"Charmayne, don't never think you have to be afraid to come and talk to me. If anything is wrong with my children, I want you all to feel comfortable in talking to me."

"Yes, ma'am I know. If we come and talk to you about what is going on with us, would you judge us?"

"Charmayne, I would not judge my kids for something they came to me with. One thing I want you to know is, I'm here for you. You don't have to be scared about talking to me about anything. Who am I to judge you, your sisters or brothers? What kind of mother would I be?"

"Well ma, me and Gram."

Before Charmayne can finish talking to her mom, the phone rang.

"I'll get it ma."

"We're going to finish our little conversation after you get off the phone."

"Yes ma'am."

Charmayne picked up the phone.

"Hello."

"Hello Charmayne, how are you?"

"Hey Gram, what's up?"

"I was just calling to make sure you didn't tell your mom about what I did to you."

"Well, I was about to tell her until you call."

"Bitch don't fucking play with me. If you tell your mom, I promise you I will kill you. Now fucking play with me and see what happen."

Charmayne was so scared, she almost dropped the phone out of her hand.

Charmayne's mom knew something was wrong with Charmayne.

"Charmayne, what's wrong with you?" You better not tell me nothing. Is that Gram on the phone?"

"Yes, ma'am."

Charmayne knew she had better hurry and come up with a quick lie to tell her mom.

"It's nothing mom. He was just telling me his dog Nookie had just got hit by a car and died in his arms. He's crazy about his dog. It got me shaken up. We just went to the store yesterday and bought her some dog food. I'm trying to calm him down on the phone."

"Oh, okay. Tell Gram I said sorry for his loss. Maybe you need to go and be with him."

Gram overheard what Charmayne's mom had said to her.

"Get dress, I'm coming to get you."

"Gram, I'll call you when I get finished cleaning up. I just got up. I haven't even taken a shower yet."

"You better keep your mouth closed, before *you* be my fake dog named Nookie."

"Okay, I'll call you."

Charmayne and Gram both hung up.

Charmayne felt tormented by Gram and his abusive behavior.

"Lord, I don't know what to do. Gram is threatening to kill me if I tell my mom or someone else. Lord, give me strength, because you know I need it right now."

Charmayne's sisters and brothers overheard what their mom and Charmayne discussed.

"Can we go with you over to Gram's house?" Asked TyMeisha.

"No, TyMeisha, stay home and clean up your room. I've already told you to stop asking me about going over to Gram's house."

"I'm sorry Charmayne." I just wanted to show my condolence to Gram and his dog.

"I don't believe TyMeisha just said she wanted to show her condolence to Gram and his dog," Rocky said. "You really need to stop acting like you know his dog."

"TyMeisha you are so extra," Grace said. "You act like Gram and his family is having a funeral for their dog."

"So I guess you want to go to the funeral huh," said Mark.

Everybody started laughing at what Mark said to TyMeisha.

"Ma, I guess we all need to get dressed for Gram's dog funeral," Miracle said.

"I wish you all would stop laughing at me. I'm serious."

"And so are we," Miracle said.

"Alright now that's enough of picking on your sister. She was just showing her condolence to Gram's dog."

"Thanks ma. My heart goes out to animals."

"Girl, you don't even like animals," Gracie said.

"I know, but I don't like to hear that somebody dog died."

"TyMeisha just go in your room and help clean up," Charmayne said. "I will let Gram know you sent your love and condolences."

They all went in their rooms to clean up.

Charmayne hated lying to her mom about her and Gram's relationship.

How can I keep lying to my mom, sisters and brothers about what Gram did to me? I hate what I'm doing to them. I know my brothers would kill him, let alone my mom. Dang, I forgot about my Uncle Smith. I definitely can't tell him. My uncle would go to Gram's house and shoot up everybody in there who try to stand in his way of getting to Gram. One thing for sure, my Uncle Smith don't play when it comes to his nieces and nephews. One day, I'm going to have to tell my family what Gram did to me. I know they would protect me.

After cleaning up her room and playing a game of match with her sisters and brother, Charmayne decided to give Gram a call.

"Charmayne, you need to go ahead and call Gram so you can be home at a decent time."

"Yes ma'am. I'm not planning on being out that late with him. I told him we need to stop spending a lot of time with each other so much."

"What did he say when you told him that?"

"I can tell he didn't like it, but he understood what I was saying. I told him I need to start spending time with my sisters and brothers."

I know my mom discerned I was lying. She was looking at me in a strange way. My mom knows when her children be lying to her. She gave me the look like, "Why are you lying to me?"

"It's getting late, let me call Gram."

Charmayne picked up the phone and called Gram.

Gram didn't answer.

As Charmayne was getting ready to go in her room, the phone rang.

"Hello."

"Hey Charmayne, what's up?"

"I was calling to let you know I'm ready."

"Okay, I'll be there shortly."

"TyMeisha told me to give you her condolences."

"Tell TyMeisha, I said thanks."

"Okay, I will." See you soon.

Charmayne hung the phone up.

"TyMeisha, Gram told me to tell you thanks."

Charmayne, her mom, sisters and brothers all headed outside to sit on the porch. Mark and Rocky went to one of their friend's house to play football.

Charmayne had a flash back when she saw Gram's car pulled in her driveway.

Gram got out and spoke to everyone.

"Hello everyone."

"Hello Gram," they all said. "Sorry for the loss of your dog."

"Thanks everyone."

"See you later Charmayne," Miracle said.

"See you all later." Call me if you need me if you need me ma.

"Okay, I will." Don't be out too late.

"Yes, ma'am I won't."

Charmayne and Gram drove out of Charmayne's drive way.

Gram tooted his horn at Charmayne mom and sisters.

"I hope you didn't tell your mom that I had slapped you."

"Gram, you don't have to keep asking me about that. I already told you I wasn't going to mention what you did to me. You don't have to keep reminding me."

"Bitch, I know you're not trying to get slick at the mouth at me. If I was you, I'll keep my mouth closed if I was you. The next slap I give you, won't be that easy."

Charmayne knew she better not say anything slick out her mouth to Gram.

Damn, I should stayed my black ass home with my family. I don't need this bullshit from him. Who do he think he is? He's not my dad that's number one, I'm not his punching bag that's number two and I'm not about to let him keep putting his hands on me that's number three. I promise you if he hits me again, I'm going to jump out his car while he's driving and run to the nearest house or store and call the damn police. I done had enough with his shit.

Charmayne and Gram stopped at a red light. A car pulled up next to Gram's car with loud playing music.

Charmayne and Gram both noticed how loud the music was.

Charmayne noticed four girls in the car next to them.

One of the girls begin rolling down her window and looking at Gram.

I hope he knows, I'm sitting in the passenger seat watching what's going on between the both of them. Gram act like I was invisible to him.

One of the girls in the car winked her eye at Gram as they drove off. Gram smiled back at the girl.

Gram looked over at Charmayne to see if she was looking at him.

"What's wrong with you?"

"Well, I guess I'm invisible to you. You showed no respect for me."

"What are you talking about I have no respect for you? All I did was smile back at her. That don't mean shit to me. Just because I smiled back at her doesn't mean I want her."

"Gram, you didn't respect me at all. Let alone, I'm your girlfriend who is in the car with you."

"And what is your point?"

"My point is, how would you feel if I did that to you?"

"If you did that to me while we're together, I would have knocked your pussy ass out. Point blank no questions asked. Anything else you want to ask me?"

"Just take me home."

Charmayne knew she had blew a fuel in Gram's brain. Instead of Gram taking Charmayne home, he went to his house instead. Gram knew nobody would be home but him.

"Gram if you don't mind, can you take me home?"

Gram got out of his car and went around to open Charmayne's door.

"I dare you to get out and run."

Charmayne did not want to get out of Gram's car. She was trying to find someone and yell out for help.

"Bitch if you do, I will cut your body in half. Don't even think about it."

Charmayne knew she had to get out of the car before Gram did-something to her.

Gram helped Charmayne out of the car. He made sure to hold Charmayne tight around her waist, so she couldn't get away from him.

Gram noticed several of his neighbors standing outside washing their cars. He kissed Charmayne passionately on her lips.

"Hey Gram, how are you doing?"

"Hey Mr. Bond, how are you?"

Charmayne was glad to see Mr. Bond outside washing his car just in case something happens to her.

"Is that Charmayne with you, Gram?"

"Yes sir, this her."

"Hey Charmayne."

"Hey Mr. Bond, how are you?"

"Tell your Uncle I need him to come over and take a look at my lawnmower."

"Okay, I will tell him.

"You two kids have fun."

They went in Gram's house and closed the door behind them.

Without any warning, Gram reached over and punched Charmayne dead in her face. He started punching Charmayne non-stop, where ever his punches landed. He did not care where he punched. He made sure however, not to punch Charmayne in her face.

"Stop it Gram, you're hurting me."

"No, this is what you want. I keep telling you about your slick ass mouth. I'm just giving you a taste of your own medicine."

Charmayne laid in the fetal position.

"Gram, please stop please. I'm sorry Gram, please stop."

Charmayne body was sore, she couldn't feel anymore of Gram's licks.

He finally stopped punching her.

"Get up, go in the bathroom, and clean yourself up before I give you some more."

Charmayne was in so much pain she had to limp to the bathroom.

Charmayne made sure her hair was in place and her clothes were neat before leaving the bathroom.

Lord, please give me the strength to leave him. If I continue to stay in this abusive relationship, he is going to kill me one day. I don't deserve this abusiveness from him. What have I done to be treated like this? All I asked him to do, is to show me some respect. This is the thanks I get for asking him to respect me?

"Get ready so I can take you home. I don't want you to call me unless I call you. Once again if you tell your mom or anyone of what I did to you, it won't look pretty on your end. Do you understand what I just said to you?"

"Yes Gram, I understand."

Gram walked over and kiss Charmayne on her lips.

Chapter 33

Pregnant With His First Child

Charmayne awoke the next morning at seven thirty-two a.m. Her sister Carla was still sleeping. She didn't want to wake her up, so Charmayne let her sleep a little while longer. Her mom was already in the kitchen cooking breakfast for them.

"Mom, thanks for putting a quilt on us," Charmayne said.

"No, problem," she replied. "That's what a mother is supposed to do. I heard you and your sister having a good time in the living room. I didn't want to intrude on what you and Carla were doing."

"Mom, you should have come and had fun with us. We would have liked that. We were pretending to be characters in the story. We played dress up with her baby dolls."

"All ten of them?" My mom asked me.

"Yes, ma'am," Charmayne said to her. "I don't know what time we fell asleep," I said. "I'm going to take a shower before she gets up and starts looking for me."

While Charmayne was in the shower she overheard her sister Carla crying. Charmayne turned off the shower and waited to hear the cry again. This time the voice was screaming. She jumped out of the shower with nothing on and opened the door to see what was going on.

"What's going on with her?" Charmayne asked her mom.

"She's crying, because she did not see you," her mom replied.

Charmayne bent down and waved for her sister to come over to her. She picked her up and began singing to her. Charmayne rocked her back and forth in her arms.

"I'm never going to leave you." Charmayne said to her sister. "I will always be by your side."

"I thought you had left me," she said.

"No, I went to take a shower," Charmayne said. "I didn't want to wake you up. You were sleeping so peacefully. I didn't wake you. I apologize for not waking you up," Charmayne said.

Her mom went in the room to get her some clothes so she can take a shower with me. After taking a shower, we both got dressed. We went in the kitchen to eat breakfast.

"I have to go to school but I'll be home as soon as I can," I said to my sister.

"Okay," she said. I gave her and my mom a hug and a kiss before heading out the door.

"Don't be late for practice," she said.

I had my life already planned out. After I graduate from college, had a full time job at a restaurant, work on weekends and holidays at a Department Store. On my first week at work, I started getting sick and feeling weak at the stomach. I didn't know what was going on with me. I was taking a customer's order and had to run straight to the bathroom. As soon as I stepped in the bathroom, I begin to vomit all over the floor. It was yellow with a bad nasty taste and a funny smell. My manager walked in the bathroom and noticed the vomit on the floor.

"Hey Charmayne are you okay?" My manager asked me.

"I don't know," I said to her. I just started feeling sick as I was taking my customer order.

"Did you have a period last month?" She asked me.

"Yes, it just went off two weeks ago," I said.

"Was your period normal?" She asked me.

"Why you're asking me about my period?" I asked to her.

"Maybe you're pregnant," she said.

"I'm not pregnant," I said to her. It's something I ate this morning. It probably didn't agree with my stomach. I grabbed some paper towels and started cleaning up my vomit. My manager started helping me. I looked at her and said, "You don't have to do this I can clean it up."

"I don't mind," she said.

"Thank you for helping me clean up this mess," I said.

"You're my girl and I love you like you're my daughter," she said.

"Get yourself together and I'll finish cleaning this up," she said. You look terrible.

"Please don't send me home," Charmayne said to her manager. "If I feel like I'm going to get sick again, I'll let you know."

"I want you to work in the stock room and help me with inventory so I can keep an eye on you," she said.

I washed my face in the sink before I went back out on the floor to work. My manager asked me again if I noticed anything different about my period.

"No," I said. "My period was normal. Nothing out of the ordinary. I really didn't pay it any attention, so it didn't bother me. Sometimes it maybe light and then sometimes it may be dark. I've noticed the color of my period for the past month, but I didn't pay it any attention. I tried to work, but I wasn't feeling well."

Charmayne picked up the phone and called Gram. As Charmayne was trying to explain to Gram what happened to her at work, Gram hung the phone up. All Charmayne heard was a dial tone.

Charmayne sat in the lobby and waited for Gram to pick her up.

"Hope you feel better one of her friends called to her."

"I'll call you when I get off," my manager said.

When Gram walked in he had a strange look on his face.

"What happened to you?" Gram asked Charmayne.

"I got sick and started vomiting," Charmayne explained. "I started feeling a little drowsy and weak. I don't know what's was wrong with me."

Gram started telling Charmayne how he started vomiting in the bathroom as well.

"It must have been something we ate the other night," Charmayne said.

"It probably was something we ate from the restaurant," he said. "We both had a rib dinner from the restaurant we normally go to."

He continued, "I was told that if you dream about fishes someone is pregnant."

"What does that mean?" Charmayne asked Gram.

"It means you might be pregnant."

"Well, don't look at me," Charmayne said. "I just had my period and you know that. You must have somebody else pregnant because it's not me," Charmayne said.

When Charmayne got home, she called her doctor's office. She told the nurse why she was calling. All she wanted was get a pregnancy test. Either she was pregnant or had a stomach virus one or the other. Charmayne was scheduled to see the doctor in the morning at nine fifteen a.m.

Charmayne arrived at the doctor's office around nine am. She signed her name on the sign in sheet and waited for her name to be called. The nurse called Charmayne's name and escorted her to the lab room. The nurse took a urine sample and drew blood. Charmayne waited anxiously for her to return with the result. Charmayne was never a nail bitter. While waiting for the nurse to come in with the results she started biting her nails until they started bleeding. Charmayne nerves were bad that day. When the nurse walked in, she seemed to have a little smirk on face.

"Congratulation are in order," the nurse said to Charmayne.

"What did you just said to me?" Charmayne asked the nurse.

"You're going to be a mother," the nurse said.

"No, you have to take it again," Charmayne said to the nurse. "There's no way I'm pregnant. We used protection every time we had sexual intercourse."

The nurse said to Charmayne, "I don't have a problem doing another pregnancy test on you, but you're going to get the same result." The second result came back the same. The test proved that Charmayne was surely pregnant.

"How many months am I?" Charmayne asked the nurse.

"You're four months pregnant," the nurse told Charmayne. Charmayne's eyes opened as big as a camel's eyes. "How can that be when I've been having my period every month?" Charmayne inquired.

"You can still get pregnant and have your period," the nurse explained.

"That doesn't make sense," Charmayne said. Charmayne could not believe what she was hearing. Every month she got a period. "This some bull shit," Charmayne murmured.

"I know you can't believe what you're hearing, but you are pregnant," the nurse said to Charmayne. Charmayne looked at the nurse with anger in her eyes not wanting to say anything inappropriate to her.

Charmayne just smiled. But she didn't know how she was going to tell her mom that she was pregnant.

Charmayne noticed her mom sitting on the porch watching her sister ride her bicycle. Charmayne plopped herself on the chair next to her mom. Not sure of what to say, she blurted out, "You're going to be a grandmother."

"I already knew it," her mom said. "I was just waiting on you to tell me."

Charmayne looked at her mom with a strange look on her face.

How did my mom knew I was pregnant?

Charmayne asked herself. I hope the nurse didn't call her. My mom caught me off guard of what she had said to me.

"How many months are you?" Her mom asked.

"The nurse told me I was four months pregnant."

"How did you know I was pregnant?" Charmayne asked.

"A mom knows when something is wrong with her children. I've been watching you lately around the house. You've been eating a lot of junk food. You can't stand the smell of certain food I cook. I guess I'll have two grandbabies running around here," Charmayne's mom sighed.

"What do you mean by that?" Charmayne asked her mom.

"Hope is pregnant too," Charmayne's mom replied. I couldn't believe Hope was pregnant too.

Charmayne decided to call Gram and let him know that she was pregnant. To Charmayne's surprise, Gram was happier than she was. Gram was ready to be a father.

"I'm on my way to your house to get you," Gram said to Charmayne. Charmayne didn't know what to think.

Why would Gram want me to go with him to tell his friends and family that I'm pregnant?

Charmayne was dressed when Gram came to picked her up. Gram wanted to everybody to know that he has a baby on the way and that he was a man.

Meanwhile Charmayne was always told. "Just because you have a girl pregnant does not mean you're a man. You become a man when you take on your responsibility."

Chapter 34

Missing In Action

On this particular day, Charmayne had a doctor's appointment at ten-fifteen a.m. Charmayne reminded Gram over and over the night before about her appointment. Gram promised Charmayne that he would take her to her doctor's appointment. Charmayne made sure to be ready by eight twenty-five a.m. She gathered all her paper work the nurse had given her to fill out the day before. She made sure everything was signed, dated, and completed. She showered, got dressed, ate breakfast, and did her little sister's hair while waiting on him.

Charmayne tried calling him, but he didn't answer. Time was approaching fast. She was determine to be on time for my doctor's appointment. Good thing she asked her mom to take her to the clinic just in case he couldn't. It's good to have another plan on hand, because you never know what might happen. She tried calling him again, but got no answer. By this time, you can imagine what she was thinking and what he was probably doing. Unfortunately, he was nowhere to be found. Instead of having her mom taking her to the clinic. She caught the city bus. she told her mother, "If he comes here, let him know I'm at the doctor's office." Charmayne was so mad at him she could've wrung his neck right off. It wasn't like he didn't know she had a doctor's appointment. She had to take a specific test the doctor had ordered for her to take. They considered her as being high risk. They didn't the baby in danger. There were certain things she was restricted to do and certain foods she couldn't eat or drink. They had to monitor her and the baby twice a week.

After walking out the doctor's office, she thought he would be in the lobby waiting for her. By the minute she was growing impatient with him.

I have had enough of his bullshit. I can't be in a relationship with someone who don't want to be in a relationship with me. I know when I do see him, he is going to give me some lame ass excuse that he has to do this for his mom or sister. All he do is tell lies after lies. I don't want to raise my child without his or her father. I always said, "If I have a child I'm going to make sure my kids have the same father." I want us to be a family not a broken home. I don't know where he was or what he was doing, but I'm not going to worry about that. I have a child to raise. I wasn't about to let him or anybody else stress me out. It's not good for me or the baby.

When Charmayne got off the bus, guess who was sitting in her driveway?

He might as well take his ass home or go wherever he just came from. I wasn't up to hearing one of his old tired out lies or one of his lame dumb ass excuses. Nothing he could say or do would make me feel any different with the way I'm feeling about him at this moment.

He was sitting on the porch talking to her mom and playing catch with her sister. When Charmayne walked up, he started smiling like everything was good. She threw him the dirtiest look she could give a stranger on the street. Her mom asked, "How come you didn't call me to come pick you up?"

"I thought he was coming up there to get me since he knew I had a doctor's appointment," She responded. "I don't mind riding the bus. It's not that bad."

"I do apologize for not calling you," Gram said. "My mom's car broke down. I had to pick her up."

"Well, if you two don't mind, I'm going in the house to rest my tired feet. She went in the house and closed the door behind her."

Charmayne didn't look back to see if anybody had said something to her or who was coming in behind her.

"What's wrong with you?" Asked Charmayne's mom.

"I'm just tired and my feet hurt."

"Charmayne he wants to talk to you for a minute. You need to go outside and listen to what he has to say."

Charmayne opened the door and sat on the chair next to him.

"Baby, can I talk to you for a minute please?" Gram asked.

"Okay, what is it that you want to talk about? Since we've been in a relationship, all you've been doing is telling me lies after lies and getting caught up in your own mess. I refuse to be in a relationship with somebody who doesn't want to be in a relationship with me. The best thing you can do for me is to leave me alone and go be with whoever you want to be with. No matter what you decide, the baby is going to be taken care of. I don't want you to think just because I'm pregnant you have to stay with me," Charmayne snapped.

"I'm not cheating on you," he said. "I wish you'd stop saying that. Yes, I cheated on you once and I regret it from the bottom of my heart. I hate what I did to you," he said. "I regret every moment of it.

"Well, you should regret what you've done to me," Charmayne said. "You've taken me through a lot of your mess and I am not going to deal with the drama anymore. I'm a big girl. I can take care of myself and my baby. I think you need to go, before I say some things that will hurt your feelings. I'm not trying to make you out to be the bad person, but I need time to think."

Good thing my sister was bouncing her ball on the side walk. I didn't want her to hear me fussing at him. She stopped kicking for a minute and looked at the both of us. I thought she had heard me fussing at him. I don't know if she heard us, but I'm praying she didn't.

Charmayne called out to her sister "Come on, so we can go in the house."

"I'll call you when I feel a little better," Charmayne said to Gram. "Right now I'm going in the house to rest my aching body."

"Don't tell me you're going to call and then you don't," he said.

"Every time I tried calling you, you don't answer any of my calls. Let's see how you feel if I don't call you."

He glared at her and left without saying a word. She was glad he did.

When they walked in the house, Charmayne's mom asked what her problem was.

"Mom, I don't have a problem. He knew I had a doctor's appointment and he never answered any of my phone calls. I kept calling and calling him. Not one time did he pick up the phone to let me know his mom's car broke down," I said. "I don't know what it is, but something is not right. He's up to his old tricks. I just don't have time for all the lies and cheating."

"Well, I think you owe him an apology," her mom said. "You don't know for sure if his mom's car broke down. Don't never think a person is doing wrong unless you can prove it," she said. "He's a good guy and whatever you need he makes sure you have it."

If only my mom knew exactly what was going on between us. I wanted to tell her, but I didn't want her to dislike him for something he did to me. I use to hear people say, "What goes around, comes around." Whatever he's doing out there with whomever would come to the light. If he thinks he's going to have unprotected sex with me, then he needs to rethink again. I'm not going to put my baby or myself at risk. If he wants to catch a disease, then he can catch all the diseases he want. I'm in love with myself. I'm not going to let him or his carelessness bring me down. I have a baby to think about. Sitting here thinking about what he's doing and who he's doing it with is a waste of my time.

Chapter 35

I Still Love Him

During the rest of her pregnancy, things between them worsened. Charmayne was fed up with his lies and cheating. She knew she loved him deeply, but this circumstance was calling for her to learn to love herself more.

"I know you're out there cheating on me. Nothing you say will convince me otherwise. I'm so tired of putting up with your bull shit. The best thing for you is leave me and this baby alone. All you have to do is be honest with me and let me make that decision if I want to be with you or not. Don't make that decision for me. Do you remember telling me how much you love and care for me?" She asked him. "You said you would never cheat on me and that you'd be here for me no matter what? All of that was a lie. I don't trust anything you say. I don't know when you're telling me the truth or when you're lying. You've lied so much to the point I believe NOTHING from you!" Charmayne was furious.

"I love you and you're not leaving me," he said.

"Boy, you can't make me be in a relationship with you when you don't want to be with me.

"I want to spend the rest of my life with you," he said.

She replied, "Boy, you need to stop playing with yourself."

"I don't want to be with no other woman but you," he stated.

"Well, you have a funny way of showing me how much you love and care about me," I said. I don't want to be in a relationship with a person I can't trust. You knew I had a doctor's appointment. Not one time did you pick up the phone and call me to let me know what was going on. I know you saw me calling you. I guess you were tied up with the other female making sure you satisfied her needs. The best thing you can do for me is to tell me the truth about what is going on. You should let me make the decision if I want to be with you or not. I don't need you to make that decision for me. People have been telling me about you messing around with other females and they caught you kissing this girl."

"Who in the hell told you?" He asked me.

"I don't care who you mess with," I said. "You're not going to keep running back in forth in my life or my son's life. I'm not trying to catch any diseases. You can leave those diseases somewhere else. I'm done talking to you and being with you. I have dreams to accomplish and a baby I have to raise and take care of. You think you can keep running back in my life when it's convenient for you. *"News Flash"* I'm not the other woman. I'm your baby's mother who supposed to be your only girlfriend. I don't need you for anything and I damn sure don't need you for this baby. I love you with everything I have. You treat me like you don't care anything about me or my feelings. I can't believe I wasted all my time with a loser like you. You deserve a gold medal for being a liar and a cheater. Thanks for boosting my head up thinking we were going to be together forever and that we were going to get married. Boy... I really deserved that."

He tried to walk closer to her. She put her hands up to block his move.

"Baby, I hate what I did to you," he said. It hurts me to see you hurting. I know what I've done was wrong. I keep beating up myself for putting you through this.

Charmayne replied, "Maybe you need to keep beating up on yourself."

"Baby, I love you unconditionally and nothing will ever take that away," he pleaded.

"What we had has gone down the drain when you started cheating on me. What we have is a bunch of lies. What we have is no longer us anymore. What we have you can kiss goodbye. Now, that's what we have."

The relationship "I thought" we had was weighing me down. I can't stand looking at him or hearing his voice. I wasn't mad at what he did to me. I'm mad that he took my love for granted and lied to me after all these years. I could've been dating someone else who really wanted to spend some time with me. I've turned down a lot of good guys I knew was loyal and true. One thing I can say is I graduated from high school, college, and had two jobs. I wasn't that type of person who lay up with this guy and that guy. I only had one boyfriend and that was him. I don't believe in going out of my relationship and cheating with someone else. I was better than that.

"In my heart I know you love me, but how can I ever forget what you did to me?"

"Baby, can you just hear me out?" He asked.

"I still love you," Charmayne said. "I wish this could work between us, but it's too late for us. I tried to please you in every way, but somewhere down the line I wasn't enough."

"Baby, I promise you. I'm not messing around with anybody else," he said. "I know it's hard for you to believe what I'm saying, but please don't give up on us. I don't want no body but you."

"You don't want me," she said. "You're the one who's cheating with God knows who."

"Baby, please listen to what I'm saying," he beckoned.

"See, that's the problem, You want me to believe every word you say. Do you honestly think I can believe anything that comes out of that-mouth?" Charmayne snapped.

"Baby, just give me a chance to prove my love to you," he said.

"Let's be honest here. Let me ask you something. What went wrong between us? What have I done to be treated like this?" she asked.

"Baby, you're a good person and nothing went wrong between us,"

"Something went wrong between us. So, don't tell me nothing went wrong."

"I love you with every air in my body."

"Well, I think you need to save every hole in your body to keep that air for yourself."

"What do you mean by that?"

"Don't stop breathing on the account of me."

I love him with everything I have. I wanted my son to be a part of his dad's life, but not like this.

She placed her hands on the side of his face.

"If I hear or see you cheating on me again, I promise you it won't be good. I want you to hear me clearly, If you get caught cheating, you will never and I mean never see your son again.

"Why would you keep my son from me?"

"So, I guess you're admitting to cheating on me?"

"No, I'm not cheating on you. I'm just letting you know that you need to believe and trust me."

"Do you actually think you're going to see your son while you're cheating on his mother? Let's be real. Well, I'm tired. I'm going to go lie down."

Before she went in the house, he reached in his pocket and gave her some money as if that was going to do the trick. She took the money told him she'd call him later, went in the house, and shut the door.

Chapter 36

Giving Birth to Your Son, Where Are You?

After getting off from work, Charmayne decided to walk to one of her friend's house down the street from her house. As she was walking, she started feeling pressure and pain between her legs. The cramps were not that bad, but painful. Soon as shestarted walking again, another pain hit. This time much worse than the first. She noticed a car stopped in the middle of the road.

"Excuse me young lady, are you okay?" A voice from the car asked.

Charmayne was bent over and could hardly say a word. "I'm just having contractions. I'm going right here to my friend's house. I pointed to my friend's house."

"Okay, I'll drive slowly to make sure you get there safe," she said to me.

Charmayne didn't know who the lady was, but she thanked her for helping out. When Charmayne arrived at her friend's house she knocked on the door. Her mom answered the door and let her in. Charmayne waved her hand at the kind lady.

"Mary, she just left to go to the store for me," her mom said.

Charmayne was in so much pain she could hardly walk. She asked her friend's mom if she could call her mom to let her know she's on her way home.

I was in a lot of pain. I didn't wait for my friend's mom to respond. I started walking fast toward my house. I knew I had to get home fast. A lot of people who knew me were stopping their cars to make sure I was okay. They wanted to make sure I got home safe. Some had me laughing to the point where I forgot I was in pain. One of my neighbors stopped the cars from passing as I crossed the street.

Her mom, sister, and auntie ran out the house looking for her. Her sister made sure to come and see about her. The pain was non-stop. Her mom ran in the house to call the paramedics. Charmayne walked in the house and headed straight to the bathroom. When the paramedics arrived, she was still on the toilet.

It felt like my bowels wouldn't stop.

"What are you doing in the bathroom?" her mom asked.

"I'm having a bowel movement," Charmayne replied.

"If you can help it, try not to push," a males voice urged.

"I'll try not to," she said.

I was glad it was over. It felt like everything I ate that morning was running through me. I wiped off real good, washed my face and made sure to sanitize my hands. I pulled up my clothes, took a deep breathe and headed into the unknown. When I opened the bathroom door they had a stretcher for me to lie on. The paramedics took my blood pressure, checked my vital signs, and monitored my contractions. Just as they were about to wheel me out the door, I had to go to the bathroom again. They would not let me get off the stretcher to go use the bathroom. They told me it was just the baby pressing down on my uterus causing me to go to the bathroom. "We need you to try not push, but to breathe slowly," one of the males said to me.

Charmayne gave her mom her boyfriend's number.

"I'll call him to let him know you had to be rushed to the hospital," her mom assured her. Her mom started dialed his number, but he didn't answer.

"You can go ahead and take her to the hospital," her mom said. "We'll meet you there." Charmayne overheard her mom tell her Auntie she was going to go by his house to let him know they had to rush her to the hospital. As they were wheeling Charmayne out the door, the phone started ringing.

"Hello," her mom answered. "The paramedics are taking her to the hospital because she's in labor."

It was Gram. They talked for a while and hung the phone up.

The ride was a bumpy one, it felt like they hit every bump in the road. The more bumps they hit on the road, the more pain they were caused Charmayne.

They wasn't making it easy for me I can tell you that. As bad as I was in pain, I couldn't even cursed them out. The pain was coming faster and harder. I felt a splash between my legs. I didn't know what it was. The lady looked at me and said, your water bag just broke.

She tapped on the driver's shoulder. "Her water bag broke," she told the driver. She radioed the hospital to let them know her vital signs had changed. The person on the other end told them to prop Charmayne's legs up. "Do you see the baby's head?" She asked them. They checked for the baby's head. Thank God the baby's head wasn't out. Charmayne let out another loud scream as the contractions intensified.

It's a good thing we were at the hospital, because I was ready to push.

When they pulled up it looked like every nurse and doctor on duty were waiting for her. When they wheeled her in to a room, she noticed about two more nurses in the room. They hooked her up to different type of machines. They explained what they were doing.

"We need to monitor you and the baby's heartbeat," one of the nurses said.

They moved her from the stretcher to a bed. They put several IV"S in her left arm. They checked her vital signs and monitored her and the baby's heartbeat. They stopped the contractions from coming fast. I knew something was wrong when they all huddled in a circle around the monitor.

"Excuse me," Charmayne kept saying to the doctors and nurses.

Finally, one of the nurses responded. "Is everything okay with you?" She asked me.

"No, I was wondering why all of you are standing over the monitoring talking and whispering."

"The doctors just want to make sure the baby's heartbeat is okay," she said. "They need you to breathe a little slower and not push when you feel a contraction."

"Is something wrong with my baby?" she asked the nurse. The doctor walked over. Just as he was about to check her private area, her family walked in. The doctor asked them if they could wait outside for a few minutes. The doctor started checking and pressing down on her stomach.

"Do you feel like walking?" The doctor asked.

"Is there a reason I need to walk?"

"You only dilated four centimeter," he said.

"Four centimeters, that's all?"

"I need you to a walk a little for me," the doctor said. "I'll check you when you come back to the room."

"How far would you like for me to walk?" she asked the doctor.

"You can walk around the nurse's station at least ten times," he said.

I had my sister and cousin to walk with me just in case something happens. I was doing okay until I had to go to the bathroom. I told my sister and cousin to wait for me by the door and not to let anyone in. "We're not going to let anyone in," they said to me. I can hear my cousin asking my sister, "Why is she always going to the bathroom?"

"I guess it's time for the baby to come out," my sister said to my cousin. I started laughing at them. I couldn't believe the words that were coming out of their mouths. I was able to wipe myself off without any help.

They resumed walking and this time something didn't feel right.

"I think we need to go back to the room." Charmayne said.

"Why do we need to go back to the room?" her sister asked.

"I'm not feeling well."

I tried to avoid the questions they were asking me. As we were walking, I felt a sharp pain below my stomach. My sister ran in the room to tell my mom. The nurse came out and helped me in the bed. The pain was coming non stop. It felt like a head was coming out. The nurse looked at the monitor. She hurried out the room to go get the doctor. There were still two other nurses in the room with me. I said to my mom, "Can you just tell them to take the baby? I'm in so much pain."

Her mom said, "That's what happens when you have unprotected sex. I'm not telling the doctors anything. You say you're a woman so take these pains."

"Momma, this is not the time to see if I'm a woman or not."

"I went through the same thing four times with you, your sisters, and brother. Back then, we didn't get shots. You had to take those pain. I have faith in you," her mom said.

"Momma, I can't take these pains."

Her aunt felt bad for her. She told her mom not to treat her like that.

"We don't know what type of pain she's in," her aunt said. "Maybe something is wrong with the baby. We don't know why she's in a lot of pain."

"Something might be wrong," my aunt continued.

Two doctors, two midwives, and one more nurse walked in the room. The midwives walked over to her. They were making sure she was breathing slowly. They showed her a breathing technique to help her with the contractions. The doctor was watching the baby monitor as he was walked towards her. He asked her to bend my legs up. When she did, he noticed she was having a contraction.

"Do not push," he told her.

The doctor begin to examine her. By the look on his face, it did not look good.

"We don't have time to shave her. We have to do an emergency surgery on her right away."

Her mom asked the doctor, "What seems to be the problem?"

"The baby swallowed some of her bowels and we need to get her to surgery right away," he said.

I started crying. My mom and aunt started praying for me. I can hear my sister telling me to be strong. They hurried up and rushed me down the hall and through some double doors. I noticed other patients in wheelchair, stretcher or just sitting in chairs waiting to be seen by a doctor.

"Clear the hallway please," one of the doctors said.

"Excuse me, we have an emergency here," one of the other nurses said. "Please move out the way."

I can hear one of the midwives telling me to hold on and that everything is going to be okay. I was not trying to hear what she or anybody else was saying to me. All I was trying to do is find out if my baby was okay.

"I'm going to place several IV's in both of your arms. I need you to try and be still. I need to make sure I don't stick you in the wrong place," When I put medicine in your IV, I need you to count backward starting at ten."

I started at ten and ended at eight. When I woke up, I didn't know where I was. I remember feeling a sharp pain in my stomach.

"Ouch," Charmayne said.

"Are you okay?" One of the nurses asked.

"Yes, I just felt a sharp pain in my stomach. I put my hand on my stomach to make sure my baby was still there. **"Lord, please let my baby be okay and in good health."** She looked up and begin praising God for bringing me out of a major surgery.

When the other nurse walked in, she walked over to her. "I'm so glad you're awake," she said. "I thought I had to give you something to wake you up."

"Excuse me, how is my baby doing?" Charmayne asked her.

"Congratulations are in order, you have a seven-pound and one ounce baby boy." she said.

Charmayne started crying. "Thank you Jesus for blessing me with a healthy baby boy."

"You have a handsome young man who is ready to meet his mom," the nurse said.

"I'm ready to meet my son as well," she said to the nurse.

"Your son is my special baby," she said.

"I don't want nobody fighting over my baby," Charmayne said to her. They both started laughing.

"I'm so happy for you," one of the other nurses said. "If you don't mind, I would like to buy him something before you two are discharged," she said.

"Thank you," Charmayne said to her.

"I hope you don't spoil him while he's in the ward."

"The other nurses are in love with him. They all took turns enjoying your bundle of joy. You have a handsome son. He has a head full of curly hair."

As, the nurse was wheeling me to my room, I noticed my mom, aunt, sister, cousin, my son's father and his family standing in my room. I looked at him with anger in my eyes. I just gave birth to my son, my mind wasn't on him. I had to think about my son and my son only. He grabbed my hand.

"I'll be in your room when they get you settled in," he said. "I'm going to go visit my son."

Charmayne was in a lot of pain. The nurse gave her some pain medicine.

"You gave us a little scare," she said. "Thank God he brought you both out of it. I'll be back to check on you later.

"Someone will be bringing the baby in so you can see him."

"Thanks for all your help," Charmayne replied. She indeed was grateful for God's hand in the midst.

"You're welcome," she replied. "That's what I'm here for. You all have a blessed day."

Chapter 37

Another of His Lies

Everybody had gone down stairs to see the baby. When her son's father walked in, it was just her and him. Charmayne wanted to curse him out, but she was in a lot of pain.

He pushed the nurse station button for me and asked the nurse if they can bring me some pain medicine. We talked for a few minutes before the nurse walked in. He was glad when she walked out. He begin telling me how sorry he was for putting me through all his mess and not being there when I needed him the most.

"No you were where you wanted to be, I'm beyond tired of your lies and cheating.

"Baby, what are you talking about?" He asked.

"You don't care about me or our relationship."

"Don't say that. I care about you, my son, and our relationship."

"I still love and care about you, but I have a son I have to take care of. Your name is nowhere on my list of responsibilities. I've tried on several occasions to make you happy and for you to love me, but something just won't let you love me back. I'd rather be happy, lonely, and sad than being with a person who don't feel the same way about me. All I asked from you was to be here when I give birth to your son."

"Baby I know," he said. "I was trying to make it here in time to see my son being born."

"My mom has been there for me when you were supposed to be there. My mom made sure I had this and that, 'But where were you?' My mom bought food, diaper, clothes, formulas and whatever else the baby or I needed. I owe you NOTHING not even my heart. All the lies you've been telling me and the things you've been doing to me are hurtful. I'm done. I can't go through this again with you. All I ask is that you be here for your son. I'm going to be okay and that you can believe. I don't want you for anything and neither will this baby. If I don't have it, I'll make sure he have it I'll go lacking before I let my son go lacking."

"Baby, if you just listen to me and stop jumping to conclusions about me cheating on you with all these different females."

"I really don't care who you're cheating with. It doesn't matter to me anymore. I'm not stupid. Do I have *Stupid Ass* written on my face?"

Before she could read him again, both of their families walked in. They put on a happy face so noone detected something was going on between us. They all started hugging and kissing.

"Did you pick a name for him yet?" One of his sister asked.

"He's going to be named after his father, the third. I'm so proud of the both of you," Charmayne's mom said.

"He sure has some big feet and lips. I can't wait to babysit him along with my other nephew," her little sister chimed in.

I was glad when the nurse brought the baby in. I made sure to sanitize my hands real good cleaning between fingers. She picked him up and placed him in my arms. I started kissing him. I was checking him to make sure he had all ten toes, fingers, eyes, ears, nose, mouth, tongue, and every other part on his body.

"Thank you Jesus," Charmayne sighed.

They were right. My baby did have big lips and feet. I know I don't have big lips and I definitely don't have a big feet. He had every features of his dad and his side of the family in him.

Everybody wanted to hold him, but I made sure they washed their hands thoroughly. I wanted me and my baby to be germs free. He's too young to get sick. I definitely didn't want the other babies in the nursery to get sick. I got a chance to see what it was like to raise a baby. My older sister had her son two weeks before I did. I enjoyed helping her raising my nephew. I kept my nephew while my mom either went to work or to the store.

"Well, I'll see you tomorrow," her mom said. "I need to get home and check on your nephew. You know how his momma is."

"I'll call you when I get home," her sister said. Her boyfriend's family left as well. He stayed and talked with her for a while before he left. The nurse came in and took the baby back to the nursery. Charmayne was feeling sleepy from the medication.

It was around eight a.m. when the nurse came in.

"Good morning," she said.

"Good morning," Charmayne replied. She tried to sit up, but the pain was unbearable.

"Be careful. You just had a major surgery," she said.

"Could you explain that to me?" Charmayne requested.

"The doctor had to cut you in order to get the baby out," she said. "You were having difficulty giving birth." The nurse walked over and pulled up her gown to show her the cut the doctor performed. It was long and felt weird. It was also painful.

"How are you feeling this morning?" She asked.

"It hurts when I try to cough," Charmaune explained to her.

"When you get ready to cough, the secret is you must hold the pillow close and tight to your cut and then cough. Try not to let it sneak up on you," she advised.

"If that happens, what do I need to do?" Charmayne asked her.

"When it does happen, it will feel like your stitches had been cut open again," she said "This is something you need to try avoid," she said.

"Well, well, well, look who's up lying in a hospital bed and making a fuss already. Girl, hush all that fussing. You just had a baby." Charmayne looked up and it was one of her friends from school.

"Well, you know I wouldn't be here if this baby wasn't trying to see what he was missing." They both smiled. She walked over and gave Charmayne a hug and a kiss on the forehead.

"So, how does it feel to be a mother?" She asked.

"I've only had a day to feel like a mothe and Ialready know I'm going to enjoy every moment with him."

"Even though, I don't like hospitals I had to come see you and my nephew," she said.

"I can't wait to get released from this hospital, go home and sleep in my own bed. I hate the way it smells in here and girl the food… The food tastes horrible."

"Girl, I know how you feel, when I had my son, I told his dad to bring me something from home or from McDonald's. I refused to eat what they had brought me to eat on my tray," she said.

"Girl, that's what I'm going to have to do. The eggs be looking old, hard and green. The grits looks stiffs and the toast be burnt. I send it all back to them when they come and pick up my tray. All I order now are fruits, cereal, and crackers," Charmayne humorously complained.

The phone rang.

"Hello," Charmayne aswered.

It was my son's father on the other end. We talked for a while. I asked him to bring me something to eat from McDonald's.

"Yes, just call me and let me know what you want to eat," he said.

"I'm glad you came by to see me and the baby. I know you're going to be the perfect auntie to your nephew.

"Thanks again for coming to see us," I said. I enjoyed your company.

"I'll call you when I get home," she said.

Chapter 38

Ready to Go Home

A week passed. The baby and Charmayne were still in the hospital waiting to be released. Charmayne was getting angrier and angrier by the day trying to figure out what was going on. When the nurse walked in, Charmayne noticed she had a tray in her hand. She had a couple of tube to draw blood with, a needle and bandages.

"How are you feeling this morning," She asked.

"I'm doing fine, just waiting to go home," Charmayne said to her.

"It looks like your doctor ordered some blood work."

"Why is that?" Charmayne asked.

"He's trying to see why your blood pressure keeps going up and down," she explained.

"They gave me some medicine to keep it from going up," Charmayne informed her.

"If you can keep the medicine down, you'll be able to go home in the next four days. "

Charmayne was glad when the nurse left out the room. She wasn't in the mood to talk or listen. She started feeling sick to her stomach.

I didn't know if it was the medicine they gave me to take by mouth or the medicine they put in my IV. I guess it was time for me to feed the baby when the nurse brought him in, but she noticed me vomiting on the floor. She hurried and pushed the baby away from me. She asked if I was okay. I couldn't reply. I was just that sick. The nurse pushed the button to the nurse station and asked a nurse to come to my room. Two nurses rushed to my bed side and begin checking my vital signs.

"What did you eat," One of the nurses asked?"

"Nothing," I said. "The doctor prescribed some medicine to control my blood pressure and that was it."

"Do you know what kind of medicine they gave you?" She asked me.

"The only thing I know the nurse gave me two pills to take by mouth and the other medicine she put in my IV," Charmayne said.

The other nurse said," Let me take a look at your chart and see what the doctor prescribed for you to take." In the meantime, one of the nurse took the baby back to the nursery. Charmayne was glad she did. Trying to feed her baby would not be the best option. Charmayne really didn't want to put him at risk.

If he becomes sick that meant he would have to stay in the hospital until he gets better. When I leave the hospital, my baby will be leaving along with me. I refuse to leave my baby in the hospital while I'm at home feeling comfortable. There's no way I was going to do that. If my son has to stay in the hospital, then I'll be staying as well.

As they were cleaning the vomit up off the floor, her mom walked in.

"What's going on in here?" She asked.

"I started vomiting when they brought the baby in to be fed."

"What did you eat?" She asked.

"Well, I haven't eating anything. The doctor prescribed medicines for me to take by mouth and through my IV. The nurse said she's trying to get in contact with the doctor."

"Please make sure the doctor comes in to see her," her mom said to the nurse. He ordered too much medications for her to take. "

"By the nurse not paying attention to her chart, she just went by what the doctor had prescribed for her," the nurse said.

"You have to make sure the patient is not allergic to the medications being prescribed for them."

"Yes ma'am," the nurse said.

"You are absolutely right about that," the nurse said. Some medications are too strong for certain people. I'm trying to get in contact with him as we speak. When I get in contact with him, I'll make sure to have him get in contact with the both of you," the nurse assured them.

I don't know who was more upset, my mom or me. My mom said everything I wanted to say to the nurse. I forgot I was sharing a room with another person. I did not want her to see me or my mom act up like this.

The phone rang.

"Hello," Charmayne's mom said.

"Hold on for a minute," she said. Her mom handed her the phone. It was my Gram.

"Hello," Charmayne said.

"Hey, I was calling to see how you and the baby were doing."

"Well, I got sick and they took the baby back to the nursery."

"When I get off, I'm going to bring you something to eat from McDonald's," he said. He asked if her mom and sister were also there.

"Yes, they're here with me," she said. They spoke a few more minutes and said their goodbyes.

Charmayne hung the phone up and started talking to her mom and sister. Charmayne was saying to her sister "even though I had a baby, I'm not going to stop spending time with you. We're still going to do what we've been doing." Her sister and she are very close.

The love my sister and I have is unbreakable. Some people have other siblings and they don't spend any time with them. I love spending time with my little sister. We have a special bond that nobody can separate. My sister looks up to me. I'm going to try my best to protect her and be there for her whenever she needs me.

It was seven p.m. when Gram came by to see her and the baby. Her mom knew she was mad.

Now, he knows visiting hours are over at eight p.m. Now he wants to show up" I know it doesn't take that long to take a shower and put on clothes. Knowing him, he probably was tricking with one of his tricks. He knew I was mad at him. He came in the room with gift bags in his hands. Little did he know, just because you brought gift bags doesn't mean you're off the hook. I didn't say anything to him. I respect my mom, sister, and roommate. If my mom, sister, or the other roommate wasn't in the room with me, I would have cursed him out and told him to go back to where he just came from. He walked in with food from McDonald's. He brought a Happy Meal for my sister, a Big Mac Meal for me, and a Fish Sandwich Meal for my mom. My sister loves to play with her toy before she eats her food. I paged the nurse station to see if they could bring the baby in.

The doctor walked. He picked up my chart and started looking over it. He walked over to where I was seated and began explaining about the medications.

"I do want to apologize for the mistake that happened to you today," he said.

"The nurse gave you too much medications. She was supposed to give you the medicine by mouth only. I do apologize for that. We value our patients. We want to ensure the patients are being taking care of while staying here, at the hospital. I do want you to know, I had to write her up on this incident. She will be suspended until further notice," he informed them.

"She needs to be suspended," her mom said. "This could've been something serious with my daughter. There's no telling what that would have done to her."

"You are absolutely right about that," the doctor said.

"Suppose I was breastfeeding my baby and he got sick from the medication she gave me. Nobody can tell me nothing when it comes to my son. There's no telling what I would have done to her. The medicine she gave me could have damaged my son's brain, lungs, heart and anything else in his body. What do you think I would've done to you, the nurse, and this hospital?" Charmayne asked him.

He acknowledged her and said, "I understand exactly what you're saying and where you're coming from. I would have done the same thing if this happened to me or my wife. I can assure you, she will be suspended until further notice. I'll make sure you have everything you need before you leave here in writing."

The nurse brought the baby in as the doctor was walking out. Her mom and sister left after they played with the baby for a while. Charmayne couldn't wait for her mom and sister to leave.

I started cursing my son's father out. I didn't care who heard what I was saying to him, not even my roommate. He swore me up and down that he's not cheating on me.

"I don't love anybody else but you," he said to her.

"Boy please, all your lies are going to catch up with you one day. I'm not pregnant anymore."

The baby started crying and he rushed over to pick the baby up. He begin rocking the baby back and forth talking to him.

Soon as he started talking to him, he stopped crying. I was like, what the hell? My mom and sister walked back in the room. I thought they left.

"I talked to the doctor to see when you and the baby will be released," she said.

"What did he say?" Charmayne asked her mom.

"He has to see what your tests look like when they come back tomorrow," her mom explained. "He' going to call me personally to let me know about your tests. I guess he's kind of shook up about what happened to you earlier today. He said he's going to have the nurse come and draw some blood from you. He needs to make sure the blood is normal." It was about nine p.m. when my mom and sister left. I told them to call me when they get home and to kiss my nephew for me.

"I can't wait for you and my nephew to come home," her sister said. "I can't wait to play with him." Before she left, she made sure to kiss Charmayne and her nephew goodnight.

Charmayne paged the nurse to come and take the baby back to the nursery so she could get some rest. A nurse walked in and introduced herself.

"I'm here to draw some blood and check your vital signs," she informed. Charmayne showed her the best arm to take the blood from and which vein was perfect to use. By now, she was not a newbie at this.

"What are you going to do when you and the baby get released from the hospital?" He asked.

"My baby and I are going home and we're not coming out until I'm able and ready to go visit people."

"I was thinking maybe you and the baby would like to go over to my grandmother's house so she can see her great grandson."

"Boy stop playing with yourself. As I said before, we are going home and we're not coming out. Do you actually think I want to be sitting at your family house with your son?" she asked him. "We both just got out of the hospital. You sound dumb right about now. When he gets his first six week checkup, than we'll see. Until then, we're not going anywhere. It's too early for him to come out."

He kissed her goodnight on the forehead. "I'll call you when I get home," he said.

Charmayne and her roommate sparked up a conversation and talked about how stupid men think women are when it comes to *our* babies. Her roommate shared how her baby's daddy got caught having sex with her best friend in her bed where they stay at.

"What did you do?" Charmayne asked her.

"Girl, I kicked her ass until she passed out."

Charmayne started laughing at her. "Girl, you a bad chick! Does your daughter belong to him?" She inquired.

"Yes, and so does my best friend's baby."

"What you mean your best friend's baby?" She asked her.

"Yes, my best friend's baby is due next month," she said.

"Baby, I feel so sorry for you. I can't imagine what you're going through." She started crying. Charmayne got out of her bed to walk over to console her. She didn't know what to say to her.

"What happened?" She asked her.

She started explaining how she trusted her relationship with her best friend. "I use to tell her about the problems we were having and the things he used to do to me," she said. "We all used to hang out together, go to clubs, out to dinner, play cards, or just hang out at my house."

Charmayne advised her, "One mistake you made was when you invited your best friend in your relationship. You don't never let your best friend hang out with you when you and your man."

"I've learned my lesson about having a friend over with me and my man. My friend did me the same way. I don't hang out with anybody, but myself. I don't need no so-called friends to be laughing in my face and stabbing me in my back at the same time."

She responded by saying "Since that happened she wants us to be friends again for the sake of their kids."

"Don't worry about that anymore," Charmayne said to her. "You have to stay focused on your daughter now."

"Yes. I know," she agreed.

"It's going to be hard for me to trust any female around my boyfriend," she shared

They talked until they felled asleep.

Chapter 39

When Enough Is Finally Enough

Thursday morning around eight thirty-nine a.m. Charmayne noticed her roommate wasn't in her bed. Just as Charmayne was getting out of bed to go to the bathroom, her doctor walked in.

"Good morning, Ms. Charmayne," he said.

"Good morning," she replied.

"I have some good news for you this morning. Your blood work all came back good and your blood pressure is normal. It looks like you and the baby will be discharged today. I know you were worrying about when you and the baby were going to be released from the hospital."

"I'm glad you know that," she said to her doctor. "You must have known I was getting tired laying up in this bed. I want to be sleeping in my own bed." They both started laughing.

"I also have some paper work for you to look over and take home with you," he said.

"What about the other paper work you said you were going to give me?" she asked. "You told me and my mom that you would give us some paper work regarding the nurse who over medicated me."

"I have them right here in my hands as well," he said. "I also need to go over them with you and your mom. The hospital has a special policy when it comes to the patients. We don't want to take any more chances of this ever happening to any of our patients. We value our patient needs. We want them to feel at ease and comfortable while being a patient here. Our patients are our number one concern. The nurse was fired for misuse of medications. After you get discharged from the hospital I need you to take it easy. Make sure you follow all directions that I'm going to give you. You had major surgery and I need you to take it easy. I had to give you an emergency cesarean section."

"Why is that?" she asked the doctor.

"You dilated only four centimeters. You have a bikini cut just below your stomach. If you have any complications, pain, or bleeding, I need for you to come back to the emergency room as soon as possible," he patiently explained. The doctor then gave her a prescription to get filled and some medications to take home.

Charmayne called her boyfriend's phone to see if he would come and pick her and the baby up. His phone just rang and rang.

I knew I can't count on him for nothing. I don't know why keep letting this man put me through this mess. I know he's nothing but a liar. All the things he's done to me I still let him back in my life. When am I going to say enough is enough? I don't want to jump to conclusions, but I already knew what he was going to say to me when I confront him about where he was.

Charmayne called her mom to pick her and the baby up.

As always, my mom were right there to pick up the missing pieces. It's not her job to make sure I and the baby have this or that, it's his job. I'm not worried about anything. I made sure to save money for me and my baby. I don't want to have to depend on my mom to do extra for me or my baby. My mom has to take care of my sister and my nephew.

Charmayne began packing her and the baby clothes. She waited for the nurse to bring her son in to get him dressed. Just as she was finishing up the last bit of stuff she had, the nurse walked in with her son.

I was so glad to see him. I couldn't wait to hold him in my arms once again. I started singing his favorite lullaby song in his ear. He love when I sing to him. I put him on my shoulder and rock him in my arms. The nurse gave me the discharged papers for me and my son to be released from the hospital.

"You're all set," she said. "Just page the nurse's station when your mom arrives, so I can have a wheelchair ready for you."

"I surely will. Thanks for taking care of my bundle of joy."

"You know the other nurses are going to want to see him before he leaves us. She said, "I have to get my personal hug from him before they come in and get their hugs."

"He'll be glad to have his other women's around him." They both laughed.

"Thanks for taking care of my son while he was in the nursery," Charmayne said to her.

"No problem," she said. "I'm going to miss my handsome young man. He was the only baby in the nursery who don't cry when you feed or change his diaper. He sleeps through everything."

"I pray he sleeps like this when I take him home. If he thinks I'm going to hold him every time he cry, he better think twice. I refused to spoil him. If he's sick or something like that, then that's a different story. I'm not going to be walking around the house with him in my arms."

"You're right," she said. "If the baby is sleep then you need to be sleep right with him. You have to set a time for him to wake up and be fed. Don't wake him up because you want to hold him. That's how you're going to end up spoiling him. I don't blame you for not spoiling him."

Her mom and sister came to pick them up. She didn't have to page the nurse's station. They recognized her mom and sister when they passed by. The nurses on the floor gave Charmayne and her son a sweet farewell. They had lots of balloons, cards, and flowers. I'm going to miss the nurses on the floor and in the nursery, but not the nasty food. The ride home was quite relaxing for Charmayne. Her son slept all the way home.

"Did you talkto his father?" her mom asked.

"No, I tried calling him, but he never picked up," Charmayne said.

I was glad to be home. Now I can sleep in my own bed. I got the baby settled in and began putting away our belongings. This is going to be a long night for me. This would be the first time my son and I were sleeping in the same room. I really didn't know how well he sleeps at night or what time he wakes up.

Some of the church members called to check on her and the baby. A lot of them wanted to know if it was okay if they came over to see him.

"Well, we just got home," Charmayne said to her mom. "I'm not ready for anybody to come over as yet. We'll start taking visitors on Saturday evening around three p.m. and they can come by then."

My mom understood what I was saying and where I was coming from. I don't want anybody coming over to my mom's house with a cold. I just don't want to take that risk. It's my duty to protect my son from any harm and danger. I have to do what's best for me and my son. I guess I'm being over protective of him, but I had too when it came to my son.

Her mom allowed some of the church members to drop by to see the baby. When they arrived, the baby was still sleep. Charmayne didn't want to wake him up. They all got a chance to see her bundle of joy. They congratulted her on having a fine and handsome son. Everyone commented how much he looked like his dad. "He favors you just a little," one of the church member said. Charmayne was glad everybody was leaving. Motherhood was hard work and she wanted to get a little rest before he woke up.

I was able to take a nap for two hours. When I woke up, my son was asleep on my mom's bed. She had changed his diaper and fed him for me. "I know you were tired," she said. *I didn't want to wake you up.*

"He sleeps well," she said.

"Did his dad called?" Charmayne asked her mom.

"No, he didn't call," she said.

"Well, I'm not going to keep wasting my time calling him," Charmayne said. "He knows he has a newborn son to take care of. That's why I saved every penny I made to support the both of us. I don't depend on anybody to take care of us. If I need help I know you're going to be there for us," Charmayne said to her mom.

Her mom gave her a hug, because she knew Charmayne was mad at him for not being there for his son.

"You can't sit here and worry about what he's not doing for him," her mom said.

"You're absolutely right mom." Charmayne agreed.

"You be the mother you can be for your son," She said. "Your son needs you. He needs to know you're going to be okay." Charmayne tried to control her tears, but she couldn't. The words her mom said were all true. All she could do was process that painful truth; if she really wanted to heal from all the hurt and abuse.

"Yes, it hurts, but I'll get over it. I'm not going to pressure my son's father to be in his life. It's his choice if he wants to be there for him."

Chapter 40

Enjoying My Bundle of Joy

It was a nice and hot Saturday morning. The sun was shining bright. The bird were chirping their songs. The baby slept all through the night. I only had to change his diaper about three times. Each time I changed his diaper, he never woke up. I was able to clean up the room, play with my nephew, take a shower, and eat breakfast before he wakes up. It was around eight-fifteen a.m. when my boyfriend decided to call me. I guess he knew I was mad by the tone of my voice. Before he can say anything, I said to him. "Do not call this number anymore." I slammed the phone down. The phone rang again. I Hurried and picked it up on the second ring. I did not want the sound of the phone to wake up my son.

"Hello," I said.

"I was calling to see how my son was doing," he said.

"Boy, what do you want?" I asked him.

"Please don't hang up on me," he said.

"And why shouldn't I?" I asked him.

"Let me explain what happened and why I couldn't answer my phone," he said.

"Well, to be honest with you, I really don't care what happened, I said to him. If you really cared about your son, you would have been at the hospital to pick him up. "Your son should be your first priority." All I want you to do is to leave me and my son the hell alone. The woman who took up your time and stopped you from coming to the hospital to see your son, you need to go back to her. You can kiss where the sun doesn't shine and you know where that is. It's like some days I'll hear from you when you want to be a boyfriend and then it's like you don't care about nobody but yourself. Your lies will eventually catch up with you," I said to him. "I hope and pray you don't get crossed up in your own web of lies." I was glad the baby started crying. I hurried up and got off the phone with him. I washed him off, put powder and lotion on him, changed his diaper and dressed him up in one of his Nike outfits I bought.

It was about twelve- twenty thirty p.m., when my son's father decided to came by my house to see his son. I walked in my room and left him to be alone in the living room with his son. I don't want to interfere with him bonding with his son. I'd rather for him to bond with his son and not have me around. I don't want him to think that we have something going on between us, because we don't. Our relationship is messy. I don't want to have anything else to do with him or this relationship. I just want him to be here for his son and his son only.

I didn't want to be rude, so I went back in the living room and sat across from him. We talked for a while and I let him have it. I said to him, "I hate the person I've became, but you made me this way." I don't trust you or anything that comes out of your mouth. I'm tired of the lies and cheating. I deserve better and so do my son. We don't have to be together to raise our son, but you need to be here for him. That one time have I ever cheated on you or gave you a reason to think I was. You took my heart and you trampled all over it like it was a piece of glass. You never cared about my feelings or what I was going through, but you want me to forgive your for all the things you've done to me.

My mom or my sister never came out their rooms to interrupt our conversations. They both respected us. I truly thank them for that. "I hate the person I've become, but you made me this way," I said to him. I don't trust you or anything that comes out of your mouth. I'm tired of the lies and cheating. I deserve better and so do my son. We don't have to be together to raise our son, but you need to be here for him." Not one time have I ever cheated on you or gave you a reason to think I was," I said to him. You took my heart and you trampled all over it like it was a piece of glass. You never cared about my feelings or what I was going through. You want me to forgive you for all the things you've done to me.

I was glad he left, I wanted to enjoy my bundle of joy. A lot of my friends and church members came by to see the baby. I thought they wanted to see me, but they came to see my son. We all had a good time laughing and talking. My mom cooked dinner and some even brought over food. They started being noisy by asking a lot of questions about my labor. They wanted to know, how long I stayed in labor. Did I have the baby natural? How many stitches I got? They were asking unnecessary questions I thought was personal. I refused to answer the ones I thought was personal to me. I made sure the ones who wanted to hold my son sanitize their hands.

Everybody was saying how handsome he was and that he looks just like his dad. I got so tired of hearing that from them. I can see a little resemblance of me in my son. Eventually things between us will get better. We have a son to raise and I want him to be a part of his son's life. I wasn't going to push the issue about him spending time with his son. I truly love him with all my heart. I just want things between us to get better. I wanted him to change his ways and for us to be a family again. I never cheated on him, lied to him, or made him believe I didn't want our relationship. I tried everything to make it work between us. I gave him another chance even when he lied to me, cheated on me, and mistreated me. I should have left him and our relationship a long time ago. I wouldn't be sitting here taking care of a baby. Here I am taking care of our son and making sure he has the proper love and care he needs. This boy had took me through the mud, yet still I love and care about him. I love him and I don't want to be without him. He's the only man I've been with. He's my first love, and the man who took my virginity.

While sitting in the living room talking, he called to talk to me. I excused myself from everyone and went in the room to talk to him. He asked me if the baby and I would like to go over to his mom's house for a while. "No," I said to him. It's too early to take the baby out in the air and around people. He didn't have his six week checkup and neither did I.

"I'll come by later and see you and the baby," he said. We hung the phone up. I went back in the living room where my friends and church members were sitting at. As time passed by, everyone was getting their belongings and leaving. They all made sure to say something to my bundle of joy. One of my closest friends stayed to help clean the house. I was glad she stayed because I needed someone to talk to. We talked for a while and she gave me some good advice. I didn't want her to leave, but I knew she had she had some business to take care. I thanked her for helping me out and making sure everything was put away neatly. We hugged each other and she left. The house was calm and quiet. My bundle of joy slept through everything that was going on inside the house. He didn't cry when my mom picked him up, bathed him, and changed his diaper. He slept through it all. I have a good son.

Later that day, his father decided to show up with bags in his hands. I was glad to see him, but I was also mad at him. I was glad he came to see his son and for the enjoyment he brought to my heart, but something didn't feel right. Watching him with our son and the love he has for him made me feel like I was over reacting in our relationship. I can't wait for him to have his six week checkup so he can see his family.

"My grandmother can't wait to see him," he said.

I said to him, "Everybody will get a chance to see him when he has his six week checkup."

"Every day she sees me, all she does is ask about you and the baby."

"Make sure you let your family know that we have to be seen by the doctor before we can come out the house like that."

"I understand," he said.

"I'm definitely not trying to get my baby sick or myself sick. I don't want anybody breathing on him or holding him at this moment. He's a new born baby and I don't want my son getting sick. I don't want to see my son back in the hospital for someone's carelessness.

I said to him, "I hope you understand what I'm saying." I'm not trying to be rude or nasty, but I'm looking out for our son.

"I agreed on what you're saying," he said. I understood how important it is to keep him safe from getting sick.

"You don't know what a person has or if that person is drunk or whatever. That's my bundle of joy and I'm going to protect him.

The bags he brought in the house had diapers, wipes, formulas, bottles, bottle cleaner, clothes, undershirts, socks, and everything a baby needs. I was surprises he had something in the bag for me. I fixed him a plate while he was holding the baby. He really didn't want to put the baby down. My mom had to make him lie the baby down next to him on the chair while he ate. He kept looking back at the baby as if he was going to miss something.

"Your son is not going anywhere," I said. You don't have to keep looking back at him. We all started laughing. My nephew was in the room asleep. One thing I can say, both my son and nephew can sleep through anything.

After he ate, my little sister put his plate in the garbage can.

"Thanks for putting my plate in the garbage," he said to my sister.

"You're welcome," she said.

I was surprised he didn't pick him up and hold him in his arms. He just let him sleep peacefully. He stayed and talked with us for another two hours before he went home.

"I'll call you when I get home," he said. He stood up and gave his son a kiss on his puffy little cheeks.

I said to him, "Don't forget to tell your family we'll be over when we get our checkup. I walked him to the door and kissed him goodnight. He made sure to call me when he got home. We talked on the phone about an hour before hanging up. I was able to take a shower and put everything away before going to bed. My son was still asleep. I woke him up to give him a bottle. He didn't like that. He doesn't like to be bothered while he's sleeping. After feeding and making him burp, he went straight to sleep and so did I.

Chapter 41

A Family Gathering

The baby and I went for our six week checkup. I was glad everything came back good for the both of us. I had to be careful because I still had stitches. The doctor told me not to lift anything heavy because it can cause me to have a setback. When we left the doctor's office I called my mom and let her know everything was good. I decided to call my boyfriend when I got home. I told him the good news. He asked me if we wanted to go over to his mom's house for a little while. "I don't care," I said to him. I don't want everybody holding him. He's still young and his cord just fell off. He can catch germs from anybody. "I don't want anything to happen to him," I said. "

"I understand," he said. I'll make sure that doesn't happen to him.

Before he came to pick us up, my mom told me to be very careful with him and don't let everybody hold him. I thought I was being over protective of my son, but my mom was too. "I don't want to see him sick and have to be admitted in the hospital for someone's carelessness. "He's still a newborn and germs are out there," she said.

"If you let anybody hold him, make sure they sanitized their hands."

"Yes, ma'am," I said to her. I'll make sure they sanitized their hands.

My baby and I were dressed when my son's father came to pick us up. Before going over to his grandmother's house, we went to his mom's house first. He unstrapped the car seat and grabbed the baby bag. His mom was so glad to see her first born grandbaby and grandson. Everybody wanted to hold him, but he told them they had to wait until he gets a little older. I was shocked at what he had said to his mother. I thought he was going to let them hold him regardless of what I had said. His mom and sisters went in the bathroom to sanitize their hands. They all took turns holding him.

We weren't in the house not even fifteen minutes and his pager went off. I looked at him while he was checking it. When he looked up, my eyes were straight on him. I had an attitude at that moment I was ready to leave. I rolled my eyes and sucked my teeth at him. I said to him, "I think you need to call your trick and let her know you're spending time with your son.

He said to me, "Girl, you don't know what you're talking about. His mom took the baby in her room. He went outside for what reason I don't know.

"I have something to show you," his younger sister said to me. Just don't tell my brother what I showed you.

"I won't say anything to him, I said to her. I got up and went in her room. She reached under her mattress and pulled out a picture of a baby boy.

She reached under her mattress and pulled out a picture of a baby boy.

"Who is this?" I asked her.

"This is his baby from another girl," she said.

"Are you fucking serious?" I asked her.

"Yes," she said.

"Do you remember when you kept calling here looking for him when you got out of the hospital?" She asked me.

"Yes, and what does that mean?" I asked her.

"Well, he was with her because she's having his baby too," she said. I got so sick to my stomach I wanted to vomit. It felt like everything in my body wanted to come out. Tears started flowing from my eyes. I felt a few teardrops falling down.

"Is this a joke right?" I asked her. All jokes on me, right.

"No, it's not a joke," she said. I thought you should know. You don't deserve to be treated like this from my brother. I don't care if he is my brother, he's dead wrong.

I said to her, "I don't understand how he can do me like this." I never cheated on your brother. He always telling me how he wants us to be a family and he loves only me.

"Are you okay?" His oldest sister asked me.

"No, I'm not alright," I said to his sister. I just found out another girl had his baby. "It's not fair to me or my son. I haven't done anything to your brother. For him to treat me like this, is wrong.

His mom walked in the room and she knew something was wrong. She apologized for her son's behavior and the way he's been treating me lately. "I'm not worried about me," I said to his mom. I can take care of myself. Since he decided to sleep around without using protection and get another girl pregnant, he needs to be with her and her child. I can't keep going through this with him. I've been faithful to your son since we've been together. Not one time have I ever cheated on him and this the thanks I get from him. I said to his mom, "I guess he's where he wants to be."

"I told my son to tell you before you find out," his mom said. He was trying to keep it a secret from you.

"He really kept that a secret from me," I said to his mom.

"His mom said, "I hate what he's done to you."

"I wish he would have told me the truth about his other son," I said to his mom. That goes to show you how much he really cares about me. I started crying. I couldn't control the tears.

His mom said to me, "Charmayne, you just had a baby." I don't want you to get sick and end up in the hospital.

"Of all people, why did this had to happen to me?" I don't deserve this. I deserve better.

"Where is he," His mom asked me.

I said to his mom, "His pager went off and he went outside to see who it was."

Knots were forming in my stomach. It felt like something was stopping me from breathing. I could hardly breathe or move my body. His sister rushed outside to get him. He rushed by my side and asked me what was wrong. I started crying. "Get my son and take us home," I said to him. I need to take my medication. I lied to him. I just wanted to go home.

I couldn't believe he was having a baby with another girl. With the lies and cheating he did to me, "How could I still be with him?" I asked myself. This man knew he had another girl pregnant and not one time did he say anything to me about it. "At least let me make my own decision if I still wanted to be in a relationship with him." Hell, he took it upon himself to make the decision for me. He wanted to take me to the hospital, but I told him to take us home.

He went to his car and opened the door for me. I placed the baby bag between my legs while he strapped the baby car seat in the back. I didn't say a word to his family. They knew I was in a lot of pain. I waved goodbye to them. They understood my pain and what I was going through. When he got in the car, "He kept asking me if I was okay." I kept my mouth closed. I didn't say a word to him. I had to control the tears from my eyes before I got home. When we arrived at my house, he got out to open his door. I said to him, "No, you don't have to get out." I can handle it from here.

"You're in a lot of pain," he said.

"I've been in a lot of pain since I've been in this relationship with you," I said to him.

"Baby, what do you mean by that?" He asked me. I don't understand. What's going on? "What happened at my mom's house?" He asked me.

"Nothing, I started getting sick and feeling nauseous that's all," I said to him. I unbuckled the seatbelt around my son's car seat, grabbed his bag, and closed the door behind me without looking back or saying anything to him.

When I went inside my house, mom knew something didn't seem right with me. She looked at me and said, "Why you are crying?" She asked me.

I said to my mom, "I just heard he has another son with some other girl." His sisters told me the day I was trying to call him, he was in the hospital with her. Now, I know why he wasn't at the hospital with me when I was giving birth to his son. He was with her and probably rubbing her stomach the same way he rubs mines. My oldest sister walked in the living room where my mom and I were sitting at. "How did you find out about the other girl and her baby?" She asked me. His sister showed me a picture of his son. I couldn't believe what I was seeing.

"Well, did you say anything to him about what you found out?" My mom asked me.

"No," I said to my mom. I promise his sisters I wouldn't say anything to him about what they showed me. I unstrapped my baby in his car seat and held him close to my heart. I needed to feel his heartbeat against mines.

Holding my baby close to me eased the pain away. I couldn't cry no more. My tears were all dried up.

I wiped him off, changed his diapers and clothes, gave him a fresh warm bottle and laid him down on the bed. I took a nice long bubble bath to relax my mind and figure out my next move. I held my head back and closed my eyes. I don't remember falling asleep in the tub. My little sister came in there to wake me up. She really scared me.

"I need to use the bathroom," she said.

"How long have I been in here?" I asked her.

"Since you laid the baby down," she said.

I was exhausted. My mind was playing tricks on me. I laid down next to my son thinking of my next move. My mom came in the room making sure I was doing okay. My mom had always been there for me when I need her the most. She never told me anything wrong. She always told me the truth. My mom said to me, "Sometimes God show us things even when we don't want to see them." God has been giving you warnings about him. You didn't take heed of what he was saying to you. Sometime you have to stop and ask yourself, "What am I doing wrong?" Listen to what God is saying to you and trying to show you. You saw it coming, but you didn't know when it was coming. All the time you've been trying to call him about your doctor's appointment, getting a ride to and from work, and wanting to spend time with him this is what he does to you. "I can't tell you what to do, but you need to make the right choice in your life," she said. You have a son to raise. You can't break down now. Your son needs you just as much as you need him.

"Thanks Mom, I needed to hear those words."

I'm not going to lie, I still love him. I know I can get over him, but it's going to be hard. I have his son. If he wants to see his son, I'll let him. I'm not going to be that spiteful. It's up to him if he wants to be a part of his son's life. "I've saved enough money just in case something like this would happen."

"I'm glad you don't depend on a man to take care of you," my mom said to me.

I said to my mom, "You and daddy (God bless the dead) taught us well." I remember Daddy telling me whatever I want in life, I have to strive for it. "Don't ever put all your trust in a man or depend on him to do anything for you. I also remember my dad telling me, "He wish I can get a good man like him who provides for his family." You don't need a man who don't mean you no good. "I'll go hungry before I let my family go hungry," my dad said to me. One thing you doesn't need is a man who don't pay bills and depend on you to take care of him. That's what you call a sorry no good man. "I don't want neither one of my daughters to get a man like that." Talking about my father brought tears to my eyes. I knew if my dad were here, he would put my son's father in his place.

The phone rang. I picked it up before it woke up the baby. "Hello," I said.

"Hey, I'm calling to see how you and the baby are doing," he said.

"I'm tired, I'll call you in the morning," I said. I hung the phone up. My mom led us in a prayer before going to bed. I laid next to my son and fell asleep.

Chapter 42

Here We Go Again

Trey and I both slept well last night. He didn't even cry for a bottle or for his diaper to be changed. When I got up, I noticed he wasn't lying next to me. I can hear people in the living room talking, but I couldn't make out the voices. I asked my oldest sister, "Did momma come and get the baby?"

"Girl, he was up since six-twenty three am. He wasn't crying. He was just lying there. Momma came in and took him in her room. She knew you were exhausted from crying last night. "How are you feeling now?" My sister asked.

I said to my oldest sister, "I don't know what I'm going to do, but I have to do something before it's too late." I have a son by him. I don't want him to not be in his son's life. Well, it doesn't matter if he sees his son or not. He has another son by someone else who, so he can spend his time with them.

"Maybe that's where he needs to be at," my sister said to me.

I kept hearing voices in the living room. I heard my mom tell someone, "She just had a baby. I don't want for her to get upset and end up back in the hospital. She needs to enjoy her son and be a good mother to him. "I can't tell her what to do or say, because she has to make her own decisions, not me."

I looked at my sister. Before I can say anything else to her, she said to me, "He called and asked Momma if he can talk to you.

"What did Momma say to him?" I asked my sister.

"She told him you were still sleep." He asked Momma if he can come by and see the baby.

"Okay and what did she say?" I asked her.

"Momma said that it was okay for him to come and see the baby."

I jumped up so fast I forgot about the stitches. "Ouch," I said in a loud voice. The pain was unbearable. I bent down with my hands on my stomach.

"Are you okay, my sister asked me?"

"Hell no," I said to my sister.

"Girl, it felt like my stitches opened back up. I asked her take a look at my womb. "Do you see blood on the gauges?" I asked her.

"You look good," she said. Go handle your business. I opened my room door. The first face I saw was his.

"Good morning everybody," I said to them.

"Good morning," they said back to me.

"Why are you here this time of morning?" I asked him.

He said to me, "I came by to drop off some stuff for the baby and give you some money just in case you need to get something else for him and yourself." I reached over and grabbed the money from him. As bad as I wanted to kick him out of my house, I remained calm as a rabbit. I wasn't about to let him know what was going on inside my head or what his family had showed me. I was playing it easy.

As I was sitting in the living room, my mind took me back to the day when I was at his house and his pager went off. I remember telling him he needed to tell his trick he's spending time with his baby. **Now, I remember. Hold on! That wasn't the first incident I had with him at his** *house when his pager going off.* I remember sitting in the living room. We were sitting on the couch talking and watching a show call "Good Time on TV. His pager went off. I remember watching him walk outside. I didn't pay any attention to it until I noticed he's been outside talking for a long time. I looked out the window and I can see a car pull in to where he was standing at. I can see him on the sidewalk talking to a girl on the driver's side. That's what made me go outside. I said to myself, **"Here I am nine months pregnant with your son and you're outside talking to another female."**

I went outside and asked him what was going on. "Oh, it's nothing, he said."

"It got to be something or you wouldn't be outside running your mouth to another female." I said to him. "Your pager goes off and then you go outside. You've been outside for fifteen minutes talking to another female, so it got to be something," I said. "I'm sitting in the house waiting on and you're outside running your mouth, so don't tell me it's nothing."

I noticed another girl on the passenger side. The girl who was driving started popping off at the mouth. I wasn't about to let that go down like that. I said to her, "Girl, I know you're not talking to me you got your peoples messed up."

"Yeah, I'm talking to you," she said.

I said to her, "Cocoa, I'll beat your ass. I don't think this is what you want. Gourmet was quiet, but I noticed something different about Gourmet."

"Well, you didn't tell her you had another girl pregnant," the girl on the passenger side said to him.

"What did you just say to him?" I asked her.

"I'm having sex with him too," she said. "I reached over and slapped him across his face."

Cocoa said to him, "She wouldn't slap me like that."

"Well, get out of the car and I'll slap you the same way I slapped him,"

I said to Cocoa. She tried to get out of the car, but he wouldn't let her.

"Girl, if you really wanted to get out of the car you can."

I said to her, "He's not your excuse of not getting out of the car."

"I tell you this, nobody is going to be slapping her," he said to Cocoa.

I said to him, "Move out the way so she can get out of the car and get slapped down. "I'm going to give you what you came here for and that's this ass whooping." I pushed him out the way so she can have enough room to get out. I let her get out of her car. As soon as she got out of the car I started punching her in her face. He tried to stop me from fighting her, but he was no win on my end. I kept on punching her. She finally landed a hit on my shoulder.

"Really!" He said to her. "You better not hit her again or you'll have to answer to me."

"I don't care if you is having sex with her," Cocoa said. "Hell, she hit me.

"Girl, shut the hell up. You're mad because you just got your ass beat up while trying to defend Gourmet's battle. Now get in the car, go on home and take your little scary ass friend Gourmet with you. You're a dummy for a dummy. Gourmet was mumbling something. I couldn't make out what she was saying to me."

"Whatever you have to say to me, speak a little louder so I can hear you," I said to her. "I don't understand quietness. You brought your friend over here to fight your battle. We're both pregnant, so what's stopping you?" I asked her. "If you want some of this, I advise you to do the same thing your dumb ass friend did and get out of the car. I'm definitely not going to feel sorry because you're pregnant. I'll give you the same ass whooping your friend just got, but yours will be a little rougher than hers."

His family came running outside upon hearing all the commotion that was going on the outside.

"What's going on out here?" His mom asked me.

I said to Joyful, "Well, Gram decided to come outside and entertain someone else."

Gourmet said out loud, "I'm having sex with him too, so you're not the only one who he's sleeping with." So, I reached over and slapped him in his face. So, Hater on the driver side went popping off at the mouth. I gave her what she was looking for. I reached in her car and slapped in her face. That's what she had wanted, so I served her.

"I don't know why she keep coming here anyway," Peachy said.

"I think you and your friend needs to leave my house," Joyful said to them. "This is his who he wants to be with and not you."

Gourmet said to Joyful, "Well, he'll be raising two babies, because I'm pregnant from him too.

"I advise you to leave my house before something really happen to you, one of his sister's said to them.

"I appreciate it if you two don't come back over here to my house," his mom said.

As they were driving off, the girl on the passenger side said, "That's why I'm pregnant by your man."

I hollered back at her, "You can have him too. He's free of charge. I looked at him with so much anger in my eyes. Only if he knew what was on my mind. "How dare you pretend that our relationship is perfect?" I made him take me home after what just happened between me and his other baby momma.

My mind came back to reality. That's when I put two and two together. Whenever I paged him before, he wouldn't answer my calls. He even had to leave early when we're together. A lot of things were beginning to make sense to me. God was showing me, but I was too blind to see what he was doing to me. I allowed this boy to make decisions for me and to fill my head up with lies. He manipulative me. He kept me in the dark for so many years and now I see why. He had his cake and ice cream too. When he leaves from being with me, he'll go and be with her. He was having unprotected sex with the both of us. How nasty and low down was that? He could have giving me something as well as her. He wasn't thinking and neither was I.

Wow, this man really had my mind gone. I'm in love with a man who doesn't care anything about me, my feelings or my heart. He took my heart and did whatever he wanted to do with it. I allowed him to take advantage of me and used me to the best of his knowledge. I can't blame anybody but myself. I have a son to raise. I have to think about him and his well-being. I'm nobody's laughing stock. Everybody in his family knew what he was doing. Not one of his family member said anything to me. How dare they be in my face laughing and talking to me?"Yeah, they were laughing, at how stupid and dumb I am when it comes to him. Now, I see what my parents were talking about, especially my dad. My parents always told me not to put all my trust in a no good man who don't mean me any good.

I glared at him with anger in my eyes. I wanted to wrap my hands around his neck and strangle the hell out of him. I made him leave my house without any warning.

"Next time you want to come over here and see Trey, you need to get my approval not my mom's approval," I said to him. "I'll let you know when you can see him. As for me and you, there is no us. Don't call me, don't come here unannounced, and don't have your people calling to check on the baby or me. Get out of my house and don't you ever come back here unless I tell you to. I don't need anybody who thinks they're going to keep treating me like I'm nothing. News flash I am somebody. You've done enough damage to me. I refuse to let you walk all over me. If I don't ever be with you again, I'm okay with that. It's time for me to love myself. I'm going to enjoy every minute of loving myself. We need to go our separate ways and meet other people," I said to him. "My bad, you already have a lot of friends from my understanding."

He left without saying a word to me. I was glad he left. I almost let the worm out of the bucket about finding out about his little secret. He was about to get his throat slashed if he would've said anything else to me out of the way. That's how much anger I had in me. What I wanted to do to him would hurt him in every way. The best thing was for him to leave, because it would have been a war in my mom's house.

The rest of my day went well. I was able to calm myself down and play with my two favorite guys. They both had gained some extra pounds and were getting healthier by the day. My sister and I both had good babies. They both went to sleep and woke up around the same time. I thought they planned this while they were in our stomach.

Later that day, Gram kept calling me. I ignored his calls. I did not feel like talking to him or listening to what he had to say to me. My mind was made up and there's no turning back. I was there for him when he needed me, "Why can't he do the same for me?" I never cheated on him or messed around with anybody else. I was faithful to him during our entire relationship. One minute he loved me and one minute he didn't. He was constantly sending me mix signals. He made me believe I was the only woman he wanted to be with, but that's was a lie.

"Yes, I was the fool in our relationship."

Now, I have proof about him having sex with another female. "How dare he do me like that?" I had to erase everything we ever did together out of my mind and focus on Trey. He'll always be a part of my life, because he's the father of my son. Somewhere down the line we still have to keep communicate with one another.

I wished I never met him and all the lies that came along with it. Trey is my #1 priority. I need to stay calm before I do something I'll regret later on.

Chapter 43

Can't Keep It in His Pants

Every ten minutes Gram was calling me. At this point, I'm not trying to hear what he had to say to me. I wanted to forget about what his sisters told me and the picture they showed me. I have a son to raise. Fighting with him or anybody else were not in my category. I made sure to put money away for rainy days like this. I don't need for him to do anything for Trey or me. Trey didn't have to want for anything. I stocked up on his diapers, wipes, clothes, bottles, and milk. He had plenty of clothes all the way up to his first year.

"Someone called here asking about Trey," my mom said to me.

"Who was it?" I asked her.

"Some special wanted to know if he could come by and bring some stuff over for the baby," my mom said.

"What did you say to him," I asked her.

"I just told him the truth," my mom said

"Thanks mom," I just don't feel like seeing him.

"I understand how you feel about what he did to you," my mom said. You have to learn to live and forgive."

"I know mom," but I never cheated on him and nor have I messed around on him. I put my trust in him and this the thanks I get from him. My mom knew I was anger at what he did to me, but she understood my pain. I wanted to spend the rest of my life with him and raise our kids together as a family, but he ruined all of that.

There was a knock on the door. "Who is it?" I asked. He said his name. I went and opened the door for him to come in. I was glad to see his dad come by my house. His dad, grandmother and I are real close. No matter what, they always show me love and has been there for me whenever I needed them. I opened the door for him to come in. We hugged each other tight. He congratulated me for giving him his first grandson. Yes, I gave him his first grandson, but he also has another grandson. My mom walked out of the room with my son in her arms. He reached his arms out to hold grandson. He was so excited, he had tears in his eyes.

We sat down on the sofa talking. I didn't tell him everything. I just told him what his daughters told me.

"Well it looks like you have another grandson," I said to him.

"What do you mean another grandson?" He asked me.

"They showed me a picture of his other son he has with another girl." "Are you serious?" He asked me. I know he didn't do that to you.

I started crying. I said to his dad, "This boy has tormented me throughout our relationship and he thinks he deserves a gold medal."

"Wait until I see him," his dad said. Trust me he's not going to be happy to what I have to say to him. I begged his father not to say anything to him.

"He doesn't know that I know he has another son with someone else," I said. That's why I'm playing it safe. I don't want his sisters to get caught up in his mess. He promised me he wouldn't say a word to his son. That was a relief to me. I didn't want to cause any more confusion between us.

He's been trying to call me, but I've been ignoring his calls. I'm not ready to talk to him. If I talk to him, I'm going to say the wrong words to him. He needs to leave me alone until I'm ready to talk to him. "If he keeps pushing my button, it might slip out my mouth about having a son by someone else."

"I don't believe my son did something like this to you," his dad said.

I looked in the bags my son's granddaddy had brought to the house. I couldn't believe my eyes. Not only did he buy my son some things, but he also bought me some things as well. "I appreciate the things you bought for my son and me," I said. I gave him a big hug and a kiss on his jaw thanking him for his generosity. His dad promised me he wouldn't mention anything I've said to him about his son's other son. He kissed the baby goodnight.

The phone was ringing. "I'll get it," I said to my mom. "Hello," I said.

"How are you doing?" my son's father asked me. I was glad nobody was sitting in the living room, but me. It gave me a chance to really say what I wanted to say to him. I decided to talk to him and put our differences aside for my son's sake. As bad as I wanted to tell him what his sisters showed me, I kept my promise not to. I wanted to see if he was going to tell me about his other son. To my surprise he kept that secret to himself. Yes, my mind was made up. I don't want to be in a relationship with him, not even for the sake of our son. What he did to me, he can never take back.

We talked for a few minutes. He tried to apologize for the mistakes he made in our relationship. I listened while he kept lying to me about this and that. I said to him, "Sooner or later your lies are going to catch up with you and you want be able to get yourself out of it."

"Baby, I love you." I know I've made some dumb and stupid mistakes in our relationship, but you're the only one who makes me happy," he said.

"You sure have a funny way in showing it," I said to him. "How are you going to have another?" Boy, I had to catch myself. I was about to tell him I know about his other son. I kept my lips sealed. Wow! "How can I be with a man who has another baby with someone else?" I asked myself. I went back to square one. I refused to let him take me out of my character. I have a son to raise. I don't want to put that stress on my son or myself.

The baby has a doctor's appointment in the morning and we need a way to the doctor's office. I asked him if he could take us.

"What time is his appointment?" He asked me. I told him the time we needed to be there. Yes, I'll be there to get you, he said.

Before I hung up the phone, he asked if he can talk to me. "I said to him, you should have talked to me when we were in a relationship." I think you're a little too late for a talk.

"Baby, I know I've messed up. "I can't take back what I've done and said to you, but give me another chance to prove my love for you and our son," he said to me.

"Our son?" Don't talk about our son, I said to him. Where were you when I was giving birth to our son? Where were you, when I needed you to be here for our son? Where were you when our son started crying for a bottle or needed his diaper changed? Where were you when our son wanted to feel his dad's heartbeat against his? You have some nerves talking to me about our son. I've been here for our son from day one. "Did you ever thought about my feelings?" I asked him. Not one time have you put my feelings into consideration? You thought about yourself and yourself only.

"Now, let's talk about your son," I said to him.

"Baby, please let me be here for the both of you," he said to me. I know I don't deserve your love, trust and honesty, but I truly do love you. He said to me, "I love you with all my heart." I don't want to be with anyone else but you.

"Well, if you wanted to be with me and our son you would have never cheated on me. Here I am fighting with another female you're messing around with. Not only that, you have another son by someone else. "What were you thinking about?" I asked him. Throughout our relationship I never lied to you, cheated on you, misused you, or mistreated you.

"All the love I have for you this is how you do me?" I asked him. Do you actually think you deserve my love, my heart let alone being a family? The best thing you can do for me, is give me my space and let me sort things out. As a matter of fact, "Why don't you go be with the woman you have a son with?" You can forget about our son and raise the son you have with her. It was quiet on the other end.

"Hello!" Hello!" Don't get quiet now this is the mess you made not me. You can at least say something. Now I see why you were never committed to me. I said to him, "You're a bad man trying to handle two women's at the same damn time." You were too busy trying to have sex with someone else other than me. "I guess you never thought about catching a disease from her or any of your other tricks." I said to him. You could have spread that disease to me and my son. "I've been your fool for too long and now it's my turn."

"Baby."

"Don't baby me," I said to him. I'm not your baby and I never was your baby. You can stop all the baby this and the baby that. I wasn't you baby when you were sleeping with another woman. He couldn't say anything. That's just how quiet he was on the phone. I got tired of listening to him breathe through the phone. What we had is long overdue. One thing I want you to know, we only have a son together and that's all. I don't want you to get the wrong idea about me and you being together again, because we're not. You lost every inch of that. "I don't think we can ever be in a relationship again," I said to him.

He said to me, "You're not leaving me."

"You're not my dad," I said to him. My dad died when I was in high school. He never signed any papers giving you permission to tell what to do or when to do it.

"I'm not trying to be your dad," he said to me. I'm your man and you heard what I've said. If you're bad the way you're talking, try and leave me and see what happens. "If you think you're going to leave me, you got another thing coming," he said to me.

"Did you think about your son when you were having sex with someone else?" I asked him. Did you think about your son when he needed you? Were you thinking about your son when you were beating up on his mother? Your son don't even know who you are. So you can stop talking about your son.

"Boy, please, you don't get that respect from me," I said to him.

"If I can't have you, no other man will and I promise you that," he said.

"And what do you mean by that?" I asked him.

"You heard what I said, so don't fucking play with me."

"I have Trey to raise. "I'm not about to listen to your mess," I said to him.

"I'm sorry, for what I've put you through, but you will not leave me." "Try to leave me and you're see what will happen to you," he said to me. He was talking like he wanted to kill me.

"Boy, stop playing with yourself," I said to him.

As I said before, you're the only woman I want to spend the rest of my life with. She doesn't mean anything to me. "Beside it was a one night stand," he said.

"Well one night, two nights or three nights, it doesn't matter," I said. You had unprotected sex with her and got her pregnant. While I was home being faithful to you and our relationship, you were out there cheating on me. Now I see why you never wanted me to go anywhere unless I was with you. You never wanted me to hang out with my friends. I couldn't go to parties, go to the stores or just ride in the car with one of my friends. You were scared I was going to catch you cheating on me. I said to him, "Yes, I was your fool as you can say."

He said to me, "You never were my fool baby." I love you with every inch of my body. "I can't live without you or my son," he said. I just got tired of hearing his lies. I was ready to hang the phone up on him.

"I'll talk to you in the morning," I said to him. I'm going to take a shower and get ready for bed.

"I'll see you in the morning," he said to me. We both hung the phone up.

Trey was already in bed sleeping peacefully. My mom always took care of Trey for me even when I didn't ask her too. Lying next to Trey was something I enjoyed doing. I laid next to him and began singing his favorite lullaby in his ear. Trey loves it when I sing to him. I set my alarm clock for seven-fifteen am.

Chapter 44

Abused By My Lover

My alarm clock went off around seven-fifteen am. I'm surprised it didn't wake up the twins. Charmayne eased slowly out of bed not trying to wake them up.

Charmayne had to finish getting herself together. She had to make sure the twins diaper bag was ready as well.

While Charmayne was in the bathroom taking a shower, the words Gram said to her was harsh. When she walked in her room to get dressed, she noticed the twins wasn't laying in their bed.

Charmayne mom had gotten the twins dressed for her.

"Thanks mom for getting them dressed for me."

"No problem," she said. That's what I'm here for. I can't do for one and don't do for the other.

By the time Gram came to pick Charmayne and the twins up, they all were dressed.

Charmayne didn't give Gram time enough to get out of the car and come knock on the door. I She grabbed the twin's baby bag while her mom grabbed their car seats and was heading out the door.

Gram got out of his car and opened the door for them.

I guess he thought that was going to win him some brownie points by opening the car door for me.

Gram strapped each one of the twins in their car seat while I put their bag in the front seat with me.

"Thanks for coming to take us to their doctor's appointment," I said to him. I'm surprised you came to pick us up since I found out about what you've done.

"I know I've made some mistake in our relationship," he said.

"You made too many mistakes in our relationship," I said to him.

He said to me, "I don't need you to keep throwing it up in my face."

"Well, I wouldn't keep throwing it up in your face if you would've never cheated on me," I said. You're the one who's been cheating, not me. Don't catch an attitude with me, because of something you did. I think we should go our separate ways. All I ask is that you be here for the twins.

He looked at me as if he wanted to knock me out.

"Don't play with me," he said. I let you do all your talking and I'm tired of your mouth. I already told you, **"If I can't have you, no other man will and that's a promise."**

"Were you being concern about when you were sleeping around with this other girl?" I asked him. You wasn't thinking about me or my feelings. How dare you tell me, "If I can't have you, no other man will?" That's what you should have been saying to yourself and not to me. You got some nerve to let those words come out of your mouth, when you're the one who's been cheating. There's no telling who else you've been sleeping with.

"I guess you're taking me as a joke," he said.

"No I'm not taking you as a joke," I said. I'm just speaking the truth.

"Charmayne, don't fucking play with me," he said. "I'll spit in your face and then kill you. I'll get amazed in watching you die," he said to me. "Don't say another word to me. I'll knock your ugly ass out."

The look Gram had on his face was scaring Charmayne.

Charmayne dared not to say another word to him.

Gram knew he had the upper hand on Charmayne. He knew she was scared of him.

Gram reached over and grabbed Charmayne by her arm. "I hope you heard what I've said to you," he said. Keep running your mouth and watch what I do to you.

"Gram just take us home," Charmayne said. I'll find a way to their doctor's appointment. You're not going to keep putting your hands on me. "I'm not your punching bag. I'm just your twin's mother.

"Don't play with me," he said. I guess you're trying me. "It look like I have to show you better than I can tell you."

By this time Charmayne was getting scared.

She didn't know if she should cry or jump out of the car and leave the twins behind. Maybe he would like that.

Charmayne refused to let a no-good man like him raise her twins.

Gram grabbed Charmayne by her neck and squeezed it hard with his hand.

Charmayne screamed out in pain.

"Bitch, close your damn mouth before you wake up my kids," he said. Don't say another word to me.

Charmayne cried in silence trying not to let a tear fall down from my eyes.

Instead of Gram taking Charmayne to the twin's doctor appointment, he took them somewhere else.

Charmayne didn't know where she was at. She really was getting scared. Gram took the twins car seat out one by one.

"Get out of my car," Gram told Charmayne.

"I just want to go home so I can take the twins to their doctor's appointment."

Charmayne refused to get out of his car. She was scared as HELL. Charmayne didn't know what else to do.

He opened the car door.

"I just told you to get out of my car."

Charmayne looked at him and rolled her eyes.

"You know they have a doctor's appointment. They need to be seen by their doctor.

"I'm going to take you to their doctor's appointment," he said. Just get out of the car and come in the house.

Charmayne had no other choice but to roll up the window and get out of the car.

As Charmayne was getting ready to step inside, Gram pushed me.

"You don't have to push me either," Charmayne said.

Just as Charmayne was about to turn around and face him, he slapped her hard against her face.

Charmayne looked at him with so much anger in her eyes.

"Man, why in the hell did you slap me for?" Charmayne asked him. I'm not your punching bag and you're not going to be putting your hands on me. You're getting mad at me for telling you the truth about what you did. You got some nerves. I'm not going to stand here and let you put your hands on me for something I didn't do. Just take us home so I can get a way to take them to their appointment.

Gram walked closer to Charmayne with anger in his eyes. He looked like he could have strangled her to death.

"Leave me alone," Charmayne said to Gram.

Just as he was about to hit me, his friend Warner walked in the house.

"He man, what's going on in here?" Warner asked Gram.

"Man Charmayne is tripping."

Gram sat down next to Charmayne like nothing was wrong between them.

"Hey Charmayne," Warner said.

Charmayne couldn't say nothing. She was too scared to open her mouth. She didn't know what Gram was going to do to her.

By that time the rest of Gram's friend walked in the house.

"Hey Charmayne," they all said in unison.

"Are the twins sleep?" Asked Duke.

"Yes, they sleep," Gram said.

Duke girlfriend Amber had walked in the house with their daughter Aleah

"Can I see the twins? Asked Amber.

"Yes you can see them," Charmayne said.

Warner knew something was wrong with me. He knew I was crying.

Charmayne was too scared to tell anyone what Gram had said and did to her.

Gram kind of knew his friends suspect something had happen between him and Charmayne.

"Gram, I hope you didn't put your hands on Charmayne," Duke said.

"Charmayne are you okay?" Asked Amber.

Charmayne started crying. She's afraid of Gram and the behavior he has toward her.

"Charmayne what just happen between you and Gram?" Asked Warner. I know something is wrong with you. So, you can stop pretending like nothing happen.

"Man listen, you need to mind your own damn business," Gram said.

"This is my business when you put your hands on her," Warner said.

"Please keep the noise down," Amber said. The babies are sleeping. No need to argue in front of them.

"Charmayne you need to stop letting him abused you," Amber said. He don't mean you or your twins any good.

"Amber, mind your fucking business. Gram said. You don't know what the fuck you're talking about.

"I know you don't love her or your twins." Now that's what Amber know.

Gram got so upset he told Charmayne to lets go.

Charmayne did as Gram told her. She grabbed the twin's baby bag.

"Go get in the car," Gram said to Charmayne.

Charmayne went outside to the car just as Gram has told her too.

There were silence in the house while Gram was getting the twin's situated.

"Man, I'll help you, Trey said.

"Thanks man I appreciate it." At least I have one true friend.

"Gram we're your friends," Scotty said. What you're doing to Charmayne and your twins are ridiculous. She doesn't need to be treated like this and neither your twins.

When Gram got in the car, he told Charmayne not to call him or ask him for anything.

"You don't have to worry about that," Charmayne said to Gram. I won't be calling you for nothing. I don't need you or your money. "You're taking your anger out on me for something I didn't even do."

Before Charmayne can say anything to him, Gram reached over and slapped her.

Charmayne grabbed her face and started crying.

"I guess this what you like for me to do to you," Gram said.

Charmayne looked at Gram with a straight face, "I'm not your fucking punching bag." You will not put your hands on me ever again. "My parents didn't beat me and neither will you," I said to him. I told you not to put your hands on me, but you did it anyway. I promise, you will regret for putting your hands on me.

"What you mean by that?" Gram asked Charmayne.

I was glad we pulled in the parking lot at the doctor's office. "I don't know how many times I keep telling you about your mouth," he said to me.

I said to Gram, "You get mad at me when one of your females can't give you what you want and need." You take your anger out on me like I did something wrong to you. Not one time have I ever cheated on you, but you did. "Now, I'm paying for the mistakes you made." My heart was racing fast. It felt like it was about to jump out of my chest.

Even though we were ten minutes late to Trey's doctor appointment, they were still able to see him. I was surprised he stayed and waited for us. After leaving the doctor's office he still had an attitude with me. I tried not to say anything to him out of the way. On the way to my house, he brought up about what happened at his house. I said to him, "I'm not going to let you treat me like I'm trash." You get mad at me for no damn reason. I haven't done anything to you, but be a good friend to you. You take your anger out on me like I did something wrong. I guess I'm the bad person. Not one time have I ever cheated on you or lied to you about anything. I don't need to be treated like this. "Can you count on your fingers how many times I cheated on you?" I asked Gram. I'm not like that. If I'm in a relationship with a person, I'm not going to go out there and mess around with someone else. I'm not that type of woman. I don't get down like that. Too many diseases are out there. I care about my body.

As I was about to open the car door, Gram grabbed my hand. He said to me, "If you think you're going to leave me, you have another thing coming." I hope you heard what I said. "Don't play with me," he said to me. I grabbed the baby bag and unstrapped his car seat. I made sure my face was clear of tears before I walked in the house.

My sister opened the door before I could unlock it with my key. I was glad to be in the comfort of my own home. My face was swollen a little but not that much. The side he slapped me on, I tried to avoid from eating on that side. I'm glad my son is in good health. He's gaining pounds rapidly. Trey didn't cry when the doctor was examining him or when he gave him a shot in his leg and arm. He cried just a little. Back to sleep he went.

I don't think my mom or sisters noticed anything different about me. I asked my baby sister to watch him while I take a shower. The water felt good against my body. My face was still sore and a little swollen. I tried to fight the tears, but I couldn't hold it in. I kept asking myself "Why I'm I with a man who beats me up?" I know I'm not a bad person. I deserved to be treated with respect. My crying got louder.

"Are you okay in there?" My mom asked me.

"I bit my tongue," I said to her. Here I am again lying to my mother. If I tell my mom what he's done to me, she'll be mad at him. The first thing my mom would say is, "He's not your father." How dare he puts his hands on you? It hurting me on the inside of not being honest with my mom about what he's doing to me. I know my mom would protect me from him. I just couldn't get the nerve to tell her everything.

When I got out of the bathroom, Gram was sitting in the living room holding my son in his arm. "What were you doing for you to bite your tongue?" She asked me. Only if my mom really knew what was going on with me and why I was crying in the bathroom. He looked at me scared in the face. I guess he thought I was going to burst his bubbles.

"I was singing my favorite church song," I said to my mom. When I started singing in alto voice, I bit down on my tongue. I looked at him with a unit on my face. He had stupid written all over his face. I know he was praying I didn't tell my mom what he did to me. He was sweating badly. He asked me if we needed anything from the store. "Yes," I said. Neither my son nor I needed anything from the store. We both had everything we needed. My baby had plenty of diapers, formulas, and wipes. I had all the snacks I wanted. Well, the baby needs more diapers, formulas, and wipes. "When you go to the store can you also get him some lotion, powder, and shampoo?" I asked him. "You can get me some snacks, fruit, and juice to drink." I'm going to teach him a lesson about putting his hands on me.

"I'll be back," he said.

My mom asked me how come I lied to him about getting me and the baby some things from the store. I had to come up with a quick lie to tell her. "You never have enough when it comes down to your baby," I said to her. I'd rather have more stuff for him than not having anything at all. "I don't want to keep running to the store to get this and that for him or myself." I couldn't tell my mom this man just jumped on me. I knew exactly what I was doing.

He called me to let me know he was standing outside with bags in his hands. I opened the door for him to come in He put the bags on his table and went back to his car. I looked in the bags he had brought in the house from the store. He brought some stuff for me and the baby. He went back to his car and brought some bags in that he had pick for us. "Thank you for buying us something to eat," my mom said to him.

"No problem," he said.

"I'll bathe and feed him while you eat," my mom said to me. He played with the baby before leaving.

"I'll call you when I get home," he said to me. "Goodnight," everyone."

"Goodnight," my mom and sister said to him.

I walked him to the door. While standing at the door, he whispered in my ear, "If I can't have you no other man will." He turned around and walked out the door without looking back at me. He was scaring me. I knew he meant every word he said to me.

His pager went off as he was getting in his car. He looked at me and dared me to say anything to him. He pointed his finger at me and said, "Don't make me knock your ass out in your yard." I looked away from him. I promise you, if he would have hit me in my yard, his momma will be burying him the same night. I would have killed him myself. I would have waited for the police to come to my house and arrest me for killing him. I would have told them all the things he's done to me. I would have showed them the bruises that he done. That night really made me think about our relationship. He was making me feel uncomfortable being around him. Let alone Trey being around him.

Chapter 45

A Bitter Love

The next day came, Charmayne still hadn't heard from Gram. She decided to call him. Charmayne was unsuccessful in reaching him.

The phone rung several times before it was answered.

"Hello, this Charmayne."

"Hey Charmayne."

"I'm trying to reach Gram, is he there."

"We haven't seen him since yesterday," Scotty said.

"Are you serious, Scotty?"

"Yes, I am Charmayne. We all been trying to call him.

"When he comes there just tell him to call me."

"Okay, I'll let him know to call you," Scotty said.

"Thanks" I said. We both hung the phone up. Can you imagine what was going through Charmayne's mind and what she was feeling on the inside?

All Charmayne could do is think about Gram cheating.

He's out there cheating on me and his son needs diapers and wipes.

Charmayne's friend Destiny called to see if she wanted to ride to the store with her.

"Not really," Charmayne said. The baby is a little cranky.

Charmayne lied to her friend Destiny.

Charmayne wanted to stay home. She waited for Gram to call her or come by her house.

Charmayne hate lying to her mom and friends. It wasn't fair to them or to Charmayne. She knew she had to put a stop to it before it gets out of hand.

Charmayne can't see herself messing around with another man knowing she's still in a relationship with her son's father. The love Charmayne has for him is much stronger than the love he has for her.

Charmayne asked her mom is she could watched the baby while she take a shower.

Charmayne went in the bathroom to take a shower to ease her mind. She knew their relationship was on the edge of a breakup.

Charmayne wanted to end her relationship with Gram.

Charmayne son is her first priority. Ending things with Gram was going to be hard. She knew Gram wasn't going to end their relationship.

"If he thinks he can have his cake and ice cream at the same time, he got it all wrong."

Charmayne refused to be the other woman.

"He acts like he don't care, so why should I?"

Charmayne mom knocked on the bathroom door to let me know Gram was on the phone.

"Tell him I'll call him when I get out of the shower."

Charmayne took her time taking a shower. She wasn't going to rush calling him back.

"Why should I call him back?" Charmayne asked herself. He didn't rush bringing my son his diapers or wipes.

Charmayne mom knocked on the bathroom door again.

"Are you dressed?" My mom asked me.

"No, ma'am." I'll be out in a minute.

"Gram wants you and the baby to be dressed when he comes and drop off the baby diapers and wipes.

Charmayne was smiling from ear to ear. She was mad, but she was glad to spend some alone time with him. This man had Charmayne's heart racing fast, she couldn't keep up with the beat.

Charmayne forgot about all the bad things he's done to her. She forgot about all the lies he use to tell her, cheating with different girls and not being there when she needed him the most.

Charmayne forgot about all the things she was going to say to him.

All Charmayne knew, she was with the man she love.

Charmayne wanted to spend the rest of my life with Gram. Nothing or nobody was going to stand in her way. She was determine to be with him. This is the man who took her virginity away. This is the man she had her first child by. A son she gave him. No Matter what he does to her, she love him.

When Gram came to drop off his son's pampers and wipes, Charmayne and the baby were dressed and ready.

Gram asked Charmayne mom if it was okay if he take all the kids sister to get some ice cream.

"Yes, they can go," Charmayne's mom said.

You all better behave yourself and listen to them.

Charmayne sisters and brothers was excited about going to get ice cream.

Charmayne sisters and brothers are real close. They look out for one another. Even though Charmayne has her own child to raise, she's still going to be there to protect her sisters and brothers.

Gram took the baby car seat to the car.

"We're be back later momma."

"Be careful." Make sure you keep an eye on your sisters and brothers.

"Yes ma'am," I will.

"Gram where were you last night?" I asked him.

"What did you just asked me?"

"You knew the baby needed pampers and wipes." Not one time has you consider me or him.

Good thing the music was playing loud. Charmayne did not want her sisters and brothers hearing them arguing.

Gram came up with some stupid excuse that he was at his cousin's house drinking.

"Charmayne I got drunk and fell asleep on his sofa." I did not feel like driving home.

"Well, I guess you think I have stupid writing all over my forehead too." He couldn't say a word.

They ended up going to their favorite ice cream shop and getting ice cream.

Gram was trying to butter Charmayne up, but she wasn't trying to hear what he was saying to her.

Gram apology or ice cream wasn't going to make Charmayne change her mind or the way she was feeling about him. After ordering everyone ice cream, they all wanted to go to the park and play for a while.

When they got to the park, they all sat at the table to eat their ice cream before going to play.

Charmayne sisters and brothers went to play on the monkey bars.

Gram went in his trunk and threw a basketball for them to play with. The girls played against the boys.

Gram tried to apologize to Charmayne about what he's done to her and his son.

"Listen, I'm just sick and tired of all your lies and cheating." You've put me through so much pain. I don't think I can take it anymore.

"You can take us home when my sisters and brothers get finished playing basketball.

"Girl, what is your problem." Don't play with me like that. I already told you what happen.

One thing I want you to remember, "Your son comes before any of your females you're messing with."

When I call you and tell your son needs this and that, you need to make sure he have it. You're not coming to see me. You're coming to see your son, so let's make that perfectly clear. You actually think I'm dumb. I know you're messing with someone else. I know I'm not the only one you're sleeping with.

Gram looked at Charmayne as if he had malice in his eyes. He looked like he wanted to snatch Charmayne up in front of my son, sisters, brothers and whomever was in the park with their children.

Charmayne was praying Gram wouldn't flip out on her.

Gram was good in showing off in front of his friends. He treated Charmayne like she didn't mean anything to him.

"I'm no longer going to sit at home waiting for you to call me while you're out there sleeping with God knows who.

Before Charmayne can anything else, he grabbed her by the arm.

"If you ever speak to me like that again, I'll knock your ass out cold."

Charmayne snatched her arm away from him.

Charmayne looked Gram straight in his eyes.

"I'm not your punching bag."

You will never put your hands on me ever again. If you ever put your hands on me again, I promise you the police will be on your ass like rice boiling in a pot.

Charmayne don't know where she got the courage from to say those words to Gram. She was surprise of her own actions.

Gram was shocked at what Charmayne had said to him.

Gram slapped Charmayne in a smooth way. He slapped her so hard in her face, she didn't see it coming. There were a lot of people in the park, but nobody saw what happened.

Gram made sure nobody saw him when he slapped Charmayne.

As Charmayne was about to get up, Gram pushed her back down.

"You better enjoy your ice cream," Gram said.

If you ever come out your mouth and talk to me like that again, you're be laying up in somebody hospital with your mouth all wired up. I've already told you not to play with me.

"I'll kill you," Gram said. I'll kill you and nobody will find your body, so don't fucking play with me.

"This fool is crazy," Charmayne said to herself.

He's cheating on me, but he wants to kill me for leaving him.

Charmayne heart was racing so fast she wasn't about to say anything else to him.

Gram came and sat closer next to Charmayne.

Gram put his arm around Charmayne and whisper in her ear.

"If I can't have you, no other man will and I promise you that".

Everything I'm saying to you, you better think twice about leaving me. I'm going to know your every move and who you're messing with.

"I'll kill the both of you," Gram said to me.

The best thing for me to do is weigh this thing out and stay in this abusive relationship. I wasn't about to tell nobody what was going on. If I did, this man is going to kill me. I didn't want my son to be without his mother. I didn't want any other woman raising my son, but me.

Charmayne was glad her sisters and brothers didn't hear what Gram had said to her.

The baby was getting a little cranky.

Charmayne face and arm wasn't bruised, but a little sore.

Charmayne just wanted to go home, take a shower and let the water soothe my pain away. She wanted to forget about what occurred at the park.

On their way home, Gram stopped at the store to buy pampers and wipes for the baby.

"Do you need anything from out the store?"

"No." I just want to go home.

Charmayne just wanted Gram to spend his money.

Charmayne made sure to stock up on pampers and wipes for her son.

Chapter 46

Brought Back to Reality

On the way to Charmayne's house, Gram turned on the radio. Their favorite song, *"You Give Good Love,"* came on the radio. Charmayne's heart remembered the first time they met. Charmayne felt all the love she had for him all over again. She wanted to feel his touch all over her body and the softness of his lips against hers.

When suddenly reality burst in and bust that bubble.

Wait! One minute he is telling me how much he loves me and that I'm the only girl he wants to be with. The next minute he's beating my ass. I'm trying to figure out what the hell is going on with him. I am getting tired of him jumping on me for no damn reason. It is wearing my body and spirit down. He beats me up like I am his punching bag. He slams me against the wall, slams me on the floor, kicks me in my ribs, and even hit me upside my head with a telephone he snatched from the wall. I allowed this man to treat me like I was nothing to him.

Gram wanted to cause Charmayne harm in any and every way he could.

Everybody was in the backseat sleep including her baby.

Charmayne sisters and brothers didn't hear anything that was being said or done to her. If Charmayne needed her sisters and brothers help they wouldn't of been able to help her. They were all fast asleep.

I don't believe Gram would never do anything out of the way in front of my brothers and sisters. he never has.

When the pulled in her driveway, she reached in the back to wake her brothers and sister up.

"I need one of you to grab the baby bag for me." Her sister Gracie is always helpful when it comes to her nephew.

"I know you're tired Gracie, but I need help. When you get in the house, you can go lay in the bed."

Gram took the baby and the baby car seat out while Charmayne brought the bags in the house.

She was glad to be home and away from Gram.

Charmayne sat down on the chair and let out a loud moan.

"Ouch."

"What's wrong with you Charmayne?" Asked Rocky.

"Oh, it's nothing Rocky. I sat on a needle."

Charmayne was back lying to her family again. She was covering up what Gram did to her.

"You must have been sliding down the sliding board with your sisters?" My mom asked me.

"No ma'am," I said. "I'm just tired."

If only my mom knew what really went on at the park with my son's father and me. I wanted to tell my mom, but I knew he would kill me. I promised him that I wouldn't say a word or anything to my mom or anyone else about his abusiveness. I hated lying to my mom. Some days I just feel like killing myself, because of the things he's doing to me.

Charmayne's brothers and sisters went into their rooms to lie down. They all were exhausted from running around with their friends.

Chapter 47

It Ends

My name is Mary C. Barron-Epps, and I am the Author of "No More Being Abused: I'm Taking My Life Back." In this book, I disclose the ordeal I endured at the hands of my abuser. I was subjected to abuse for eleven and a half years, a pain so unbearable that I could no longer tolerate it. Did I leave him? "No." I remained with him for a while, because I didn't want another woman to raise my kids.

I managed to finally break free from the relationship the day he struck me on the head with a chrome gun in front of my children. As my house phone rang, he inquired about the caller. I lied, saying it was my mom calling for me to pick her and my sister up from the Greyhound Station. He doubted me. I suggested he could accompany me if he wished, silently hoping he wouldn't accept. My head was pounding, and the pain was almost unbearable. I dressed my kids and myself quickly.

When I mentioned going to the station, his first words were, "You better not go to the Police Station."

I reassured him that I wasn't headed there. I secured my children in their car seats, locked the child safety locks, and made sure my car doors were locked too. With one foot on the brake and the other on the ground, I yelled, "By the way, I'm going to the Police Department." He rushed out, attempting to enter my car. I backed up swiftly, without caring if he stumbled.

I headed straight to the Police Department, where an officer noticed the large bump on the back of my head. I provided details of the incident, including my address, the vehicle he was driving, and his description. I also shared the addresses of his mother and another woman he was involved with. At that moment, I felt indifferent. The violence he inflicted by hitting me on the head in front of my children shattered my resolve. I never imagined God would grant me the strength to break free from that toxic relationship.

The police arrested him and took him to jail. I relocated, completely cutting off all contact with him and his family. I started a new relationship where I was treated like a queen. I had difficulty opening up to him at first, due to my past traumas. I also landed a teaching job that brought me immense joy.

One early morning, around four or five o'clock, I heard a knock at my door. Assuming it was my friend, I peeked out and saw their dad standing there in an orange jumpsuit, having ridden a bicycle to my house. Reluctantly, I opened the door.

"What are you doing here?" I asked.

"I came to see you and the kids," he replied.

"How did you find out where I live?"

"It doesn't matter. I just want to apologize for everything I did to you and our kids."

"You should have thought about that when you were assaulting me all these years."

"I know, but I wasn't thinking then. Those other women didn't mean anything to me."

"Lower your voice; the kids are sleeping and have school tomorrow."

My children woke up and greeted their dad eagerly.

"Hey dad, we miss you. When are you coming home?" they asked.

"Your dad can't come back to live with us. We'll co-parent, and that's it," I said. The children were thrilled to see their dad, and I didn't want to spoil the moment. I asked him to leave to avoid trouble.

"You need to know that I am dating someone, and there's nothing you can do about it. Any attempts to cause trouble will lead to you being cut off from your kids. Do not send your family to my house, or there will be consequences. Contact between us is not allowed, and I can have you arrested. I'm in charge now, not you.

For the sake of the kids, I permit you to visit them. They love you, and I don't want to disrupt the bond you share with them. However, you could not have that bond with me. If you can't visit, at least write them a letter to show that you think about them.

I permitted him to visit the kids and never interfered with their bond. He eventually got married, and we went our separate ways. I don't hate him, but I resent the abuse he subjected me to for eleven and a half years. He robbed me of my youth, isolating me from others except his family.

When we parted ways, it was like a breath of fresh air.

Finally, I could breathe freely without someone constantly monitoring me, interrogating me, physically abusing me, taking my money, or cheating on me. I could speak my mind, enjoy my freedom, and live my life.

If you find yourself struggling in toxic/abusive relationships, make an exit strategy and keep the affirmations on the next page somewhere you can safely read them regularly to remind yourself and to imprint in your mind the qualities you seek in a healthy, vibrant, supportive relationship.

I'm Taking My Life Back
DAILY AFFIRMATIONS

- I am worthy of love, affection, and respect.
- I attract healthy and fulfilling relationships into my life.
- I am deserving of a partner who cherishes and values me.
- I no longer tolerate any form of abuse or mistreatment
- I surround myself with supportive and loving individuals.
- I prioritize my happiness and well-being in all my relationships.
- I choose partners who uplift and empower me.
- I am deserving of a relationship built on trust, loyalty, and mutual respect.
- I am a strong and confident individual who deserves love and kindness.
- I attract partners who appreciate and honor my boundaries.
- I choose relationships that enhance my personal growth, my happiness and overall well-being.
- I release any toxic or abusive relationships from my life.
- I am deserving of love that is gentle, kind, nurturing, and understanding.
- I deserve to be with someone who values and supports my dreams and aspirations.
- I will not settle for anything less than the love and respect I deserve.
- I am surrounded by positive and loving energies in my relationships.
- I attract partners who recognize and appreciate the incredible person I am.
- I deserve to be loved, cherished, and respected, without being battered.
- I require a supportive partner who will stand by me and allow me to be the woman God has destined me to be.
- I desire a relationship where I have the freedom to spend time with my friends and not be stifled.
- I deserve to be treated like a QUEEN.

About the Author

Mary C. Barron-Epps

I am a domestic violence survivor. I come from a good Christian family who loves attending church and serving God. There was a time I thought I could not see myself without my abuser, but I was wrong! I found out that I can happily survive on my own. Today, I am living my life to the fullest and sharing my story in hopes of encouraging other battered women to walk away from the anguish of abuse. Once I left that abusive relationship I met a man who loves me unconditionally and appreciates me for who I am. I thank God each and every day for the beautiful love we share for one another.